# OBJECT-ORIENTED PROGRAMMING: FROM PROBLEM SOLVING TO JAVA

# OBJECT-ORIENTED PROGRAMMING: FROM PROBLEM SOLVING TO JAVA

**José M. Garrido**

FIREWAL MEDIA
(An Imprint of Laxmi Publications Pvt. Ltd.)
BANGALORE • CHENNAI • COCHIN • GUWAHATI • HYDERABAD
JALANDHAR • KOLKATA • LUCKNOW • MUMBAI • RANCHI
NEW DELHI

*Published by :*
**FIREWAL MEDIA**
(*An Imprint of Laxmi Publications Pvt. Ltd.*)
113, Golden House, Daryaganj,
New Delhi-110002

*Phone* : 011-43 53 25 00
*Fax* : 011-43 53 25 28

www.laxmipublications.com
info@laxmipublications.com



*Economy Edition Price* : **Rs. 295.00** *Only.* *Edition* : 2010

**OFFICES**

| | | | |
|---|---|---|---|
| ✆ **Bangalore** | 080-26 61 15 61 | ✆ **Chennai** | 044-24 34 47 26 |
| ✆ **Cochin** | 0484-237 70 04, 405 13 03 | ✆ **Guwahati** | 0361-254 36 69, 251 38 81 |
| ✆ **Hyderabad** | 040-24 65 23 33 | ✆ **Jalandhar** | 0181-222 12 72 |
| ✆ **Kolkata** | 033-22 27 43 84 | ✆ **Lucknow** | 0522-220 95 78 |
| ✆ **Mumbai** | 022-24 91 54 15, 24 92 78 69 | ✆ **Ranchi** | 0651-221 47 64 |

FOB-2767-295-OBJ ORI PRO PROB S JAVA-GAR **C—507/09/08**

*Printed at* : Sanjeev Offset Printers, Delhi.

**I dedicate this book to my wife Gisela and my two sons, Maximiliano and Constantino, for their love and support.**

# CONTENTS

# PREFACE

The main goal of this book is to present the basic concepts and techniques for object-oriented modeling and object-oriented programming principles. Because solution design is a creative activity, this book attempts to exploit the creative and critical thinking capacity of students in finding solutions to problems and implementing the solutions applying high-level, object-oriented programming principles.

The fundamental principles of problem solving techniques and illustrations of these principles are introduced with simple problems and their solutions, which are initially described mainly in pseudo-code. In the first few chapters, emphasis is on modeling and design. The principles of object-oriented modeling and programming are gradually introduced in solving problems. From a modeling point of view, objects are introduced early and represented in UML diagrams.

This book avoids stressing the syntax of the programming language from the beginning. This helps students in dealing with the difficulty of understanding the underlying concepts in problem solution and later programming.

The main conceptual tools used are modeling diagrams, pseudo-code, and some flowcharts that are applied to simplify the understanding of the design structures. The overall goal is to provide an easier way to understand problem solving by developing solutions in pseudo-code and implementing them as working programs. This also enhances the learning process as the approach allows one to isolate the problem solving and programming principle aspects from the programming language (Java™) to be used for final implementation of the problem solution.

When implementing problem solutions, students can construct working programs using the Kennesaw Java Preprocessor (KJP) programming language, and then convert to Java with the KJP translator. Compilation and execution of Java programs is carried out with the standard SDK Java software from Sun Microsystems. All Java classes can be used with KJP. This helps the students in their transition from object-oriented modeling and design to implementation with Java.

Standard pseudo-code constructs are explained and applied to the solution design of various case studies. General descriptions of the data structures needed in problem solutions are also discussed. The KJP language is introduced, which is a slightly enhanced pseudo-code notation. The KJP translator tool is used to convert (translate) a problem solution described in pseudo-code into Java. The assumption here is that, even after they learn Java, students will always use pseudo-code in the design phase of software development.

KJP is a high-level, programming language that facilitates the teaching and learning of the programming principles in an object-oriented context. The notation includes conventional pseudo-code syntax and is much easier to read, understand, and maintain than standard object-oriented programming languages.

The KJP translator tool carries out syntax checking and automatically generates an equivalent Java program. The KJP language has the same semantics as Java, so the transition from KJP to Java is, hopefully, very smooth and straightforward. The main motivation for designing the KJP language and developing the KJP translator was the quest for a higher-level language to teach programming principles, and at the same time, to take advantage of the Java programming language for all the functionality and capabilities offered.

The overall goal is to help students reason about the problem at hand, design the possible solutions to the problem, and write programs that are:

- Easy to write
- Easy to read
- Easy to understand
- Easy to modify

For most of the topics discussed, one or more complete case studies are presented and explained with the corresponding case study in pseudo-code. The KJP software tool used for converting a problem solution to Java is applied in the lab exercises. Appendix A explains the usage of the KJP translator and the jGRASP™ development environment (Auburn University); Appendix B briefly lists the contents of the included CD-ROM. The most recent version of the KJP software and the various case studies are available from the following Web page:

`http://science.kennesaw.edu/~jgarrido/kjp.html`

The important features of the book that readers can expect are:

- The emphasis on starting with modeling and design of problem solution and not programming with Java. The syntax details are not initially emphasized.
- The use of pseudo-code to describe problem solution, KJP as the high-level programming language, and Java as the ultimate implementation language. Java is chosen as the implementation language because it is one of the most important programming language today.
- When used as a teaching tool, the facilitation of understanding large and complex problems and their solutions, and gives the gives guidance on how to approach the implementation to these problems.
- The practical use of object-oriented concepts to model and solve real problems.
- A good practical source of material to understand the complexities of problem solving and programming, and their applications.

Instead of presenting examples in a cookbook manner that students blindly follow, this book attempts to stimulate and challenge the reasoning capacity and imagination of the students. Some of the problems presented at the end of the chapters make it necessary for students to look for possible solution(s) elsewhere. It also prepares students to become good programmers with the Java programming language.

I benefitted from the long discussions with my colleagues who are involved directly or indirectly in teaching the various sections of CSIS 2301

(Programming Principles I), CSIS 2302 (Programming Principles II), and related courses in the Department of Computer Science and Information Systems at Kennesaw State University. I am thankful to Mushtaq Ahmed, Ray Cobb, Richard Gayler, Hisham Haddad, Ben Setzer, Chong-Wei Xu, and Richard Schlesinger.

I am especially thankful to Mushtaq Ahmed for his help with the chapter on recursion, and to Chong-Wei Xu for his help with the chapter on threads. I am also thankful to the students in the pilot section of CSIS 2300 (Introduction to Computing) who have used the first six chapters of the book. The graduate students in the course IS 8020 (Object-Oriented Software Development) applied and reviewed most of the material in the book. I want to thank David Pallai and Bryan Davidson of Charles River Media for their help in producing the book.

J. M. Garrido

Kennesaw, GA

# 1 COMPUTER SYSTEMS

## 1.1 INTRODUCTION

A computer (or computer system) is basically an electronic machine that can carry out specific tasks by following sequences of instructions. A program includes such a sequence of instructions together with data definitions. The computer executes the program by performing one instruction after the other in the specified order.

The first part of this chapter describes the general structure of a computer system, which includes its hardware and software components. The programs constitute the software components. Most of this book is about constructing user computer programs, so the second part of the chapter explains program compilation and program execution.

## 1.2 COMPUTER SYSTEMS

The computer is a machine that can perform various tasks under control of the software. The programmer needs knowledge of the basic computer architecture concepts to clearly understand the structure of the computer to be able to develop solutions to problems, and to use the computer as a tool to execute the solutions to problems.

The computer system consists of two important types of components:

- Hardware components, which are the electronic and electromechanical devices, such as the processor, memory, disk unit, keyboard, screen, and others
- Software components, such as the operating system and user programs

All computer systems have the fundamental functions: processing, input, and output.

- Processing executes the instructions in memory to perform some transformation and/or computation on the data also in memory. This emphasizes the fact that the instructions and data must be located in memory in order for processing to proceed.
- Input involves entering data into the computer for processing. Data is entered into the computer with an input device (for example, the keyboard).
- Output involves transferring data from the computer to an output device such as the video screen.

### 1.2.1 Hardware Components

The computer is a system in which programs (software) can execute with appropriate input data and produce desired results. The basic structure of a computer, also known as the computer architecture, is illustrated in Figure 1.1. The most important hardware components are

- The central processing unit (CPU)
- Main memory, also known as random access memory (RAM)
- The storage devices
- The main input/output (I/O) devices connected to the communication ports
- Other devices

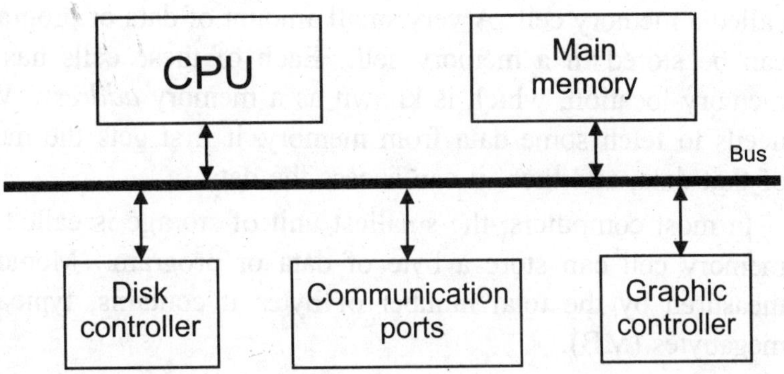


**Figure 1.1** Basic hardware structure of a computer system.

#### 1.2.1.1 CPU

The CPU is capable of executing the instructions that are stored in memory, carrying out arithmetic operations, and performing data transfers. Larger computers have several processors (CPUs).

NOTE *In order for the CPU to execute an instruction, the program must be specified in a special form called machine language. This is a notation that is specifically dependent on the type of CPU. To execute a program, the source program is translated from its original text form into a machine language program.*

An important parameter of the computer is the speed of the CPU, usually measured in MHz or GHz. This is the number of machine cycles that the CPU can handle. Roughly, it indicates the time the CPU takes to perform an instruction. On small systems such as small servers and personal computers, the CPU is constructed on a tiny electronic chip (integrated circuit) called a microprocessor. This chip is placed on a circuit board that contains other electronic components, including the memory chips. Two typical CPUs found in today's personal computers are the Intel Pentium™ 4 with 2.4 GHz and the AMD Athlon XP™ 2400.

#### 1.2.1.2 Main Memory

The main memory of a computer is also called *random access memory* (RAM). It is a high-speed device for temporary storage of data and programs. Memory consists of a large number of storage cells; each one is called a memory cell. A very small amount of data or program instructions can be stored in a memory cell. Each of these cells has an associated memory location, which is known as a memory *address*. When the CPU needs to fetch some data from memory, it first gets the memory location of that data, and then, it can access the data.

In most computers, the smallest unit of storage is called a *byte*. Every memory cell can store a byte of data or program. Memory capacity is measured by the total number of bytes it contains, typically about 512 megabytes (MB).

Another important characteristic of main memory is the access time. This affects the performance of a computer system if the amount of data to store or retrieve to and from memory is large. The access time is the time interval that the CPU takes to fetch some data from a memory cell, or to store some data to a memory cell. Main memory is considered a nonpermanent storage device; all data and programs in memory are lost when the power is disconnected.

#### 1.2.1.3 Storage Devices

There are other storage devices that are used to store programs and massive amounts of data; these devices are the disks and tape units. They provide permanent storage until the user decides to erase the data and/or programs. The unit of capacity for these devices is the byte, usually megabytes (MB) and gigabytes (GB). A typical hard disk can have a storage capacity of 60 GB. These storage devices are much slower than main memory; the CPU takes much more time to access data on a disk device than data on main memory. Compact discs (CD) devices are based on laser technology, and are smaller in size and capacity compared to hard disks; they provide a very convenient media to transport data and programs to computer systems.

Magnetic tape devices are much slower than disks but are less expensive and more convenient to exchange data and/or programs between different computers. These devices are used mainly to back up large files or databases on larger computers. Magnetic tape devices are serial devices because the access is sequential only. To access some data anywhere in the magnetic tape, the unit must be fast-forwarded to the position of the specified data. The various disk and tape devices are connected to the disk and tape controllers (see Figure 1.1).

#### 1.2.1.4 Input Devices

Input devices are hardware units for entering data and/or programs into the computer. On a personal computer, the main input device is usually the keyboard. The user types the values of data required by the program on the keyboard. A storage device such as a disk can also be assigned as an input device. The mouse is a pointing device that is indirectly used as an input device. A modem is a communication device that can also be assigned as an input device.

#### 1.2.1.5 Output Devices

Output devices are the units for transferring data from inside the computer to the outside world. The main output device is the screen, the video unit. With this device, data is sent from inside the computer to the screen for the user(s).

In most applications, the input and output devices mentioned are used when the program maintains a dialog with the user while executing. This computer-user dialog is called user interaction. The input and output devices are connected to the communication ports in the computer (see Figure 1.1). For graphic applications, a video display device is connected to the graphic controller, which is a unit for connecting one or more video units and/or graphic devices.

#### 1.2.1.6 Other Devices

Additional hardware devices include floppy disk drives, CD-ROM drives, mice, scanners, digital cameras, microphones, speakers, modems, and others. Diskettes are the most popular portable media for permanent storage and exchange of small amounts of data and programs. The standard capacity of a diskette is 1.44 MB. The compact disc read only memory (CD-ROM) is another portable media for storing data and/or programs. The capacity of a CD-ROM is about 650 MB. A similar device is the CD-Rewritable (CD-RW). These CD media can be erased and reused.

All the hardware components are interconnected via electronic paths called a bus. Data and controlling signals are normally transferred to or from the CPU to the appropriate device through the bus. The speed capacity of the bus is another important parameter that affects the overall performance of a computer system.

## 1.2.2 Computer Networks

A computer network consists of two or more computers interconnected in such a way that they can exchange data and programs. On a small network, sometimes known as a local area network (LAN), several small computers are connected to a larger computer called a server that stores the global files or databases and may include one or more shared printers. A local area network is limited to a relatively small geographical area, such as a building, a floor, or a university campus. Figure 1.2 shows the simplified structure of a local area network. This example is a client-server system with one server.

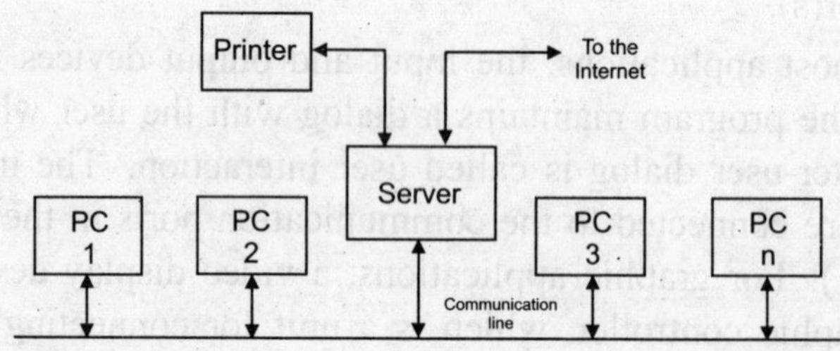


**Figure 1.2** Basic structure of a local area network.

A wide area network (WAN) covers a large geographical region and connects local area networks located in various remote places. The Internet is a public, international wide area network.

## 1.2.3 The Internet

The Internet is an international network of smaller networks. On a university campus, a typical user is connected to a computer on the campus local area network. Access to the Internet is provided through a special communication device called a router. Figure 1.3 shows this type of connection to the Internet.

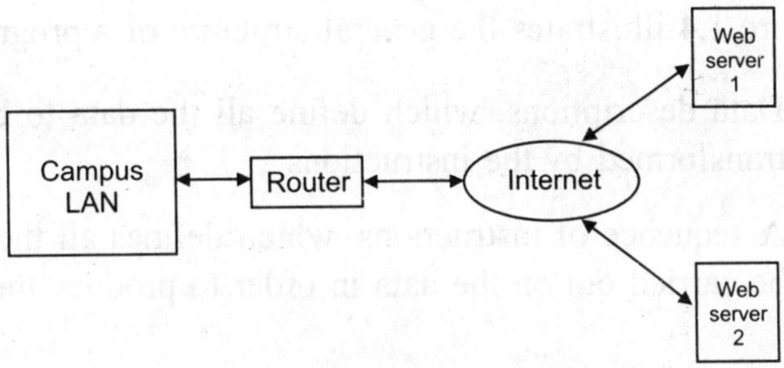


**Figure 1.3** A LAN connected to the Internet.

The Internet provides various services, the most common of which are electronic mail, remote login, file transfer, and the World Wide Web. The Web allows the sharing of information across the Internet to be very convenient and simple. It is based on the concepts of hypertext and hypermedia.

Hypertext presents the documents in such a way that they can be linked according to the user needs. Hypermedia allows the inclusion of other media, such as graphics, animations, video, and sound.

Web servers host various types of documents, and a Web browser, which is a software component installed in a client machine, can load, format, and display a Web document. These documents are formatted using the HTML language, which is a notation that allows the Web browser to display the document. Java programs can be embedded in HTML documents and executed by the Web browser.

Every computer connected to the Internet has a unique Internet Protocol (IP) address, or Internet address. This address can be represented symbolically by the computer name and the domain name. For example, a symbolic Internet address is:

```
cs3.kennesaw.edu
```

### 1.2.4 Software Components

The hardware components are driven and controlled by the software components. The software components consist of the set of programs that execute in the computer. These programs control, manage, and carry out important tasks.

Figure 1.4 illustrates the general structure of a program. It consists of:

- Data descriptions, which define all the data to be manipulated and transformed by the instructions
- A sequence of instructions, which defines all the transformations to be carried out on the data in order to produce the desired results

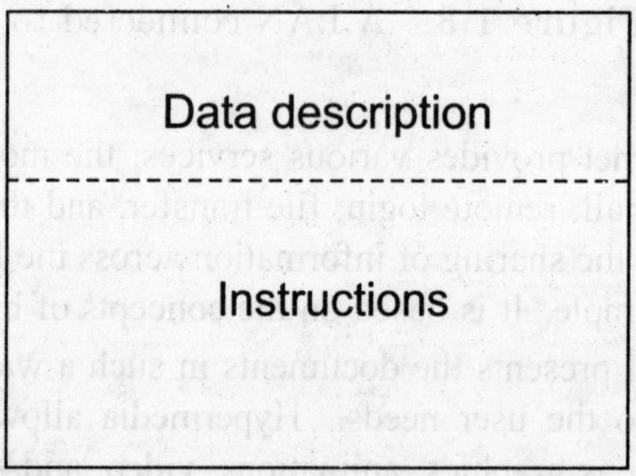


**Figure 1.4** General structure of a program.

There are two general types of software components:

- System software
- Application software

The system software is a collection of programs that control the activities and functions of the various hardware components. An example of system software is the operating system, such as Unix, Windows, MacOS, OS/2, and others.

Application software consists of those programs that solve specific problems for the users. These programs execute under control of the system software. Application programs are developed by individuals and organizations for solving specific problems.

## 1.3 PROGRAMMING LANGUAGES

A programming language is a formal notation that is used to write the data description and the instructions of a program. The language has a well-defined set of syntax and semantic rules. The programming language's syntax rules describe how to write sentences. The semantic rules describe the meaning of the sentences. These two types of rules must be consistent.

### 1.3.1 Machine Languages

Historically, the first group of programming languages that were developed were the machine languages for the various computers. Until the early fifties, this was the only category of programming languages available. The human representation of a program was a sequence of ones and zeros (or bits). Program development was extremely difficult, tedious, and error prone. These programming languages were very low-level because they consisted of symbolic machine instructions used to express very detailed manipulation at the hardware level and consequently, were hardware dependent.

### 1.3.2 Assembly Languages

The next group of programming languages includes the symbolic machine languages (also called assembly languages). These languages were developed to ease and improve the construction of programs. In these languages, various mnemonic symbols represent operations and addresses in memory. These languages are also low-level and hardware dependent; there is a different assembly language for every computer type. Assembly language is still used today for detailed control of hardware devices; it is also used when extremely efficient execution is required.

### 1.3.3 High-Level Programming Languages

The purpose of a programming language is to allow a human to write instructions to the computer in the form of a program. A programming language must be expressive enough to help the human in the writing of programs for a large family of problems.

High-level programming languages are so called because they are hardware independent and closer to the problem (or family of problems) to be solved.

NOTE *High-level languages allow more readable programs, and are easier to write and maintain. Examples of these languages are Pascal, C, Cobol, FORTRAN, Algol, Ada, Smalltalk, C++, Eiffel, and Java.*

These last four high-level programming languages are object-oriented programming languages. These are considered slightly higher level than the other high-level languages.

The first object-oriented language, Simula, was developed in the mid-sixties. It was used mainly to write simulation models. The language is an extension of Algol. In a similar manner, C++ was developed as an extension to C in the early eighties.

Java was developed by Sun Microsystems in the mid-nineties, as an improved object-oriented programming language compared to C++. Java has far more capabilities than any other object-oriented programming language to date.

Languages like C++ and Java can require considerable effort to learn and master. There are several experimental, higher-level, object-oriented programming languages. Each one has a particular goal. One such language is KJP (Kennesaw Java Preprocessor); its main purpose is to make it easier to learn object-oriented programming principles and help students transition to Java.

### 1.3.4 Compilation

The solution to a problem is implemented in an appropriate programming language. This becomes the source program written in a high-level programming language, such as C++, Eiffel, Java, or others.

After a source program is written, it is translated to an equivalent program in machine language, which is the only programming language that the computer can understand. The computer can only execute instructions that are in machine language.

The translation of the source program to machine language is called *compilation*. The step after compilation is called *linking* and it generates an executable program in machine language. For some other languages, like Java, the user carries out two steps: compilation and interpretation. This last step involves direct execution of the compiled program.

Figure 1.5 shows what is involved in compilation of a source program in Java. The Java compiler checks for syntax errors in the source program and then translates it into a program in bytecode, which is the program in an intermediate form.

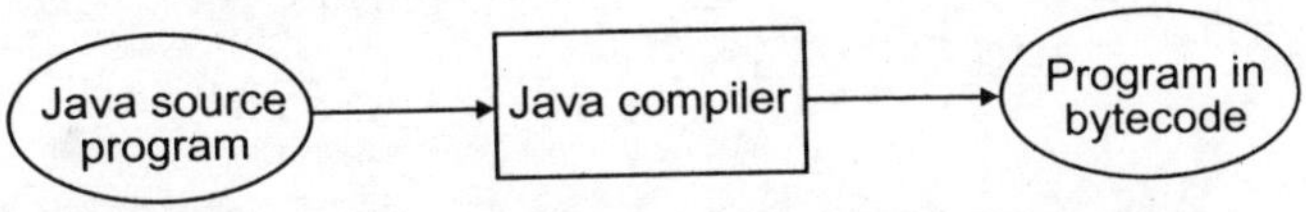


**Figure 1.5** Compiling a Java source program.

*The Java bytecode is not dependent on any particular platform or computer system. This makes the bytecode very portable from one machine to another.*

Figure 1.6 shows how to execute a program in bytecode. The Java virtual machine (JVM), which is another software tool from Sun Microsystems, carries out the interpretation of the program in bytecode.

**Figure 1.6** Executing a Java program.

### 1.3.5 Converting from KJP to Java

For programs written in KJP (an object-oriented language that is higher level than Java), the KJP language translator is needed for the conversion from KJP to Java. This translator software is freely available from the KJP Web page:

`http://science.kennesaw.edu/~jgarrido/kpl.html`

The conversion is illustrated in Figure 1.7. Appendix A explains in further detail how to use the KJP translator.

**Figure 1.7** Conversion from pseudo-code to Java.

### 1.3.6 Program Execution

*Before a program starts to execute in the computer, it must be loaded into the memory of the computer. The program executing in the computer usually reads input data from the input device and after carrying out some computations, it writes results to the output device(s).*

When executing in a computer, a program reads data from the input device (the keyboard), then carries out some transformation on the data, and writes the results on the output device (the video screen). The transformation also produces intermediate results.

In a personal computer system, the input data typically originates from the user keyboard. Similarly, the output data list is directed to the computer screen. A program reads data from the input list, carries out some transformation on this data, and writes output data (results) to the output list.

The instructions in a program define a set of transformations on the input data. These transformations together with the data description represent the program, which implements the solution. Figure 1.8 shows a typical application program in execution; reading input data and producing output data (results).

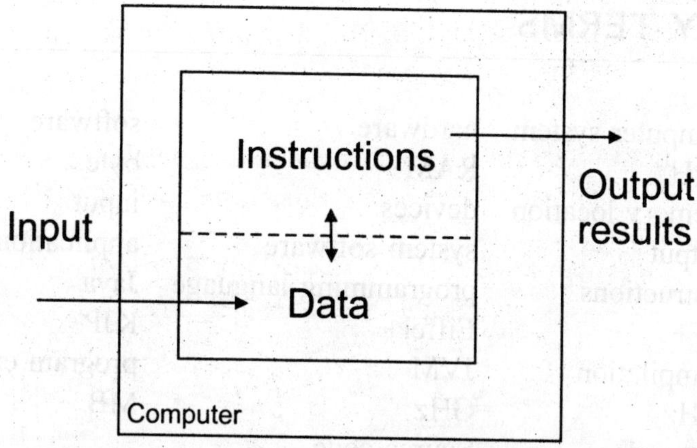


**Figure 1.8** An executing program.

## 1.4 SUMMARY

A computer system consists of several hardware and software components. The I/O devices are necessary to read or write data to and from memory to the appropriate external device. Application software is a related set of programs that the user interacts with to solve particular problems. System software is a set of programs that control the hardware and the application software.

Compilation is the task of translating a program from its source language to an equivalent program in binary code (possibly machine language). When the program executes in a computer, it reads the input data, carries out some computations, and writes the output data (results).

To fully understand the development process, it is necessary to have some knowledge about the general structure of a computer system.

## 1.5 KEY TERMS

| | | |
|---|---|---|
| computer system | hardware | software |
| CPU | RAM | byte |
| memory location | devices | input |
| output | system software | application software |
| instructions | programming language | Java |
| C++ | Eiffel | KJP |
| compilation | JVM | program execution |
| MHz | GHz | MB |
| bytecode | Source code | |

## 1.6 EXERCISES

1. Explain the relevant differences between hardware and software components. Give examples.
2. List and explain the hardware parameters that affect the performance of a computer system.
3. Why is the unit of capacity for memory and for the storage devices the same? Explain with an example.
4. Which is the main input device in a personal computer (PC)? What other devices are normally used as input devices?
5. Which is the main output device in a personal computer? What other devices are normally used as output devices?
6. Can a disk device be used as an input device? Explain. Can it be used as an output device? Explain.
7. What is a programming language? Why do we need one? Why are there so many programming languages?
8. Explain the purpose of compilation. How many compilers are necessary for a given application? What is the difference between program compilation and program execution? Explain.

9. What is the real purpose of developing a program? Can we just use a spreadsheet program such as MS Excel to solve numerical problems? Explain.

# 2 PROGRAM DEVELOPMENT

## 2.1 INTRODUCTION

Computer problem solving involves a series of tasks or phases, such as understanding the problem, finding the solution(s) to the problem, and then using the computer to write, compile, and execute the corresponding program(s). To carry out these tasks for developing programs in an appropriate manner, basic knowledge of the software development process is essential. One of the reasons for carefully following the software development process is to increase the quality of software produced at a reasonable cost. The main goal of this chapter is to explain the program development process.

## 2.2 PROBLEM SOLVING

The ultimate goal of developing a computer program is to solve some real-world problem. The real challenge is to find some method of solution or some way to approximate a solution to the problem at hand. If the method of solution to a problem cannot be found (not even an approximation), then there is no point in attempting to construct a program. In reality, there are many types of problems with no known method of solution discovered to date.

### 2.2.1 Problem Solving Process

Computer problem solving is a creative process; in a simple manner, it involves:

1. Describing the problem in a clear and unambiguous form
2. Finding a solution to the problem
3. Developing a computer implementation of the solution

In order to design the solution to a problem, one has to identify the major parts of a problem:

- The given data
- The required results
- The necessary transformation to be carried out on the given data to produce the final results

### 2.2.2 Algorithm

In a broad sense, the transformation on the data is described as a sequence of operations that are to be carried out on the given data in order to produce the desired results. Figure 2.1 illustrates the notion of transformation. This is a clear, detailed, precise, and complete description of the sequence of operations. The transformation of the data is also called an *algorithm*. The algorithm is a formal description of how to solve the problem.

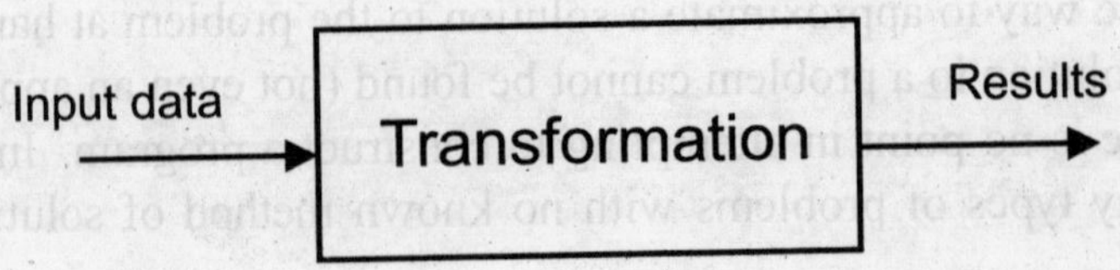


**Figure 2.1** Transformation applied to the input data.

A *program* consists of a group of data descriptions and one or more sequences of instructions to the computer for producing correct results when given appropriate data. The program is written in an appropriate programming language, and it tells the computer how to transform the given data into correct results. Software development is a process for producing a program that implements the solution on a computer.

## 2.3 SOFTWARE DEVELOPMENT PROCESS

As mentioned previously, computer problem solving involves finding one or more possible solutions to a problem, and describing the solution(s) in an appropriate form to implement the solution in a computer. Software engineering attempts to guide the developer into a well-defined process to be carried out in a disciplined manner, and to accomplish development of correct software. The life cycle is used to organize and manage the software development process and the phases to maintain and retire the software. The overall goal is to produce a quality software product at a reasonable cost. This is one of the basic issues in software engineering.

### 2.3.1 Software Life Cycle

The entire development process consists of a sequence of activities or phases that are carried out by a team of developers. These activities represent the complete life of the software from birth to retirement. In most cases, the development process is also known as the *system life cycle*.

The life cycle of a software system can be broadly divided into four groups of activities:

1. Software development, which includes all the phases necessary to carry out the initial development of the software product
2. Using the developed software, which includes the activities that support the software in production
3. Maintenance, which includes the activities that report defects in the software and the subsequent fixes and releases of new versions of the software product

4. Retirement, which takes the software off production when it can no longer be maintained

The software maintenance is the most expensive, difficult, and time-consuming of these groups of activities. To minimize this, it is important that the development process be well planned and well carried out.

One of the earliest and simplest models for the software life cycle is the *waterfall model*. This model represents the sequence of activities to develop the software system up to installation for using the software. In this model, the activity in a given stage or phase cannot be started until the activity of the previous phase has been completed.

Figure 2.2 illustrates the sequence of activities or phases involved in the waterfall model of the software life cycle.

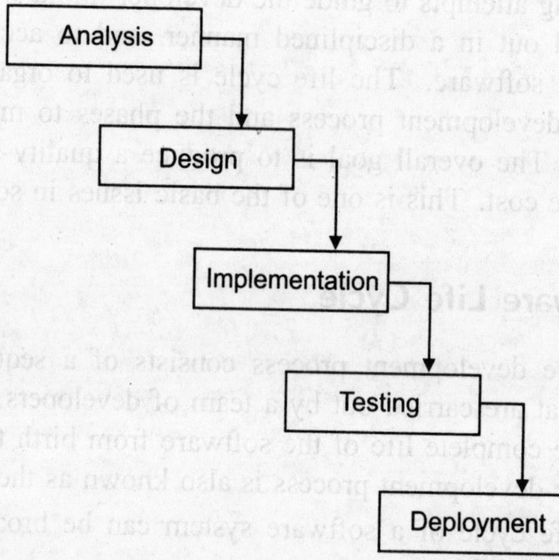


**Figure 2.2** The waterfall model of development process.

### 2.3.2 Tasks in the Software Development Process

Starting with the description of the initial problem statement, the general sequence of tasks that need to be carried out for developing a correct program is:

1. Analysis describes what the problem solution is supposed to accomplish. The outcomes of this phase are the various requirement documents, which include specifying the requirements of the problem in a more complete, precise, clear, and understandable form.

2. Design describes the detailed structure and behavior of the components of the system model. The outcome of this phase is a detailed description of the data structures and algorithms in each component of the model.

3. Implementation includes the translation of the design solution into a programming language, followed by the compilation of the code written. This is the actual construction of the program(s) for the application. The outcome of this phase is the set of programs constructed.

4. Testing verifies the program(s) works according to requirements with appropriate data according to the set of examples provided. This phase includes unit testing, which involves the testing of individual components (modules), and integration testing, which involves testing all the components together. The outcome of this phase is the verified application software.

5. Deployment includes delivery and installation of the program in the user environment.

The overall outcome of this process is a well-documented computer program (software application) that has been tested in the computer with appropriate data and that produces reliable results.

The analysis phase details the requirements of the problem and entails a thorough understanding of the problem and describing in a very precise manner of what the problem is, and what is to be done. It can be argued that this is the most critical phase of program development, because if not done well, the rest of the phases are fruitless.

The analysis phase produces the description of the product in a form that is clear, precise, easy to understand, complete, and consistent.

The decomposition of the software into smaller parts is usually part of the preliminary design. The rationale for this step is that it is much easier to manage small pieces of the software instead of the whole product.

The detailed design may be the most intellectually challenging in program development. In this step, one or more solutions to the problem are investigated. The data structures and the algorithms are designed, written in some appropriate notation (i.e., pseudo-code and/or flowcharts), and documented.

The implementation phase is what is normally called coding, or *programming*. The implementation phase consists of converting the solution to a suitable programming language and then compiling the corresponding modules of the program.

**NOTE** *For large programs, it is necessary to follow the life cycle as a process. This allows for the program construction to be accomplished in an organized and disciplined manner. Even for small programs, it is good practice to carry out these activities in a well-defined development process.*

## 2.3.3 Other Development Approaches

The main limitation of the waterfall model is that it is not iterative, which is extremely necessary in practice. There are some variations proposed for the waterfall model. These include returning to the previous phase when necessary. Recent trends in system development have emphasized the iterative approach. In this approach, previous stages can be revised and enhanced.

The *spiral model* of software development is a more complete model that incorporates the construction of prototypes in the early stages. A prototype is an early version of the application that does not have all the final characteristics. Other development approaches involve prototyping and rapid application development (RAD).

In carrying out the tasks in the software development process, the following general practices have been proposed:

- For the design task, the strategy called design refinement has proven very useful. You start with a general, high-level and incomplete design (no details); it provides a big picture view of the solution. Next, work through a sequence of improvements or refinements of the design, each with more detail, until a final design that reflects a complete solution to the problem is obtained.

- For the implementation task, a similar strategy is followed. This is sometimes called incremental development. This captures the importance of the modular decomposition of the software system. At each step, a single module is implemented (and tested). This practice is sometimes called continuous integration.

## 2.4 SUMMARY

Program development involves finding a solution to a problem and then writing the problem solution in a programming language to produce a computer program. The program development process is a well-defined sequence of activities carried out by the programmer. The outcome of this process is a correct and good-quality program.

The software development process can be considered as part of the software life cycle. Two important and widely known models for the software life cycle are the *waterfall* and the *spiral* models.

The software development process is a well-defined sequence of tasks that are carried out to produce a program that is a computer solution to the given problem. It is strongly recommended to follow a software development process even for small programs.

## 2.5 KEY TERMS

| | | |
|---|---|---|
| transformation | problem solving | development process |
| requirements | analysis | design |
| decomposition | implementation | testing |
| maintenance | retirement | algorithm |
| waterfall model | spiral model | software life cycle |

## 2.6 EXERCISES

1. Give valid reasons why the first phase of the program development process needs to be strict with respect to ambiguity, clarity, and completeness in describing the problem.
2. In very simple terms, what is the difference between the algorithm and the program?
3. Give valid reasons why the design phase of the program development process is needed. Can you write the program without a design?
4. Explain when the analysis phase ends and the design phase starts. Is there a clear division? Is any overlapping possible?
5. Is there a clear difference between the software development process and the software life cycle? Explain.
6. Is the goal for using a development process in developing a small program valid? Explain. What are the main advantages in using a process? What are the disadvantages?

# 3 OBJECTS AND CLASSES

## 3.1 INTRODUCTION

A real-world problem consists of several collections of entities interacting with one another and with their surroundings. When solving a real-world problem, a simplified representation of the problem is used to study the problem and construct a solution. This representation is called a model of the problem. A model is composed of objects, each one representing a real-world entity. The model includes descriptions about these objects and their interactions.

In developing object-oriented applications, one of the main goals is to construct abstract representations in software of some aspect of the real world. An abstract representation is a simplified description with only the relevant or essential properties of part of a real system. A model is an abstract description of some part of the problem domain. The task of designing and constructing a model is called modeling.

This chapter introduces the concepts of objects, classes, and modeling. It also introduces the Unified Modeling Language (UML) diagrams to describe simple classes and the basic structure and behavior of objects.

## 3.2 OBJECTS AND PROBLEM SOLVING

Chapter 2 introduced problem solving as the general philosophy of the program development process. A simplification of this process is shown in Figure 3.1.

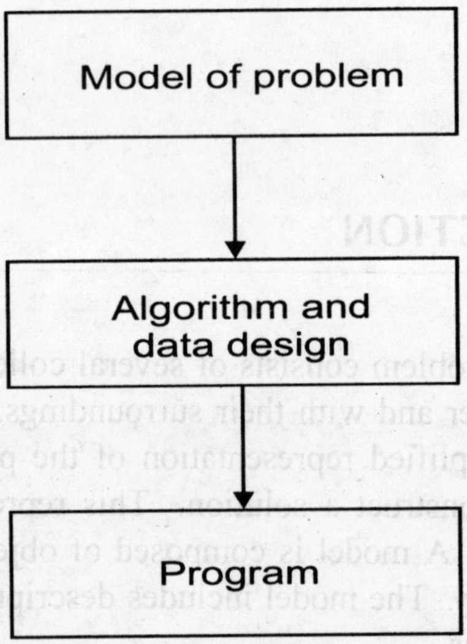


**Figure 3.1** Traditional simplified problem-solving process.

This figure starts with a model of the problem, which is derived from the initial description and analysis of the real-world problem. The figure refers to the overall process of problem solving. With the object-oriented approach, all phases of the process are based on objects. Figure 3.2 shows the inclusion of objects in the problem-solving process.

## 3.3 OBJECTS AND MODELING

Objects are the central focus of the object-oriented approach to problem solving. Objects are given the responsibility of carrying out specific tasks of the solution. Objects are models of the real-world entities identified in

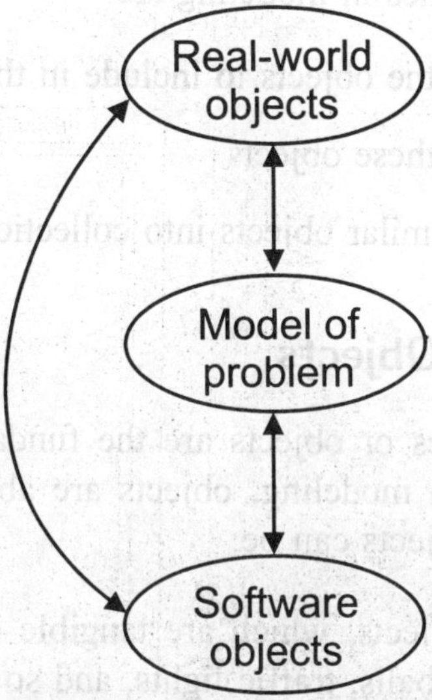


**Figure 3.2** Object-oriented approach for problem solving.

the real-world environment of the problem. Objects with similar characteristics are grouped into collections, also known as *classes*.

### 3.3.1 Models

NOTE *The concept of* abstraction *is applied in describing the objects of a problem. This involves the elimination of unessential characteristics. A model includes only the relevant aspects of the real world pertaining to the problem to solve.*

As mentioned previously, *modeling* is the task of designing and building a model. The result of modeling is that only the relevant objects and only the essential characteristics of these objects are included in the model.

There are several levels of abstraction and these correspond to the different levels of detail needed to completely define objects and the collections of objects in a model. An important and early task of the modeling process is to identify real-world *objects* and *collections* of similar objects within the boundaries of the problem.

Three basic issues in modeling are:

1. Identifying the objects to include in the model
2. Describing these objects
3. Grouping similar objects into collections

### 3.3.2 Describing Objects

Real-world entities or objects are the fundamental components of a real world system. In modeling, objects are abstract representations of real-world entities; objects can be:

- Physical objects, which are tangible objects, such as persons, animals, cars, balls, traffic lights, and so on
- Nontangible objects, which are not directly visible, such as contracts, accounts, and so on
- Conceptual objects, which do not clearly exist but are used to represent part of the components or part of the behavior of the problem. For example, the environment that surrounds the problem and that affects the entities of the problem

An object is a dynamic concept because objects exhibit independent behavior and interact with one another. They communicate by sending messages to each other; this way all objects collaborate for a common goal. Every object has:

- State, represented by the set of properties (or attributes) and their associated values
- Behavior, represented by the operations, also known as methods, of the object
- Identity, which is a property that can help identify an object

A simple example of an object is an object of class `Ball`. Its identity is an object of class `Ball`. The attributes of this object are *color*, *size*, and *move_status*. Figure 3.3 shows the UML diagram for two `Ball` objects and illustrates their structure. The diagram is basically a rectangle divided into three sections. The top section indicates the class of the object, the middle section includes the list of the attributes and their current values, and the bottom section includes the list of operations in the object.

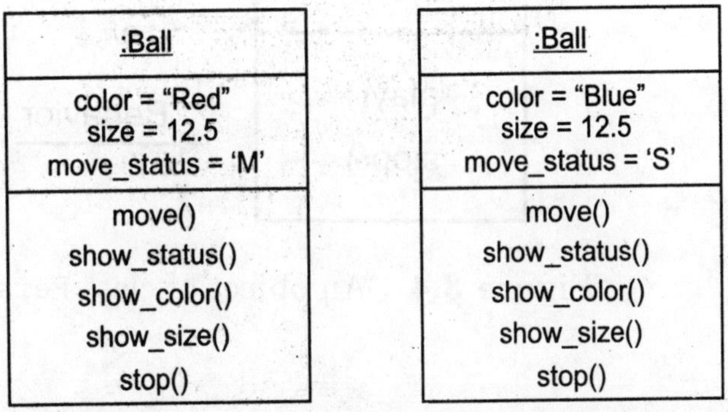


**Figure 3.3** Two objects of class `Ball`.

The values of the attributes of an object of class `Ball` are of varied types. The value of attribute *color* is a text string, which is enclosed in quotes. The value of attribute *size* is a numeric value. The value of attribute *move_status* is a single text character, which is enclosed in apostrophes. The two objects of class `Ball` are in different states because their attributes have different values.

An object of class `Person` is shown in Figure 3.4. This object has only two attributes, *name* and *age*, and two operations, *play* and *stop*. The values of these attributes are also shown. The behavior of this object is simple; the object can only start playing (with operation *play*) or stop playing (with operation *stop*).

Another simple example of an object is one of class `Automobile`. The properties are *value*, *color*, *weight*, *size*, *year*, *model*, *make*, *number of miles* (or kilometers) in the speedometer, *fuel capacity* (in gallons or liters), and the *fuel consumption* per mile (or per kilometer).

The behavior of the automobile object is defined by several operations, such as *fill_fuel_tank*, *update_value*, *move*, *show_fuel_level*, and *show_odometer*. The state of the automobile object changes when at least one of its attributes changes value.

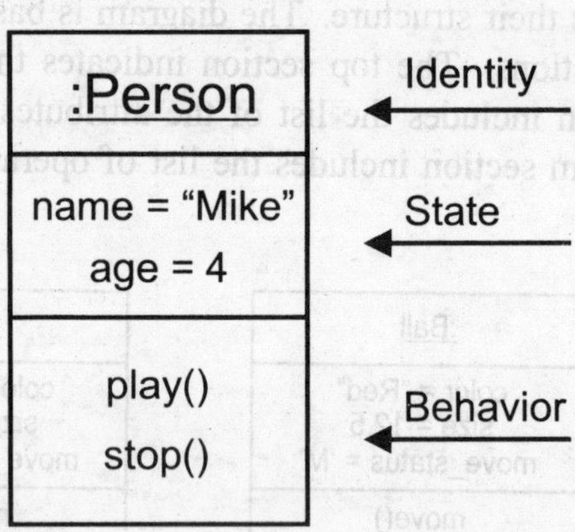


**Figure 3.4** An object of class `Person`.

### 3.3.3 Object Interactions

Suppose there is a scenario in which a child called Mike plays with two balls of the same size, one red and the other blue. The child is represented by an object of class `Person`. The balls are represented by two objects of class `Ball`. When the object of class `Person` needs to interact with the two objects of class `Ball`, the object of class `Person` invokes the *move* operation of each object of class `Ball`. Another possible interaction is the object of class `Person` invoking the *show_color* operation of an object of class `Ball`.

NOTE *Objects interact by* sending messages *to each other. The object that sends the message is the requestor of a service that can be provided by the receiver object.*

A message represents a request for service, which is provided by the object receiving the message. The sender object is known as the *client* of a service, and the receiver object is known as the *supplier* of the service.

The purpose of sending a message is the request for some operation of the receiver object to be carried out; in other words, the request is a call to one of the operations of the supplier object. Objects carry out operations in response to messages.

These operations are object-specific; a message is always sent to a specific object. This is also known as *method invocation*. A message contains three parts:

- The operation to be invoked or started, which is the service requested and must be an accessible operation
- The input data required by the operation to perform, which is known as the arguments
- The output data, which is the reply to the message and is the actual result of the request

To describe the general interaction between two or more objects (the sending of messages between objects), a UML diagram known as a *collaboration diagram* is used to describe the interaction. For example, to describe the interaction among an object of class `Person` with the two objects of class `Ball`, a simple collaboration diagram is drawn. Figure 3.5 shows a collaboration diagram with these three objects. In this example, the `Person` object invokes the *move* operation of the `Ball` object by sending a message to the first `Ball` object, and as a result of this message, that object (of class `Ball`) performs its *move* operation.

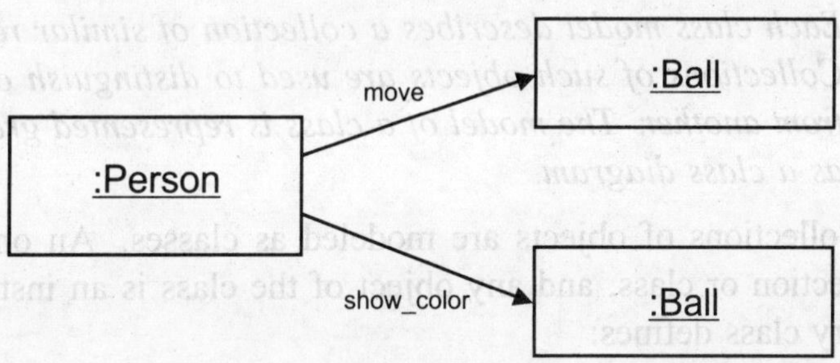


**Figure 3.5** Collaboration diagram with three objects.

## 3.4 CLASSES

In the real-world problem, a class describes a *collection* of real-world entities or objects with similar characteristics. The abstract descriptions of the collections of objects are called classes (or class models).

Figure 3.6 illustrates the identifying of two collections of real-world objects, the modeling of the classes, and the software implementation of these classes.

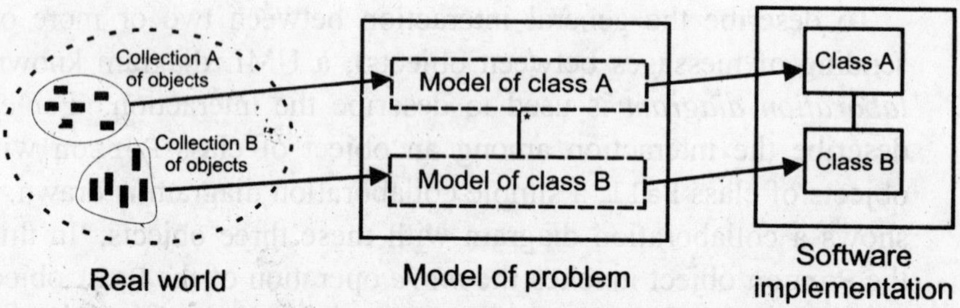


**Figure 3.6** Collections of real-world objects.

*Each class model describes a collection of similar real-world objects. Collections of such objects are used to distinguish one type of object from another. The model of a class is represented graphically in UML as a class diagram.*

Collections of objects are modeled as classes. An object belongs to a collection or class, and any object of the class is an instance of the class. Every class defines:

- Attributes (data declarations)
- One or more operations (also known as functions and methods)

A complete object-oriented model of an application consists of a description of all the classes and their relationships, the objects and their interactions, and a complete documentation of these.

A class defines the attributes and behavior for all the objects of the class. Figure 3.7 shows the diagram for class `Person`. Figure 3.8 shows the UML diagram for class `Ball`.

**Figure 3.7** Class `Person`.

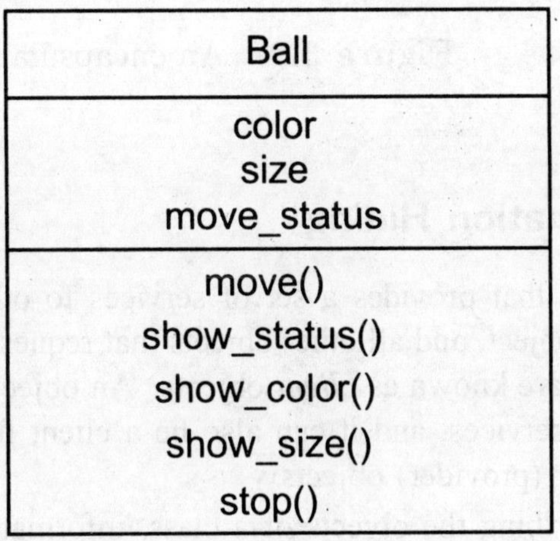


**Figure 3.8** Class `Ball`.

### 3.4.1 Encapsulation

The encapsulation principle suggests that an object be described as the integration of attributes and behavior in a single unit. There is an imaginary wall surrounding the object to protect it from another object. This is considered an encapsulation protection mechanism. To protect the features of an object, an access mode is specified for every feature.

When access to some of the attributes and some operations is not allowed, the access mode of the feature is specified to be *private*; otherwise, the access mode is *public*. If an operation of an object is public, it is accessible from other objects. Figure 3.9 illustrates the notion of an object as an encapsulation unit.

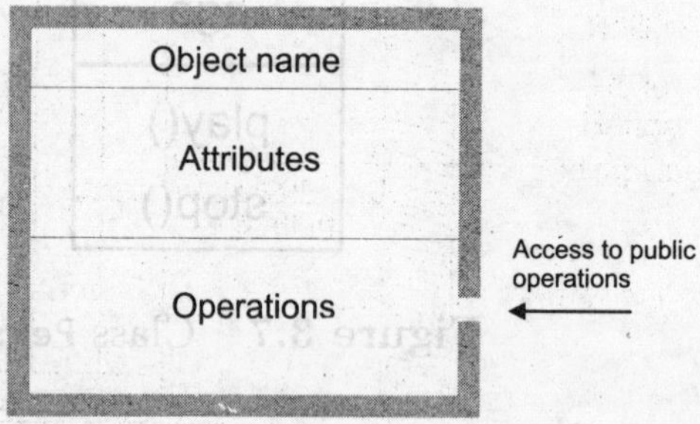


**Figure 3.9** An encapsulation unit.

### 3.4.2 Information Hiding

An object that provides a set of services to other objects is known as a *provider* object, and all other objects that request these services by sending messages are known as *client* objects. An object can be a service provider for some services, and it can also be a client for services that it requests from other (provider) objects.

In describing the objects of a class, information hiding is the principle of only showing what services the object provides and hiding all implementation details. In this manner, an *object presents two views*:

1. The external view of the object can be shown to all client objects. This view consists of the list of services (or operations) that other objects can invoke. The list of services can be used as a service contract between the provider object and the client objects.

2. The internal view presents the implementation details of the data and the operations of the object. This information is hidden from other objects.

These two views of an object are described at two different levels of abstraction. The external view is at a higher level of abstraction.

The external view implies that information about an object is limited to that only necessary for the object's features to be invoked by another object. The rest of the knowledge about the object is not revealed. As mentioned earlier, this principle is called *information hiding* or data hiding.

NOTE *In the class definition, the external view of the objects should be kept separate from the internal view. The internal view of properties and operations of an object are hidden from other objects. The object presents its external view to other objects and shows what features (operations and attributes) are accessible.*

The public features of an object are accessible to other objects, but the implementation details of these features are kept hidden. In general, only the headers, that is, the specification, of the operations are known. Similarly, only the public attributes are the ones accessible from other objects.

The models of objects are represented using the Unified Modeling Language (UML), the standard graphical notation introduced previously in this chapter. A basic part of this notation is used in this book to describe object-oriented models. Because every object belongs to a class, the complete description of the objects is included in the corresponding class definitions.

## 3.5 RESPONSIBILITIES OF OBJECTS

An object-oriented application is driven by a set of collaborating objects, each one of which has some responsibility to fulfill. The application delegates to each object its own share of the overall task to be accomplished. Typically, the application starts by delegating the overall task to one or more objects. This means that the program starts by requesting some service(s) from these objects.

These objects carry out their responsibilities, and can delegate part of their work to other objects. The chain of delegations continues until there is no more work needed to delegate.

This approach of object-oriented design is called the responsibility-driven design because the responsibilities of the objects are identified first in the software development process. The principle of information hiding supports this design approach. Every object advertises the task it can carry out but without revealing how it will implement the task.

## 3.6 SUMMARY

In modeling object-oriented applications, one of the first tasks is to identify the objects and collections of similar objects in the problem domain. An object has properties and behaviors. The class is a definition of objects with the same characteristics.

A model is an abstract representation of a real system. Modeling is the process of constructing representations of objects and defining the common characteristics into classes. Modeling involves what objects and relevant characteristics of these objects are to be included in the model.

Objects collaborate by sending messages to each other. A message is request to to carry out a certain operation by an object. Information hiding emphasizes the separation of the list of operations that an object offers to other objects from the implementation details that are hidden to other objects.

## 3.7 KEY TERMS

| | | |
|---|---|---|
| models | abstraction | objects |
| collections | real-world entities | object state |
| object behavior | messages | attributes |
| operations | methods | functions |
| UML diagram | interactions | method invocation |
| classes | encapsulation | information hiding |
| private | public | responsibilities |
| delegations | collaboration | |

## 3.8 EXERCISES

1. Explain and give examples of the difference between classes and objects. Why is the object considered a dynamic concept? Why is the class considered a static concept? Explain.
2. Explain why the UML class and object diagrams are very similar. What do these diagrams actually describe about an object and about a class? Explain.
3. Explain and give examples of object behavior. Is object interaction the same as object behavior? Explain and give examples. What UML diagram describes this? If an object-oriented application has only one object, is there any object interaction? Explain.
4. What are the differences between encapsulation and information hiding? How are these two concepts related? Explain.
5. From the principle of information hiding, why are the two views of an object at different levels of abstraction? Explain. How useful can this principle be in software development?
6. Consider an automobile rental office. A customer can rent an automobile for a number of days and with a finite number of miles (or kilometers). Identify the type and number of objects involved. For every type of object, list the properties and operations. Draw the class and object diagrams for this problem. As a starting point, use class `Automobile` described in this chapter.
7. For the automobile rental office, describe the object interactions necessary. Draw the corresponding collaboration diagrams.
8. Consider a movie rental shop. Identify the various objects. How many objects of each type are there? List the properties and the necessary operations of the objects. Draw the corresponding UML diagrams for this problem.
9. For the two problems described in Exercises 7 and 8, list the private and public characteristics (properties and operations) for every type of object. Why do you need to make this distinction? Explain.

# 4 OBJECT-ORIENTED PROGRAMS

## 4.1 INTRODUCTION

Object-oriented design and programming enhances the decomposition of a problem. Classes are the principal decomposition units. Therefore, a class is a module, or a decomposition unit. A class is also a type for object reference variables.

The first part of this chapter describes the basic structure of a class. The emphasis is on the static view of a program. The general structure of a function is also discussed. The second part of this chapter presents an introduction to data descriptions and construction of simple object-oriented programs.

## 4.2 OBJECT-ORIENTED PROGRAMS

An object-oriented program is an implementation of all the collections of objects that were modeled in the analysis and design phase of the software development process. Figure 4.1 illustrates part of the development process: the grouping of similar real-world objects into collections of objects, the modeling of these collections, and the software implementation of the corresponding classes. When the program executes, objects of these classes are created and made to interact among themselves.

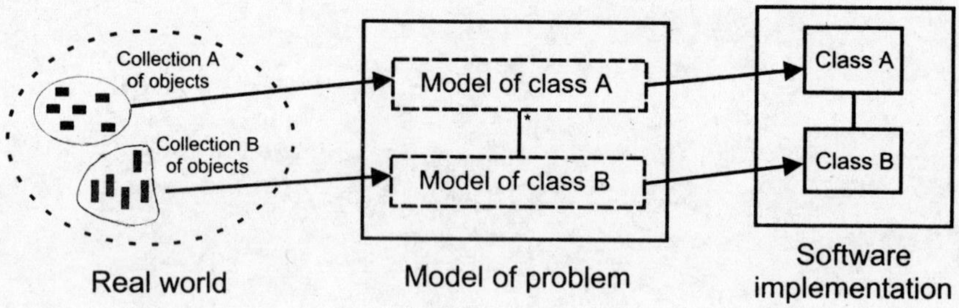


**Figure 4.1** Collections of real-world objects.

There are two views for describing an object-oriented program:

- The static view describes the structure of the program. Programs are composed of one or more modules called *classes*.
- The dynamic view describes the behavior of the program while it executes. This behavior consists of the set of *objects*, each one exhibiting individual behavior and its interaction with other objects.

## 4.3 MODULES

A problem is often too complex to deal with as a single unit. A general approach is to divide the problem into smaller problems that are easier to solve. The partitioning of a problem into smaller parts is known as *decomposition*. These small parts are called modules, which are easier to manage.

Program design usually emphasizes modular structuring, also called modular decomposition. A problem is divided into smaller problems (or subproblems), and a solution is designed for each subproblem. Therefore, the solution to a problem consists of several smaller solutions corresponding to each of the subproblems. This approach is called modular design.

Object-oriented design enhances modular design by providing classes as the most important decomposition (modular) unit. As an example, Figure 4.2 shows a program that consists of four modules.

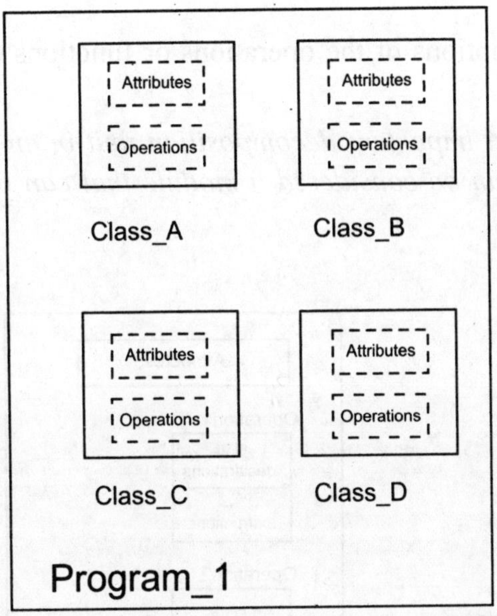


**Figure 4.2** General structure of program.

## 4.4 CLASSES AS MODULES

In object-oriented modeling and programming, there are various levels of modularity. Modules can be packages or classes. A *package* is a grouping of classes, and a class consists of one or more operations or functions.

An object-oriented program contains one or more classes, and each class defines a collection of similar objects. Therefore, from the static view, a program is an assembly of classes. For example, Figure 4.2 shows a program with four classes. The four classes are *Class_A*, *Class_B*, *Class_C*, and *Class_D*. This just illustrates that any object-oriented program is decomposed into one or more classes.

As explained before, a class defines the structure and the behavior of the objects in that class. The software definition of a class consists of:

- Descriptions of the data, which are the attribute declarations of the class
- Descriptions of the operations or functions of the class

NOTE

*The most important decomposition unit in an application is the class, which can be considered a module that can be reused in another application.*

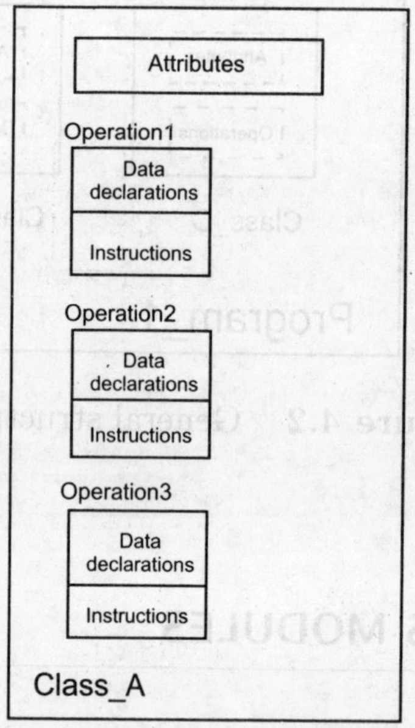


**Figure 4.3** General structure of a class named `Class_A`.

Data descriptions represent the declarations of the attributes for the objects of the class. Descriptions of the operations represent the behavior for the objects of the class. Figure 4.3 illustrates the structure of a class named `Class_A`. This class consists of the declarations of the attributes and the definitions of three operations: *Operation1*, *Operation2*, and *Operation3*. Each of these operations consists of its local data declarations and its instructions.

An operation, also known as a function or method, is the smallest modular unit; it carries out a single task. Functions are not standalone units because every function belongs to a class; a function is an internal decomposition unit.

## 4.5 DATA DEFINITIONS

Data definitions appear in the classes as attribute declarations. Similar data definitions appear within the functions (or methods); these are known as *local* data declarations. There are two general types of data definitions:

- Declarations of simple variables
- Declarations of object variables, also known as object references

Simple variables are those of simple or primitive types; these store small and simple data items like integer values, floating-point values, and others. Object variables (or object references) are variables that can store the reference to objects when they are created. The only way to manipulate objects is by using their references, because in Java and KJP objects do not have an identifier directly associated with them.

## 4.6 ALGORITHMS

The basic definition of an algorithm is a detailed and precise description of the sequence of steps for the behavioral aspect of a problem solution. This algorithm is normally broken down into smaller tasks, each carried out by an object and defined in the classes. In the design phase of software development, the detailed design of the classes includes descriptions of these smaller algorithms.

In an object-oriented program, every object carries out some particular task. The collaboration of all the objects in a program will accomplish the complete solution to the problem. As mentioned in previous chapters, the overall design involves detailed design of the classes in the problem. The design of a class describes the data and the tasks that the objects of the class will carry out.

Because the class is the main decomposition unit in a program, the overall algorithm for a problem has been decomposed into smaller algorithms, each described in the design of the class. The algorithm of a class is further decomposed into each operation in the class. This is the second level of decomposition for algorithms.

In object-oriented design and programming, the algorithms are described at the level of the operation. At this level, traditional structured design and programming techniques can be applied.

NOTE *An algorithm is normally described in an informal notation, such as pseudo-code, a flowchart, or English.*

## 4.7 SOFTWARE IMPLEMENTATION

The translation of a complete detailed design (algorithm and data descriptions) into a suitable programming language is called implementation. Pseudo-code is an intermediate notation between the modeling diagrams and the implementation programming language. In this book, KJP is used for writing the design and implementation, the translation to the Java programming language is carried out automatically by the KJP translator.

### 4.7.1 KJP and Java

Programming languages, including Java and KJP, have well-defined syntax and semantic rules. The syntax is defined by a set of grammar rules and a vocabulary (a set of words). The legal sentences are constructed using words in the form of statements. The set of words is divided into two groups:

1. Reserved words have a predefined purpose in the language and are used in most statements with precise meaning, for example, `class`, `inherits`, `variables`, `while`, `if`, and others.

2. Identifiers are names for variables, constants, functions, and classes that the programmer chooses, for example, *salary*, *age*, and *employee_name*.

The attributes in a class are defined as variable declarations. The data definitions inside a function are written as local variable declarations. Object-oriented programs include the following kinds of statements:

- Class definitions
- Declaration of simple variables
- Declaration of object references
- Definition of functions
- Creation of objects
- Manipulation of the objects created by calling (or invoking) the functions that belong to these objects

NOTE

*In Java and KJP, the functions or operations are known as methods. Objects do not directly have names, instead, object reference variables are used to reference objects when they are created.*

### 4.7.2 Definition of Classes

A class definition in KJP includes several sections. These must be written in the following order:

1. The *description* statement encloses a textual description of the purpose of the class, author, date, and any other relevant information. This section ends with a star-slash (*/).
2. The *class* statement defines the name of the class and other information related to the class.
3. The *private* section includes declarations of the private attributes of the class and definitions of the private operations.
4. The *public* section includes definitions of the public operations of the class.

5. The *endclass* statement ends the class definition.

The general syntactic definition of a class is:

```
description

class ⟨ class_name ⟩ is
   private
      constants
         . . .
      variables
         . . .
      objects
         . . .
   public
         . . .
endclass ⟨ class_name ⟩
```

## 4.8 DESCRIBING DATA

Data consists of one or more data items. For every computation, there is one or more associated data items (or entities) that are to be manipulated or transformed by the computations (computer operations). The input data is the set of data items that are transformed in order to produce the desired results.

Data descriptions are necessary together with algorithm descriptions. The algorithm is decomposed into the operations that manipulate the data and produce the results for the problem. For every data item, its description is given by:

- The data item type
- A unique name to identify the data item

- An optional initial value

The name of a data item is an identifier and is given by the programmer; it must be different from any keyword in KJP (or in Java). The type defines:

- The set of possible values that the data item may have
- The set of possible operations that can be applied to the data item

### 4.8.1 Names of Data Items

Text symbols are used in all algorithm descriptions and in the source program. The special symbols that indicate essential parts of an algorithm are called *keywords*. These are reserved words and cannot be used for any other purpose. The other symbols used in an algorithm are the ones for identifying the data items and are called *identifiers*. The identifiers are defined by the programmer.

A unique name or label is assigned to every data item; this name is an identifier. The problem for calculating the area of a triangle used five data items, *x, y, z, s*, and *area*.

The data items usually change their values when they are manipulated by the various operations. For example, the following sequence of instructions first gets the value of *x* then adds the value *x* to *y*:

```
read x          // read value of x from keyboard
add x to y
```

The data items named *x* and *y* are called *variables* because their values change when operations are applied on them. Those data items that do not change their values are called *constants*, for example, *Max_period*, *PI*, and so on. These data items are given an initial value that will never change.

When a program executes, all the data items used by the various operations are stored in memory, each data item occupying a different memory location. The names of these data items represent symbolic memory locations.

### 4.8.2 Data Types

There are two broad groups of data types:

- Elementary (or primitive) data types
- Classes

Elementary types are classified into the three following categories:

- Numeric
- Text
- Boolean

The numeric types are further divided into three types, *integer*, *float*, and *double*. The noninteger types are also known as fractional, which means that the numerical values have a fractional part.

Values of *integer* type are those that are countable to a finite value, for example, age, number of automobiles, number of pages in a book, and so on. Values of type *float* have a decimal point; for example, cost of an item, the height of a building, current temperature in a room, a time interval (period). These values cannot be expressed as integers. Values of type *double* provide more precision than type *float*, for example, the value of the total assets of a corporation.

Text data items are of two basic types: *character* and type *string*. Data items of type *string* consist of a sequence of characters. The values for these two types of data items are textual values.

A third type of variables is the one in which the values of the variables can take a truth-value (true or false); these variables are of type *boolean*.

Classes are more complex types that appear as types of object variables in all object-oriented programs. Data entities declared (and created) with classes are called *objects*.

### 4.8.3 Data Declarations

The data descriptions are the data *declarations*. Each data description includes the name of every variable or constant with its type. The initial values, if any, for the data items are also included in the data declaration. There are two general categories of variables:

- Elementary
- Object variables (references)

NOTE *Object-oriented programming is mainly about defining classes as types for object variables (references), and then declaring and creating objects of these classes. The type of an object reference is a class.*

#### 4.8.3.1 Variables of Elementary Types

In KJP, the declaration of variables of elementary types has the following basic syntactic structure:

⟨ *elementary type* ⟩ ⟨ variable_name ⟩

The following are examples of data declarations of elementary variables of type *integer*, *float*, and *boolean*:

```
variables
    integer count
    real salary
    boolean active
```

#### 4.8.3.2 Object References

As mentioned previously, an object reference is a variable that can refer to (point to) an object. The KJP statement for declaration of object references has the following structure:

**object** ⟨ *object_ref_name* ⟩ **of class** ⟨ *class_name* ⟩

For example, consider a program that includes two class definitions, Employee and Ball. The declarations of an object reference called *emp_obj* of class Employee, and an object reference *ball1* of class Ball are:

```
objects
     object emp_obj of class Employee
     object ball1 of class Ball
```

### 4.8.4 Scope and Persistence

When identifying data items in software development, there are two important concepts to consider:

- The *scope* of a data item is that portion of a program in which statements can reference that data item
- The *persistence* of a data item is the interval of time that the data item exists—the lifetime of the data item

## 4.9 DEFINITION OF FUNCTIONS

A program is normally decomposed into classes, and the classes consist of data declarations and definitions of functions (or methods).

Functions are the internal decomposition units. A function represents a small task in the overall solution. Figure 4.4 illustrates the general structure of a function. The body of a function consists of two basic parts:

- The data declarations
- The instructions that manipulate the data

The data declared within a function is known only to that function—the scope of the data is *local* to the function. Every function has its own data declaration and instructions that manipulate the data. The data in a

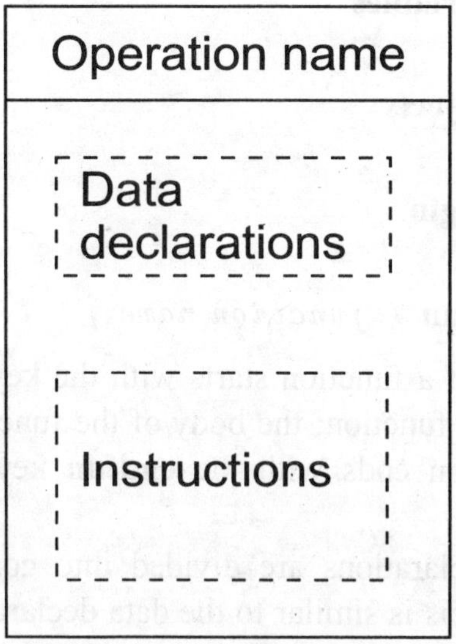


**Figure 4.4** General structure of a function.

function only exists during execution of the function; their persistence is limited to the lifetime of the function.

The purpose of the function is described in the paragraph that starts with the keyword **description** and ends with a star-slash (*/). The paragraph contains mainly text that explains the purpose of the function. Other comments can be included at any point in the function to clarify and/or document the algorithm. Line comments start with a double forward slash (//) and end with the line.

Every function has a name, which must be meaningful and should be the name of the task carried out by the function. The name of the function is declared in the *function* statement. This name is used when the function is called or invoked by some other function. The following KJP code defines the basic structure of a function. As before, the keywords are in boldface.

```
description
   . . .
function ⟨ function_name ⟩ is
constants
   . . .
```

**variables**

. . .

**objects**

. . .

**begin**

. . .

**endfun** ⟨ *function_name* ⟩

The header of a function starts with the keyword **function** followed by the name of the function; the body of the function starts with the keyword **is**. The function ends with the **endfun** keyword and the name of the function.

The data declarations are divided into constant, variable, and object declarations. This is similar to the data declarations in the class. Constant, variable, and object declarations are optional. The instructions in the body of the function appear between the keywords **begin** and **endfun**.

One of the classes in every program must include a function called *main*. This function starts and terminates the execution of the entire program; it is the control function of the program.

In very simple and small programs that have only one class, the algorithm for the problem is implemented in function *main*—all the instructions for the solution of the problem are located in this function.

## 4.10 CREATING OBJECTS

After declaring object references, the corresponding objects can be created. The KJP statement to create objects has the following structure:

**create** ⟨ *object_ref_name* ⟩ **of class** ⟨ *class_name* ⟩

For example, assume that the program described previously is to create an object for each of the two class definitions, `Employee` and `Ball`. The declarations of the object reference called *emp_obj* of class `Employee`, and the object reference *ball1* of class `Ball` were previously provided. The KJP statements for creating the two objects are:

```
create emp_obj of class Employee
create ball1 of class Ball
```

## 4.11 WRITING OBJECT-ORIENTED PROGRAMS

Object interaction was explained in Chapter 2. When one object sends a message to another object, the first object invokes or calls a function of the second object. In the class definition of the second object, this function must have been defined as *public*; otherwise, the function is not accessible to other objects.

Function *main* is special; execution of the entire application starts in this function, and terminates here. In a typical program (or application), function *main* carries out the following general sequence of tasks:

1. Declares constants, simple variables, and object variables, as necessary
2. Creates one or more objects of the previously defined classes
3. Invokes one or more methods of the various objects. This delegates the tasks and subtasks to the objects for carrying the complete solution of the application.

### 4.11.1 A Simple Object-Oriented Program

Consider a definition of class `Ball`, similar to the one presented in Chapter 3. The attributes of the class are:

- *size* of type *real*; represents the diameter of the object in inches
- *color* of type *character* (not string); the possible values are 'B' for blue, 'R' for red, 'Y' for yellow, 'W' for white, and 'O' for orange
- *move_status* of type *character*; represents the state of the ball object. 'M' is the value of this attribute if the ball is moving. 'S' is the value of this attribute if the ball object is not moving and/or has been stopped.

The methods (functions) of this class are:

- *move*, which starts movement of the ball object
- *stop*, which stops the movement of the ball object
- *show_status*, which displays the values of the attributes *color* and *move_status*
- *get_color*, which reads the value of attribute *color* from the console
- *get_size*, which reads the value of attribute *size* from the console

The program has two classes: `Ball` and `Mball`. The second class (`Mball`) is the class with function *main*. This function is defined to carry out the following sequence of activities:

1. Declare two object variables, *obj_1* and *obj_2*, of class `Ball`.
2. Create the two objects.
3. Invoke functions *get_color* and *get_size* for each object.
4. Invoke function *show_status* for each object.
5. Invoke functions *move* and then *show_status* for each object.
6. Terminate execution of the entire program.

ON THE CD

*The complete definition of class* `Ball` *in KJP follows and is stored in the file* `Ball.kpl` *on the CD-ROM that accompanies this book.*

```
description
  This is a simple class. The attributes are color,
  size, and move_status. Nov 2002, J Garrido    */
class Ball is
  private
  // attributes
  variables
      character color
      character move_status
```

```
    real size
public
// public methods
description
  This method reads the value of attribute color
  from the console  */
function get_color is
begin
  display "type single-character color value "
  read color
endfun get_color
description
  This method reads the value of attribute color
  from the console. */
function get_size is
begin
  display "type value of size "
  read size
endfun get_size
description
    This function displays the color, status,
    and size of the object. */
function show_status is
  begin
    display "Color of ball object: ", color
    display "Size of ball object: ", size
    display "Status of ball object: ", move_status
endfun show_status
description
    This function changes the move_status of the
    object.       */
function move is
  begin
    set move_status = 'M'
endfun move
description
    This function changes the move_status of the
```

```
        object      */
      function stop is
        begin
          set move_status = 'S'
      endfun stop
    endclass Ball
```

ON THE CD

*The implementation in KJP of class* Mball *is stored in the file* Mball.kpl. *The two Java classes produced by the KJP translator are stored in the files* Ball.java *and* Mball.java. *The complete definition of class* Mball *follows.*

```
description
   This program illustrates the general structure
   of a KJP program. It creates two objects of
   class Ball, and invokes some of their methods. */
class Mball is
  public
    description
       This function controls the program.     */
    function main is
      objects
         object obj_1 of class Ball
         object obj_2 of class Ball
      begin
         display "Creating object 1"
         create obj_1 of class Ball
         display "Creating object 2"
         create obj_2 of class Ball
         display "Invoking methods of object 1"
         call get_color of obj_1
         call get_size of obj_1
         display "Invoking methods of object 2"
         call get_color of obj_2
         call get_size of obj_2
         // to starting moving the ball objects
         call move of obj_1
```

```
            call move of obj_2
            call show_status of obj_1
            call show_status of obj_2
            // now stop moving the objects
            call stop of obj_1
            call stop of obj_2
            call show_status of obj_1
            call show_status of obj_2
        endfun main
    endclass Mball
```

The details for some of the KJP statements used in this example are explained in Chapters 5 and 6. Appendix A contains detailed explanations on compiling and executing KJP and Java programs with jGRASP. Figure 4.5 shows the main jGRASP screen with class `Mball`.

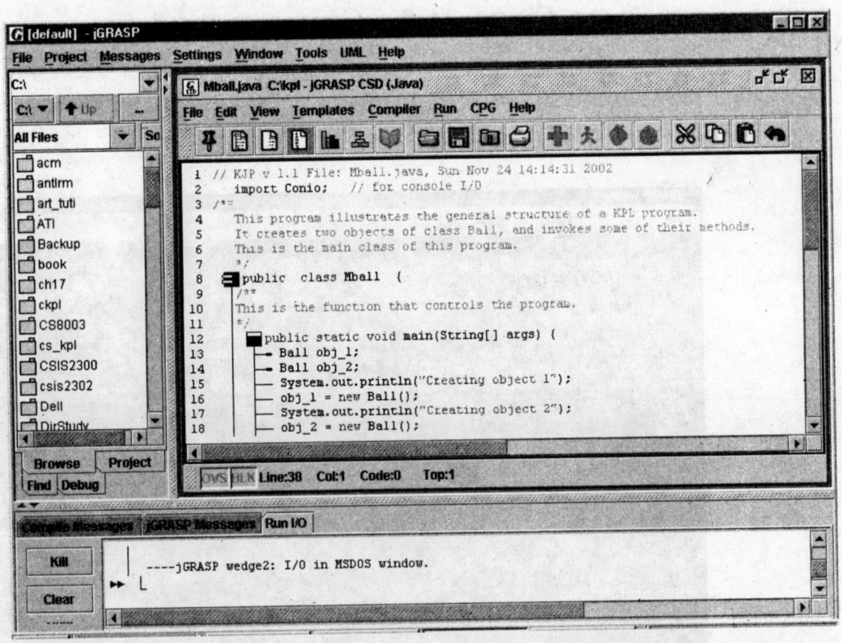

**Figure 4.5** jGRASP with class `Mball` on the main window.

Figures 4.6 and 4.7 show the console input and output produced during execution of the program.

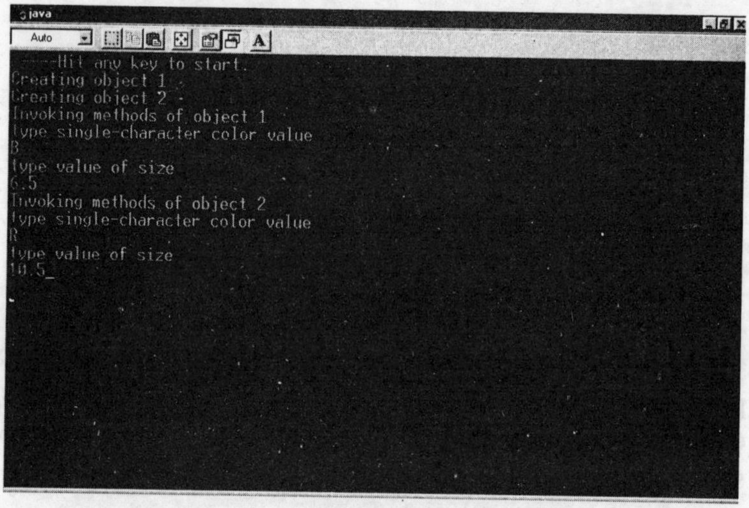


**Figure 4.6** Console input data.

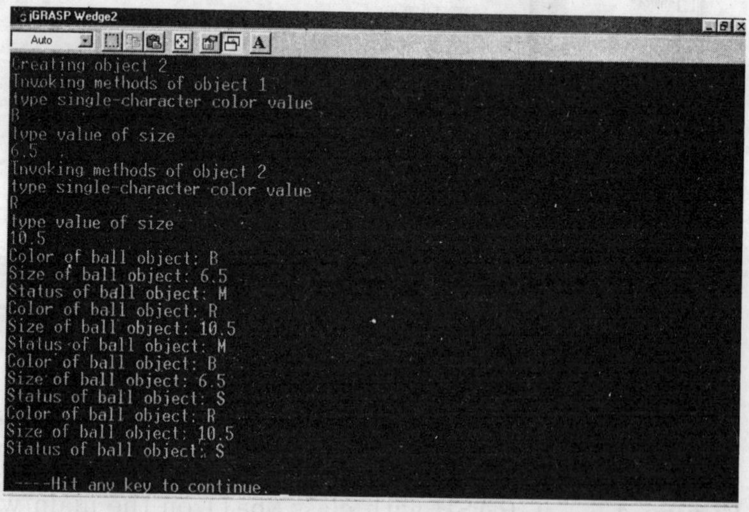


**Figure 4.7** Console output data.

## 4.11.2 A Single-Class Program

This section presents a complete and extremely simple KJP program with only one class and only one function. This is an extreme case of a simple program. No objects are necessary in this program because the entire task is carried out in function *main*.

Because this program does not involve objects, it is not a real object-oriented program. The program consists of a single-class called `Salary1`.

ON THE CD *The KJP code for class* `Salary1` *follows and is stored in the file* `Salary1.kpl`.

```
description
    This program computes the salary increase for
    an employee. If his/her salary is greater than
    $45,000 the salary increase is 4.5%; otherwise,
    the salary increase is 5%.  */
class Salary1 is
  public
  description
      This function computes the salary increase
      and updates the salary of an employee.  */
  function main is
    constants
      real percent1 = 0.045   // percent increase
      real percent2 = 0.05
    variables
      real salary
      real increase
    // body of function starts
    begin
      display "enter salary: "
      read salary
      if salary > 45000 then
         set increase = salary * percent1
      else
         set increase = salary * percent2
```

```
            endif
            add increase to salary
            print "increase: ", increase,
                         " salary: ", salary
        endfun main
    endclass Salary1
```

## 4.12 SUMMARY

The static view of a program describes the program as an assembly of classes. A class is a decomposition unit—a basic modular unit that allows breaking a problem into smaller subproblems.

A class is also a type for object reference variables. It is also a collection of objects with similar characteristics. A class is a reusable unit; it can be reused in other applications.

An algorithm is a complete, precise, detailed description of the method of solution to a problem. Because a problem is broken down into subproblems, the solution is sought for each of the subproblems. In practice, the algorithm for the complete problem is broken down and designed in each class and in each function.

The general structure of a class consists of data definitions and function definitions. A class is decomposed into data definitions and functions. Data declarations exist in the class to define the attributes; data declarations also appear in the functions to define the function's local data. A function includes data definitions and instructions.

Data definitions consist of the declarations of constants, simple variables, and object variables (references). The data declarations require the type and name of the constant, variable, and object reference. After object references are declared, the corresponding objects can be created.

The definition of classes in KJP and other object-oriented programming languages is accomplished by writing the program using the language statements and following a few rules on how to structure the program.

Two complete programs were presented in this chapter. The first program consists of two class definitions (`Ball` and `Mball`). Two objects of class

Ball are created and function *main* sends several messages to each object.

## 4.13 KEY TERMS

| | | |
|---|---|---|
| static view | dynamic view | decomposition |
| modules | units | class reuse |
| package | devices | data declaration |
| variables | constants | simple types |
| algorithms | structured programming | object references |
| class description | local data | initial value |
| data types | scope | persistence |

## 4.14 EXERCISES

1. Explain the reason why a class is an appropriate decomposition unit. What other units are possible to consider?

2. Explain why object-oriented programs need a control function such as *main*.

3. The entire algorithm for a problem is decomposed into classes and functions. Explain this decomposition structure. Why is there a need to decompose a problem into subproblems?

4. KJP programs do not allow public attribute definitions in classes. Explain the reason for this. What are the advantages and disadvantages? *Hint*: review the concepts of encapsulation and information hiding.

5. The dynamic view of a program involves the objects of the problem collaborating to accomplish the overall solution to the problem. Where are these objects created and started? Explain.

6. Consider the first complete program presented in this chapter. Add two more functions to class Ball. Include the corresponding function calls from class Mball. For example, add another attribute *weight*

in class `Ball`. The additional functions would be *get_weight* and *show_weight*.

7. Analyze the second KJP program presented in this chapter, which calculates the salary increase for employees. Follow the same pattern to write another program to compute the grade average per student. The data for each student is student name, grade1, grade2, grade3, and grade4.

8. Restructure the second program, and convert it to an object-oriented program, similar to the first program presented.

9. What are the main limitations of the programs with a single class and a single function? Explain.

# 5 OBJECTS AND METHODS

## 5.1 INTRODUCTION

A function, also known as a method, is the smallest modular unit; it carries out a single subtask in a class. Recall that classes are reusable units, which means that they can be used in another application. Functions are not reusable units because every function belongs to a class. From this point of view, a function is an internal decomposition unit.

A function can receive input data from another function when invoked; the input data passed from another function is called a parameter. The function can also return output data when it completes execution.

In its first part, this chapter describes class and function decomposition. The second part of the chapter discusses the basic mechanisms for data transfer between two functions; several examples are included.

## 5.2 CLASSES

In Chapter 3, the model of an object is described as an *encapsulation* of the attributes and behavior into a single unit. When access to some of the attributes and some operations is not allowed, the access is said to be *private*; otherwise, the access mode is *public*. This is considered an encapsulation protection mechanism.

A class defines the attributes and behavior of the objects in a collection. In other words, every collection of entities is defined by describing the attributes and behavior of these entities. The attributes are defined as data declarations, and the behavior is defined as one or more operations (methods or functions). As an example, Figure 5.1 shows the general structure of a class.

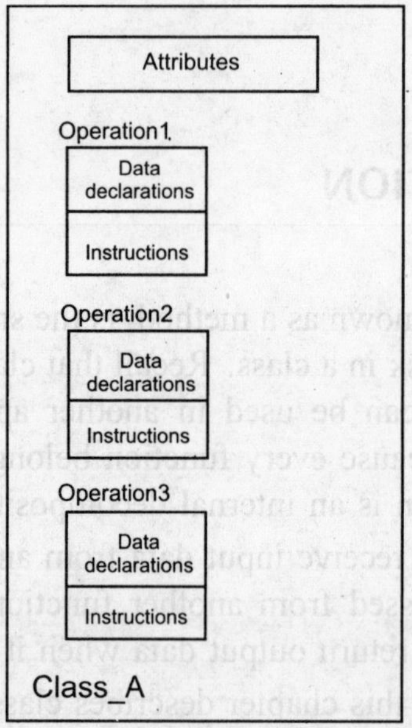


**Figure 5.1** General structure of a class named *Class_A*.

Applying the principle of information hiding, knowledge about an object is limited; only the knowledge necessary for the features of an object to be accessed by another object is made available. The rest of the knowledge about the object is not revealed. The internal details of how the various operations are carried out are not made available to other objects.

If a function of an object is *public*, it is accessible from another object; the implementation details are kept hidden. In general, only the function headers (also known as function specifications) are known to other objects.

The software definition of a class consists of:

- The data declaration of the attributes of the class
- A set of method or function definitions

## 5.3 METHODS

As mentioned in Chapter 4, a program is normally decomposed into classes, and classes are divided into methods or functions. Methods are the smallest decomposition units. A function represents a small subtask in the class. Figure 5.2 illustrates the general structure of a function. This structure consists of:

- The local data declarations
- A sequence of instructions

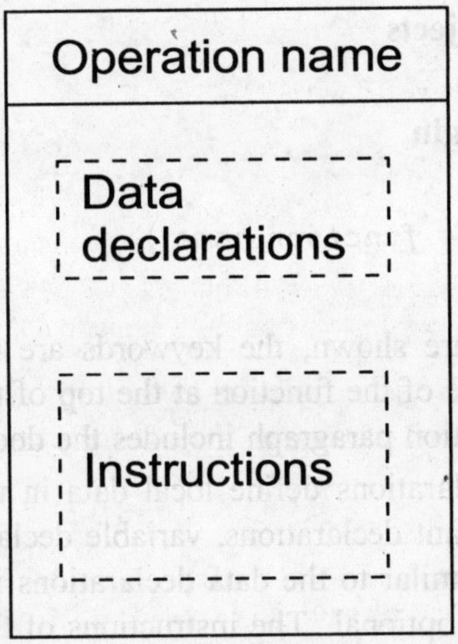


**Figure 5.2** General structure of a function.

The data declared within a function is known only to that function—the scope of the data is *local* to the function. The data in a function only exists during execution of the function; their persistence is limited to the lifetime of the function.

Every function has a name, which must be meaningful and should be the name of the subtask carried out by the function. The name of the function is used when it is called or invoked by some other function. The purpose of the function is described in the description paragraph, which ends with a star-slash (*/). The KJP statement that defines the basic structure of a function is:

```
description
    */
function ⟨ function_name ⟩ is
    constants
        . . .
    variables
        . . .
    objects
        . . .
    begin
        . . .
endfun ⟨ function_name ⟩
```

In the structure shown, the keywords are in boldface. The first line defines the name of the function at the top of the construct. In the second line, the description paragraph includes the documentation of the function.

The data declarations define local data in the function. These are divided into constant declarations, variable declarations, and object declarations. This is similar to the data declarations in the class. The local data declarations are optional. The instructions of the function appear between the keywords **begin** and **endfun**. The following KJP code shows a simple function for displaying two text messages on the screen.

```
description
```

```
    This function displays the initial message for
    the program on the screen. */
function display_message is
  begin
    print "Starting program."
    print "Computing standard deviation of rainfall
                                                 data"
  endfun display_message
```

## 5.4 EXECUTION OF FUNCTIONS

In every function call (or method invocation), the function that calls another function is known as the calling function; the second function is known as the called function. When a function calls or invokes another function, the normal execution flow of control in the first function is interrupted. The flow of control is altered and the second function starts execution. When the called function completes execution, the flow of control is transferred back (returned) to the calling function. This function continues execution from the point after it called the second function.

### 5.4.1 Object Interactions

The calling function and the called function can belong to two different objects, or to the same object. Objects interact with one another by *sending messages*. The object that sends the message is the requestor of a service that can be provided by the receiver object. A message represents a request for service, which is provided by the object receiving the message. The sender object is known as the client of a service and the receiver object as the supplier of the service.

The purpose of sending a message is to request some operation of the receiver object to be carried out; in other words, the request is a call to one of the operations of the supplier object. This is also known as *method invocation*. Objects execute operations in response to messages and the operations carried out are object specific.

For example, an object of class `Person` sends a message to an object of class `Ball`. In this message, some function (operation) of the first object calls function *move* of the second object. A message is always sent to a specific object, and it contains three parts:

- The function (operation) to be invoked or started, which is the service requested; this must be a public function if invoked by another object
- The input data required in order for the operation to start; this data is known as the arguments
- The output data, which is the reply to the message; this is the actual result of the request

To describe the general interaction between two or more objects (the sending of messages between objects), one of the UML diagrams used is the collaboration diagram; see Figure 5.3 as an example. Another UML diagram used to describe object interaction is the sequence diagram.

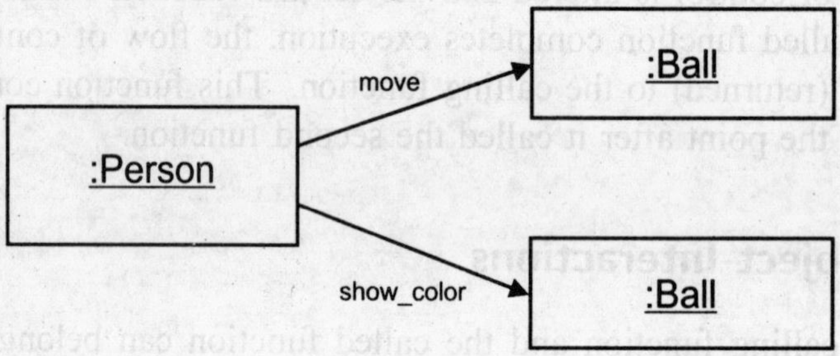


**Figure 5.3** Collaboration diagram with three objects.

### 5.4.2 Categories of Functions

The most obvious categories of functions discussed so far are the private and public functions. Only the public functions of an object can be invoked from another object. The private functions are sometimes called internal functions because they can only be invoked by another function of the same object.

The instructions in a function start execution when the function is called or invoked. After completion, the called function may or may not return a value to the calling function. From the data transfer point of view, there are three general categories of functions:

1. Simple (or void) functions do not return any value when they are invoked. The previous example, function *display_message*, is a simple or void function because it does not return any value to the function that invoked it.
2. Value-returning functions return a single value after completion.
3. Functions with parameters require one or more data items as input values when invoked.

The most general category of functions is one that combines the last two categories just listed—functions that return a value and that have parameters.

Another important criterion for describing categories of functions depends on the purpose of the function. There are two such categories of functions:

- Accessor functions return the value of an attribute of the object without changing the value of any attribute(s) of the object. For example, the following are accessor functions: *get_color*, *get_size*, and *show_status* of class `Ball` in Section 4.11.1.
- Mutator functions change the state of the object in some way by altering the value of one or more attributes in the object. Normally, these functions do not return any value. For example, the following functions are mutator functions: *move* and *stop* of class `Ball` in Section 4.11.1.

It is good programming practice to define the functions in a class as being either accessor or mutator.

### 5.4.3 Invoking a Simple Function

A simple (also called void) function does not return a value to the calling function. The simplest function of this kind is function *display_message*, discussed previously. There is no data transfer to or from the function. The KJP statement to call or invoke a void function that is referenced by an object reference is:

**call** ⟨ *function_name* ⟩ **of** ⟨ *object_ref* ⟩

For example, suppose the function *display_message* that belongs to an object referenced by *myobj* is invoked from function *main*, the call statement is:

**call** `display_message` **of** `myobj`

Figure 5.4 shows the calling mechanism. In the figure, the calling function is *main*, and the called function is *display_message*. After completing its task, the called function returns the flow of control to the calling function.

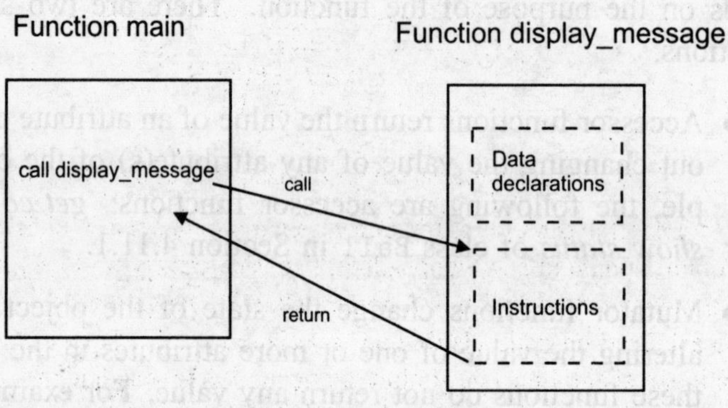


**Figure 5.4** Calling a function.

## 5.5 DATA TRANSFER WITH FUNCTIONS

A more complex mechanism in calling a function involves data transfer between the calling and the called function. This data transfer is possible in two directions, from the calling function to the called function and from the called function to the calling function. The simplest data transfer involves value-returning functions in which the direction of the data transfer is from the called function to the calling function.

## 5.5.1 Value-Returning Functions

In value-returning functions, some value is calculated or assigned to a variable that is returned to the calling function. Note that the return value is a single value; no more than one value can be returned.

### 5.5.1.1 Defining Value-Returning Functions

A type is defined in the called function, which is the type of the return value. This return value is actually the result produced by the called function. After the called function completes, control is returned with a single value to the calling function. The general structure of a value-returning function in KJP is:

```
description
    . . .
  */
function ⟨ function_name ⟩ of type ⟨ return_type ⟩ is
    . . .
  return ⟨ return_value ⟩
endfun ⟨ function_name ⟩
```

The value in the return statement can be any valid expression, following the **return** keyword. The expression can include constants, variables, object references, or a combination of these.

For example, suppose a function with name *get_val* displays a message on the console asking for an *integer* value; this value is read from the console and is returned to the calling function. In the header of the function, the type of the value returned is indicated as *integer*. The KJP code for this function definition is:

```
description
   This function asks the user for an integer
   value, then this value is returned. */
      function get_val of type integer is
      variables
         integer local_var
      begin
         display "Please enter an integer value: "
         read local_var        // read value from console
         return local_var      // return value read
      endfun get_val
```

NOTE *One difference of the value-returning function with a simple (or void) function is that the type of the value returned is indicated in the function statement. Another difference is that a return statement is necessary with the value to return.*

#### 5.5.1.2 Invoking Value-Returning Functions

The calling function can call a value-returning function, and the value returned can be used in one of the following ways:

- A simple assignment statement
- An assignment with an arithmetic expression

In a simple assignment, the value returned by the called function is used by the calling function by assigning this returned value to another variable. For example, suppose function *main* calls function *get_val* of an object referenced by *myobj*. Suppose then that function *main* assigns the value returned to variable *y*. The KJP code statement for this call is:

```
set y = call get_val of myobj
```

This *call* statement is included in an assignment statement. When the call is executed, the sequence of activities that are carried out is:

1. Function *main* calls function *get_val* in object referenced by *myobj*.

2. Function *get_val* executes when called and returns the value of variable *local_var*.

3. Function *main* receives the value returned from function *get_val*.

4. Function *main* assigns this value to variable *y*.

Using the value returned in an assignment with an arithmetic expression is straightforward after calling the function. For example, after calling function *get_val* of the object referenced by *myobj*, the value returned is assigned to variable *y*. This variable is then used in an arithmetic expression that multiplies *y* by variable *x* and adds 3. The value that results from evaluating this expression is assigned to variable *zz*. This assignment statement is:

```
set zz = x * y + 3
```

## 5.5.2 Functions with Parameters

Most useful functions can receive data values when called from another function. These data values are treated as input values by the called function. The data definitions for these input values are called parameter declarations and are similar to local data declarations. Local data has a local scope and the persistence is for the duration of the function execution. If the called function returns a value, it can be of any legal type but not of type `void`.

### 5.5.2.1 Calling Functions with Parameters

The calling function supplies the data values to send to the called function. These values are known as *arguments* and can be actual values (constants) or names of data items. When there are two or more argument values in the function call, the argument list consists of the data items separated by commas. The KJP statement for a function call with arguments is:

**call** ⟨ *function_name* ⟩ **of** ⟨ *object_ref* ⟩
  **using** ⟨ *argument_list* ⟩

For example, consider a call to function *min_1* that belongs to an object referenced by *obj_a*. The function calculates and prints the minimum value of the two given arguments *x* and *y*. This call statement in KJP is:

```
call min_1 of obj_a using x, y
```

*The difference with the previous function call is that the name of the object reference is followed by the keyword* **using** *and this is followed by the list of arguments, which are values or names of the data items.*

#### 5.5.2.2 Defining Functions with Parameters

The definition of the called function includes the declaration of the data items defined as parameters. For every parameter, the function declares a type and a name. The general structure of a function with parameter definition is:

```
description
  . . .
  */
function ⟨ function_name ⟩
      parameters ⟨ parameter_list ⟩ is
  . . .
endfun ⟨ function_name ⟩
```

The following example uses this syntax structure with a function named *min_1*. The complete definition of function *min_1* in KJP is:

```
description
  This function calculates the minimum value of
   parameters a and b, it then prints the result
   on the screen.
  */
function min_1 parameters real a, real b is
```

```
variables
  real min                  // local variable
begin
  if a < b then
    set min = a
  else
    set min = b
  endif
  display "Minimum value is: ", min
  return
endfun min_1
```

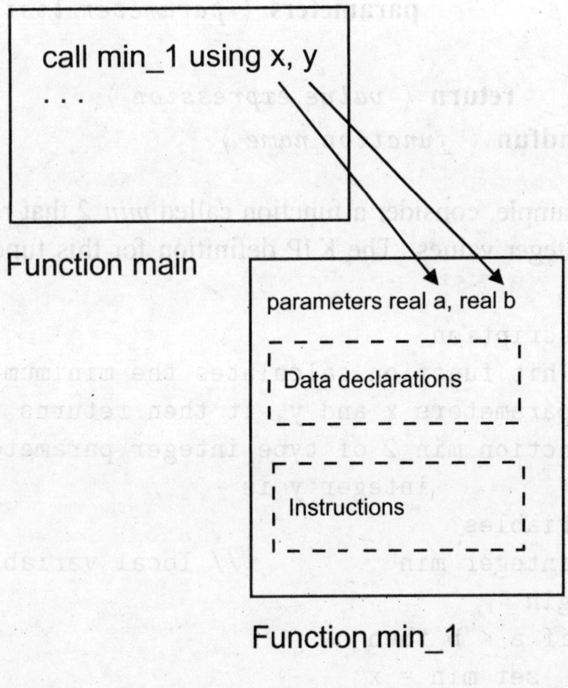


**Figure 5.5** Transferring arguments in a function call.

The definition of function *min_1* declares the parameters *a* and *b*. These parameters are used as placeholders for the corresponding argument values transferred from the calling function. Figure 5.5 illustrates the calling of function *min_1* with the transfer of argument values from the calling function to the called function.

In the call to function *min_1* shown in Figure 5.5, the value of argument *x* is assigned to parameter *a*, and the value of argument *y* is assigned to parameter *b*. The arguments and the parameters must correspond in type and meaning, so the order of arguments in the argument list depends on the parameter list definition. The general structure of a value-returning function with parameter definition is:

**description**
    . . .
    */
**function** ⟨ *function_name* ⟩ **of type** ⟨ *return_type* ⟩
        **parameters** ⟨ *parameter_list* ⟩ **is**
    . . .
    **return** ⟨ *value_expression* ⟩
**endfun** ⟨ *function_name* ⟩

For example, consider a function called *min_2* that returns the minimum of two integer values. The KJP definition for this function is:

```
description
  This function calculates the minimum value of
  parameters x and y, it then returns this value. */
function min_2 of type integer parameters integer x,
           integer y is
variables
  integer min            // local variable
begin
  if a < b then
    set min = x
  else
    set min = y
  endif
  return min
endfun min_2
```

The call to function *min_2* should be in an assignment statement, for example, to call *min_2* with two constant arguments, *a* and *b*, and assign the return value to variable *y*:

```
set y = call min_2 of obj_a using a, b
```

## 5.6 INITIALIZER FUNCTIONS

A class definition normally includes one or more initializer functions, also known as *constructors*. These constitute a special group of functions that are called when creating objects of the enclosing class. The main purpose of an initializer function is to set the object created to an appropriate (initial) state. It carries this out by assigning initial values to the attributes of the object.

The following example includes the declaration of two attributes, *age* and *obj_name* of a class named `Person`.

```
class Person is
  private
  variables            // variable data declarations
      integer age
      string obj_name
```

**NOTE:** *If no initializer function is defined in the class, the default values set by the compiler are used for all the attributes.*

If no initializer function is included in the class definition, the default values are set by the Java compiler (zero and empty) for the two attributes.

It is good programming practice to define at least a default initializer function. For example, in class `Person` the default values for the two attributes are set to 21 for *age* and "`None`" for *obj_name*. This function is defined as:

```
description
  This is the default initializer method.
  */
function initializer is
  begin
    set age = 21

    set obj_name = "None"
endfun initializer
```

Recall that the general structure of the statement to create an object is:

**create** ⟨ *object_ref_name* ⟩ **of class** ⟨ *class_name* ⟩

This statement implicitly uses the default initializer function in the class. A complete initializer function sets the value of all the attributes to the values given when called. These values are given as arguments in the statement that creates the object. The general statement to create an object with given values for the attributes is:

**create** ⟨ *object_ref_name* ⟩ **of class** ⟨ *class_name* ⟩
  **using** ⟨ *argument_list* ⟩

A second initializer function is included in class `Person` to set given initial values to the attributes of the object when created. For example, suppose there is an object reference *person_obj* of class `Person` declared, to create an object referenced by *person_obj* with initial value of 32 for *age* and `"J. K. Hunt"` for the *obj_name*:

```
create person_obj of class Person
                        using 32, "J. K. Hunt"
```

The definition of this complete initializer function in class `Person` includes parameter definitions for each attribute:

```
description
  This is a complete initializer, it sets the
  attributes to the values given when an object
  is created.
  */
function initializer parameters integer iage,
         string iname is
begin
  set age = iage
  set obj_name = iname
endfun initializer
```

*The definition of two or more functions with the same name is known as* overloading. *This facility of the programming language allows any function in a class to be overloaded. In other words, it is a redefinition of a function with another function with the same name, but with a different number of and types of parameters.*

It is very useful in a class to define more than one initializer function. This way, there is more than one way to initialize an object of the class. When a class defines two initializer functions, the compiler differentiates them by the number of and the type of parameters.

## 5.7 A COMPLETE PROGRAM

This section presents the complete definition of class `Person`. This class includes two initializer functions (also called constructors). Two objects are created from function *main*, one created with the default initializer function, and the other created with the complete initializer function. The KJP code for class `Person` is as follows:

```
description
  This is the complete definition of class Person.
  The attributes are age and name.
  */
```

```
class Person is
  private
  // attributes
  variables              // variable data declarations
      integer age
      string obj_name
  // no private methods in this class
  public
  description
    This is the default initializer method.
    */
  function initializer is
    begin
      set age = 21
      set obj_name = "None"
  endfun initializer
  //
  description
    This is a complete initializer function, it
    sets the attributes to the values given on
    object creation.
    */
  function initializer parameters integer iage,
                              string iname is
  begin
    set age = iage
    set obj_name = iname
  endfun initializer
  //
  description
      This accessor function returns the name of
      the object.
      */
  function get_name of type string is
    begin
      return obj_name
  endfun get_name
```

```
//
description
    This mutator function changes the name of
    the object to the name in variable new_name
    This function has type void.
    */
function change_name parameters
                            string new_name is
  begin
    set obj_name = new_name
endfun change_name
//
description
   This accessor function returns the age of
   the Person object.   */
function get_age of type integer is
  begin
   return age
endfun get_age
//
description
   This mutator function increases the age of
   the person object when called.
   */
function increase_age is
  begin
   increment age
endfun increase_age
endclass Person
```

ON THE CD *The complete KJP implementation of class* Person *is stored in the file* Person.kpl.

The instructions in function *main* start and control the execution of the entire program. The following KJP code (in file Mperson.kpl) implements class Mperson that contains function *main* for the creation and manipulation of two objects of class Person.

```
      description
         This is the main class in the program. It
         creates objects of class Person and then
         manipulates these objects.  */
      class Mperson is
        public
        description
          This is the control function.  */
        function main is
         variables               // data declarations
           integer lage
           string lname
         objects
           object person_a of class Person
           object person_b of class Person
         begin
           display
               "Creating two objects of class Person"
           create person_a of class Person
           create person_b of class Person using 37,
                                        "James Bond"
           call change_name of person_a using
                                        "Agent 008"
           set lname = call get_name of person_a
           set lage = call get_age of person_a
           display "First object: ", lname,
                                     " age: ", lage
           set lname = call get_name of person_b
           set lage = call get_age of person_b
           display "Second object: ", lname,
                                     " age: ", lage
           call change_name of person_a using
                                        "Agent 009"
           set lage = call get_age of person_a
           set lname = call get_name of person_a
           display "First object: ", lname,
                                     " age: ", lage
```

```
  endfun main
endclass Mperson
```

ON THE CD

*The two KJP classes discussed are stored in the files* `Person.kpl` *and* `Mperson.kpl`*; the corresponding Java classes are stored in the files* `Person.java` *and* `Mperson.java`.

After translating and compiling both classes (`Person` and `Mperson`) of the problem, the execution of class `Mperson` gives the following output:

```
Creating two objects of class Person
First object: Agent 008 age: 21
Second object: James Bond age: 37
First object: Agent 009 age: 21
```

The Java implementation of class `Person`, generated by the KJP translator from `Person.kpl`, is the following:

```
// KJP v 1.1 File: Person.java, Sun Dec 01
                                  18:25:45 2002
/**
  This is the complete definition of class
  Person. The attributes are age and name.
  */
public  class Person   {
  // attributes
  // variable data declarations
  private int  age;
  private String  obj_name;
  /**
    This is the default initializer method.
    */
  public Person() {
    age =  21;
    obj_name =  "None";
```

```
} // end constructor
/**
   This is a complete initializer function, it
   sets the attributes to the values given on
   object creation.
   */
public Person(int  iage, String  iname) {
  age =  iage;
  obj_name =  iname;
} // end constructor
/**
    This accessor function returns the name of
    the object.   */
public String  get_name() {
  return obj_name;
}  // end get_name
/**
    This mutator function changes the name of
    the object to the name in variable new_name.
    This function has type void.
    */
public void  change_name(String  new_name) {
  obj_name =  new_name;
}  // end change_name
/**
   This accessor function returns the age of
   the Person object.   */
public int  get_age() {
  return age;
}  // end get_age
/**
   This mutator function increases the age of
   the person when called.
   */
public void  increase_age() {
  age++;
}  // end increase_age
```

```
} // end Person
```

ON THE CD

*The Java implementation of class* Mperson, *generated by the KJP translator from* Mperson.kpl, *is stored in the file* Mperson.java, *and the code is as follows:*

```
// KJP v 1.1 File: Mperson.java, Sun Dec 01
                               19:00:02 2002
/**
     This is the main class in the program. It
     creates objects of class Person and then
     manipulates the objects.    */
public  class Mperson {
  /**
     This is the control function.      */
  public static void main(String[] args) {
     // data declarations
     int  lage;
     String lname;
     Person person_a;
     // body of function starts here
     Person person_b;
     System.out.println(
         "Creating two objects of class Person");
     person_a = new Person();
     person_b = new Person(37, "James Bond");
     person_a.change_name("Agent 008");
     lname =  person_a.get_name();
     lage =  person_a.get_age();
     System.out.println("First object: "+ lname+
              " age: "+ lage);
     lname =  person_b.get_name();
     lage =  person_b.get_age();
     System.out.println("Second object: "+ lname+
              " age: "+ lage);
     person_a.change_name("Agent 009");
```

```
            lage =  person_a.get_age();
            lname =  person_a.get_name();
            System.out.println("First object: "+ lname+
                 " age: "+ lage);
        } // end main
    } // end Mperson
```

## 5.8 STATIC METHODS AND VARIABLES

If a method does not belong to an object, but it is defined in a class, the method is normally called with the class name, a dot, and then the method name. No object needs to be referenced when calling such a method. For example:

```
set y = Math.sin(x) + 109.5
```

In this case, `sin` is a static method of the Java class `Math`. To define a static method, the keyword `static` is written before the name of the method. For example:

```
function static mymethod is
. . .
endfun mymethod
```

Static variables are not associated with any object. These variables should normally be private and should be accessed and/or updated using accessor and mutator functions. To declare a static variable in a class, the keyword `static` is written before the normal variable declaration. For example, the following statement declares a static variable named *num_var* and initializes it to zero value.

```
static integer num_var = 0
```

For every declaration of a static variable, there is only one copy of its value shared by all objects of the class.

A static method cannot reference nonstatic variables and cannot include calls to nonstatic methods. The basic reason for this is that nonstatic variables and methods belong to an object, static variables and methods do not.

Often, static variables are also known as class variables, and static methods as class methods.

## 5.9 SUMMARY

Two levels of program decomposition are discussed in this chapter, classes and functions. Classes are modular units that can be reused (in other applications), whereas functions are internal decomposition units. Most often, the function call depends on the manner in which messages are sent among objects.

Simple functions do not involve data transfer between the calling function and the called function. Value-returning functions return a value to the calling function; these functions have an associated type that corresponds to the return value. The third type of function is the one that defines one or more parameters. These are values sent by the calling function and used as input in the called function.

Other categories of functions group functions as accessor and mutator functions. The first group of functions access and return the value of some attribute of the object. The second group changes some of the attributes of the object.

Initializer functions are also known as constructors and are special functions that set the attributes to appropriate values when an object is created. A default initializer function sets the value of the attributes of an object to default values.

A complete program is included in this chapter. The program consists of two classes, `Person` and `Mperson`. Two objects of class `Person` are created, and then these are manipulated by invoking their functions.

Static variables and methods are associated with the class that defined them and not with its objects. The value of a static variable is shared by all objects of the class.

## 5.10 KEY TERMS

| | | |
|---|---|---|
| functions | operations | methods |
| function call | messages | object reference |
| object creation | object manipulation | local declaration |
| return value | assignment | parameters |
| arguments | local data | default values |
| initializer | constructor | |

## 5.11 EXERCISES

1. Explain the reason why a function is a complete decomposition unit. What is the purpose of a function?
2. Explain why function *main* is a special function.
3. Why is it necessary to carry out data transfer among functions? How is this accomplished?
4. Design and write a function definition in KJP that includes two parameters and returns a value.
5. Explain the reason why more than one initializer function (constructor) is normally necessary in class.
6. In the complete program presented in this chapter, add two attributes, salary and address, and two or more functions to class `Person`. Include the corresponding function calls from class `Mperson`.
7. Modify the program that computes the salary increase of employees presented in Chapter 4. Design and write two classes, `Employee` and `Memployee`. All the computations should be done in class `Employee`, and function *main* should be defined in class `Memployee`.

8. Design and write a program that consists of three classes: `Person`, `Ball`, and `Mperson`. An object of class `Person` interacts with two objects of class `Ball`, as briefly explained in Chapter 3. Redesign of these classes is needed.

# 6 DATA AND ALGORITHMS

## 6.1 INTRODUCTION

Computer problem solving is the process of designing a solution to a problem, and converting that solution into a program. An algorithm is a detailed and precise sequence of activities that accomplishes a solution to a problem. The solution includes the data description for the data to be manipulated and the data produced. A program is a computer implementation of data description and the corresponding algorithm. Problem solving involves finding a solution to a problem and describing that solution as an *algorithm*.

Computer programming is the translation of an algorithm into a program using appropriate programming language statements. The *program* consists of a group of data descriptions and instructions to the computer for producing correct results when given appropriate data. The program tells the computer how to transform the given data into correct results. The algorithm has to be broken down by decomposition into classes and functions.

An algorithm must be designed for each function in a class. This chapter explains the general structure of an algorithm using flowcharts and pseudocode. A general introduction to the four design structures for describing algorithms is presented. These structures are sequence, selection, repetition, and input/output. Two of these, sequence and input/output, are explained in some detail and are applied in the case studies.

## 6.2 DESCRIBING DATA

An introduction to data description was presented in Chapter 4. For a given problem, data consists of one or more data items. The input data is the set of data items that is transformed in order to produce the desired results.

*For every computation, there is one or more associated data items (or entities) that are to be manipulated or transformed by the computations (computer operations). Data descriptions are necessary, because the algorithm manipulates the data and produces the results of the problem.*

For every data item, its description is given by:

- A unique name to identify the data item
- A type
- An optional initial value

The software developer defines the name of a data item and it must be different than the keywords used in the programming language statements.

### 6.2.1 Names of Data Items

Text symbols are used in all algorithm descriptions and in the source program. The special symbols that indicate key parts of an algorithm are called *keywords*. These are reserved words that cannot be used for any other purpose. The other symbols used in an algorithm are for identifying the data items and are called *identifiers*. As mentioned previously, the programmer defines the identifiers.

A unique name or label is assigned to every data item; this name is an identifier. The problem for calculating the area of a triangle uses five data items, *x, y, z, s*, and *area*.

### 6.2.2 Data Types

There are two broad groups of data types:

- Elementary (or primitive) data types
- Classes

Elementary types are classified into the following three categories:

- Numeric
- Text
- Boolean

The numeric types are further divided into three types *integer*, *real*, and *double*. The second type is also called fractional, which means that the numerical values have a fractional part. Type *real* is also called *float*. Type *double* provides more precision than type *real*.

Text data items are of two basic types: *character* and type *string*. Data items of type *string* consist of a sequence of characters. The values for these data items are textual values.

A third type of variables is type *boolean*, in which the values of the variables can take a truth-value (true or false).

Classes are more complex types that appear in all object-oriented programs. Data entities declared with classes are called *object variables* or object references.

Aggregates are more advanced types that define data structures as collections of data items of any other type, for example, an array of 20 integer values.

The data items usually change their values when they are manipulated by the various operations. For example, assume that there are two data items named *x* and *y*; the following sequence of instructions in pseudo-code first gets the value of *x*, and then adds the value *x* to *y*:

```
read value of x from input device
add x to y
```

The data items named *x* and *y* are called *variables*, because their values may change when operations are applied on them. Those data items that do not change their values are called *constants*, and their names are usually denoted in uppercase, for example, *MAX_PERIOD*, *PI*, so on. These data items are given an initial value that will never change.

In every program that executes, all the data items used by the various operations are stored in memory, each data item occupying a different memory location. The names of these data items represent symbolic memory locations.

### 6.2.3 Data Declarations

The data descriptions written in a programming language are called data *declarations*. This includes the name of every variable or constant and its type. The initial values, if any, for the data items are also included in the data declaration.

There are two general categories of variables:

- Elementary
- Object references

Elementary (or simple) variables are those whose type is elementary (also called primitive). Variables *x* and *y* defined previously are examples of elementary variables.

Object-oriented programming is mainly about defining classes as types for object references, and then declaring and creating objects of these classes. The type of an object is a class.

Aggregate variables are declared as arrays of elementary types or declared as arrays of object reference variables of some class type.

The following are examples of data declarations in KJP of two constants of types *integer* and *double*, followed by three elementary variables of type *integer*, *float*, and *boolean*.

```
constants
    integer MAX_PERIOD = 24
    double PI = 3.1416
```

```
variables
    integer count
    real salary
    boolean active
```

The following is an example of a data declaration of an object reference. Assume that there is a class definition called `Employee` with two object references, one called *emp_obj* and the other called *new_emp*; the declaration is:

```
objects
    object emp_obj of class Employee
    object new_emp of class Employee
```

## 6.3 ALGORITHM DESIGN

As discussed earlier, an algorithm describes the method of solution to a problem in a precise, clear, and complete form. Algorithm design is carried out in the design phase of the software life cycle, and it is the most challenging task in the entire process. Various kinds of notations are used to describe an algorithm, such as informal English, flowcharts, and pseudo-code.

### 6.3.1 General Solution

In designing and writing an algorithm, the most general solution is the one that should be used. The intent is to describe the solution for a group of very similar problems. Sometimes, this group is called a family of problems.

Consider the problem of calculating the area of a triangle. Given the three sides of a triangle, compute its area. In this case, the algorithm should describe not only the solution to a particular triangle, with sides 3, 7, and

12, but also a solution to any triangle. Therefore, the solution sought is the one for a family of very similar problems; this case is the area of a triangle.

### 6.3.2 Algorithm for the Area of a Triangle

Consider the design of a solution for the problem of calculating the area of a triangle, described previously. The problem is to design an algorithm to calculate the area of a triangle, using the values of its three sides *x, y*, and *z*. The algorithm in informal pseudo-code is:

1. Read the value of side *x* from the input device (keyboard).
2. Read the value of side *y* from the input device (keyboard).
3. Read the value of side *z* from the input device (keyboard).
4. Compute $s = 0.5(x + y + z)$, as an intermediate result.
5. Compute $area = \sqrt{s(s-x)(s-y)(s-z)}$.
6. Print value of *area* to the output device (video screen).

Note that the algorithm is written in a very informal notation, and the value of the sides of a triangle must represent a well-defined triangle. This description of the algorithm is written in an informal pseudo-code notation.

## 6.4 NOTATIONS FOR DESCRIBING ALGORITHMS

An algorithm describes the data and the transformation of that data. The transformation part of a problem solution consists of a sequence of detailed instructions. The order of how the instructions are to be carried out is very important.

A notation is some syntax convention used for the informal description of an algorithm. Two well-known design notations to describe algorithms are:

- Flowcharts
- Pseudo-code

### 6.4.1 Flowcharts

A flowchart is a visual notation for describing a sequence of instructions, in a precise manner. Flowcharts consist of a set of symbols connected by arrows. These arrows show the order in which the instructions are to be carried out. The arrows also show the flow of data.

Figure 6.1 shows some of the basic symbols used in a flowchart, and the arrows that connect these symbols. A flowchart that describes a problem solution always begins with a *start* symbol, and always ends with a *stop* symbol. The start symbol always has an arrow pointing out of it, and the stop symbol always has one arrow pointing into it. A well-defined flowchart must have a starting point represented by a start symbol and a terminating point represented by a stop symbol.

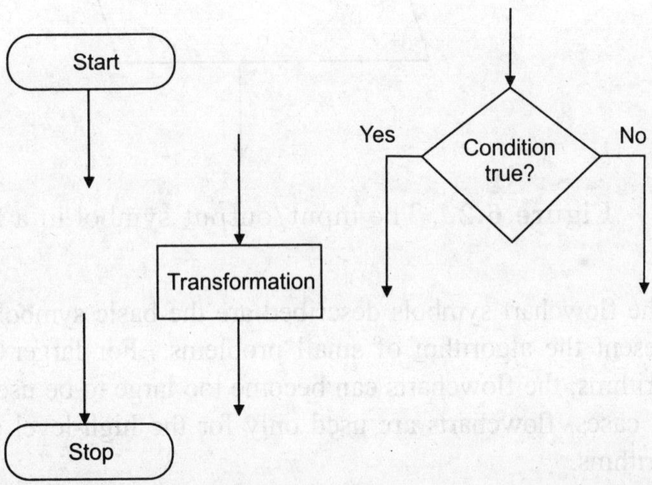


**Figure 6.1** Basic symbols used in flowcharts.

The most general symbol is the *transform* symbol, also called a *process* symbol. The symbol is represented as a rectangle and represents any computation or sequence of computations carried out on some data. There is one arrow point in and one arrow point out of the symbol. In a flowchart, a rectangle is usually called a process block or simply a block of instructions.

The symbol on the right of Figure 6.1 has the shape of a vertical rhomb (or diamond), and it represents a selection of alternate paths in the sequence.

Sometimes, this symbol is called a decision block or a conditional block because the sequence of instructions can take one of two directions in the flowchart, depending on the outcome of the condition.

Another basic symbol in a flowchart is the one that represents the input or output operation on the data. This symbol is shown in Figure 6.2. There is one arrow pointing into the block and one arrow pointing out from the block.

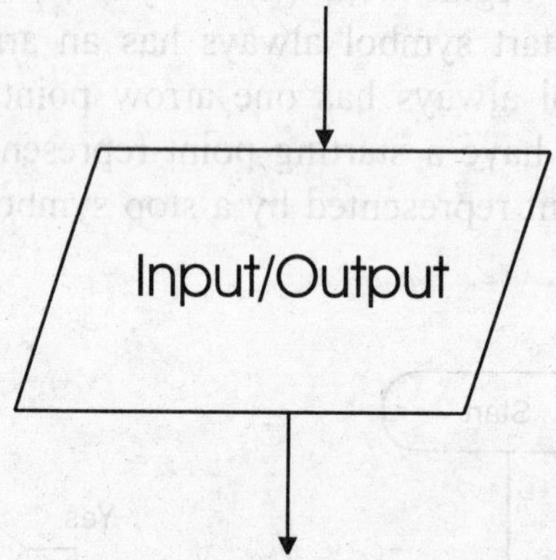


**Figure 6.2** The input/output symbol in a flowchart.

The flowchart symbols described are the basic symbols that are used to represent the algorithm of small problems. For larger or more complex algorithms, the flowcharts can become too large to be used effectively. For such cases, flowcharts are used only for the high-level description of the algorithms.

Figure 6.3 shows a sequence of three instructions, each in a separate flowchart box. The arrows precisely illustrate the order in which the instructions must be executed.

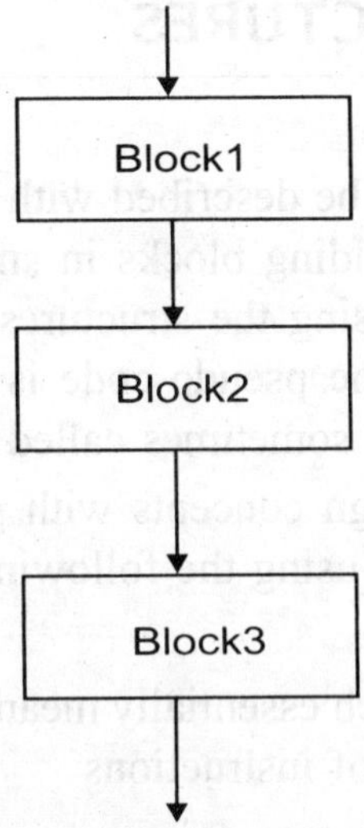


**Figure 6.3** Flowchart of a sequence of three blocks of instructions.

### 6.4.2 Pseudo-code

Pseudo-code is structured notation that can be very informal; it uses an English description of the set of transformations that define a problem solution. It is a natural language description of an algorithm.

NOTE *Pseudo-code is much easier to understand and use than an actual programming language. It can be used to describe relatively large and complex algorithms.*

If a few design rules are followed, another advantage is that it is almost straightforward to convert the pseudo-code to a programming language like KJP. The notation used in a programming language is much more formal and allows the programmer to clearly and precisely describe the algorithm in detail.

Various levels of algorithm descriptions are normally necessary, from a very general level for describing a preliminary design, to a much more detailed description for describing a final design. Thus, the first level of description is very informal, and the last level is formal.

## 6.5 DESIGN STRUCTURES

Every algorithm can be described with four logic structures, and these can be used as basic building blocks in small and in very large and complex algorithms. When using the structures in a disciplined manner, the algorithm described in the pseudo-code is called a structured algorithm, and the design process is sometimes called structured design.

Using simple design concepts with pseudo-code and flowcharts, an algorithm can be built using the following basic design structures:

- Sequence, which essentially means a sequential ordering of execution for the blocks of instructions
- Selection, also called alternation or conditional branch; the algorithm must select one of the alternate paths to follow
- Repetition, also called loops, which is a set (or block) of instructions that are executed zero, one, or more times
- Input-output, which means the values of indicated variables are taken from an input device (keyword) or the values of the variables (results) are written to an output device (screen)

NOTE

*All problem solutions include some or all of these structures, each appearing one or more times. To design problem solutions (algorithms) and programs, it is necessary to learn how to use these structures in flowcharts and in pseudo-code.*

### 6.5.1 Sequence

Figure 6.3 illustrates the first structure, a simple sequence of three blocks of instructions. This is the most common and basic structure. The problem for calculating the area of a triangle is solved using only the sequence and input-output structures. The simple salary problem, which is discussed at the end of this chapter, also uses only these structures.

### 6.5.2 Selection

Figure 6.4 illustrates the selection structure. In this case, one of two alternate paths will be followed based on the evaluation of the condition. The instructions in *Block1* are executed when the condition is true. The instructions in *Block2* are executed when the condition is false.

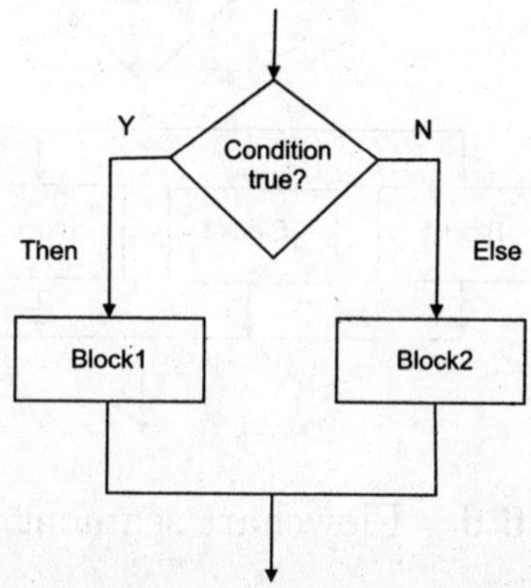


**Figure 6.4** Flowchart segment that shows alternate flow of execution for the instructions in Block1 and Block2.

An example of a condition is $x > 10$. A variation of the selection structure is shown in Figure 6.5. If the condition is false, no instructions are executed, so the flow of control continues normally.

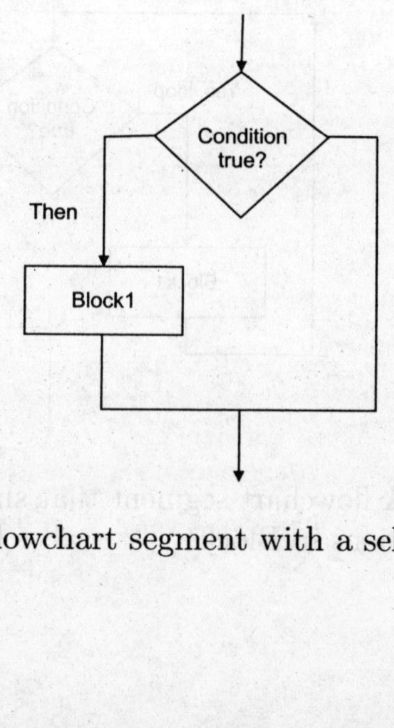


**Figure 6.5** Flowchart segment with a selection structure.

The *case* construct has multiple alternate paths, each one depends on the value of a variable. Figure 6.6 illustrates this construct.

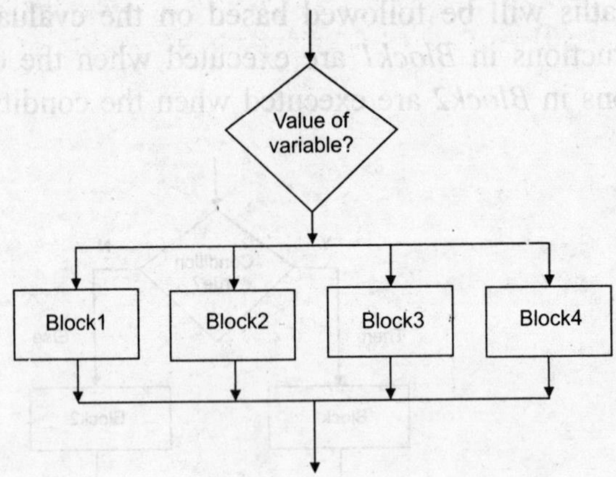


**Figure 6.6** Flowchart segment with multiple paths.

### 6.5.3 Repetition

Figure 6.7 shows the repetition structure. The execution of the instructions in *Block1* is repeated while the condition is true.

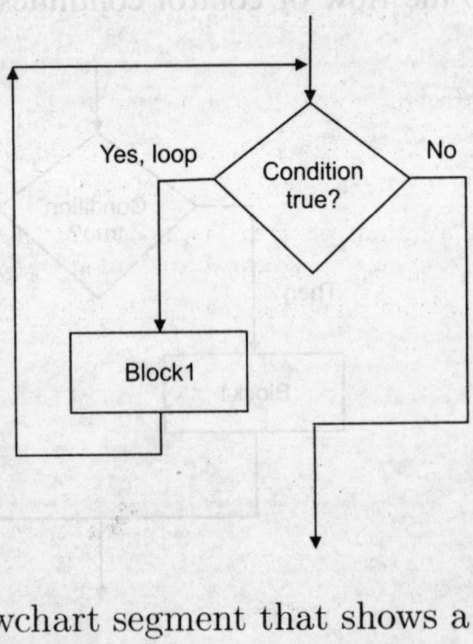


**Figure 6.7** A flowchart segment that shows a structure for repeating the instructions in Block1.

Another form for this structure is shown in Figure 6.8. The instructions in *Block1* are repeated until the condition becomes true.

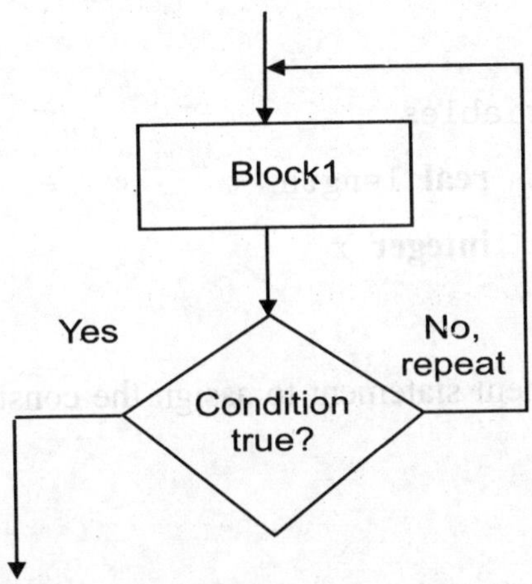


**Figure 6.8** Flowchart segment that shows another structure for repeating the instructions in Block1.

## 6.6 STATEMENTS IN KJP

In programming languages, statements are used for data declarations and for writing the instructions. KJP is an object-oriented programming language that is an enhancement of informal pseudo-code. This section mainly deals with the assignment and I/O statements.

### 6.6.1 Assignment and Arithmetic Expressions

An assignment statement is used to give a value to a variable, and this means that during execution of a program, the value of the variable changes. The keyword **set** must be included at the beginning of the assignment statement. There are two basic ways to give a new value to a variable:

1. Simple assignment
2. The result of evaluating an expression is assigned to a variable

The first kind of assignment statement simply gives a constant value to a variable. For example, given the following declarations:

```
variables
    real length
    integer x
```

The assignment statement to assign the constant value 45.85 to variable *length* is:

```
set length = 45.85
```

In a similar manner, the assignment statement to give the value 54 to variable *x* is:

```
set x = 54
```

In writing an assignment statement, the variable that is receiving the new value is always placed on the lefthand side of the equal sign, the assignment operator.

The second kind of assignment statement is a more general assignment, and is used when the value assigned to a variable is the result of evaluating an expression. For example, the value that results from evaluating the expression $x + 4.95z$ is assigned to variable *y*. The assignment statement is:

```
set y = x + 4.95 * z
```

### 6.6.2 I/O Statements

For console applications, the two simple statements for input/output require the keywords **read**, for input, and **print**, for output. The input statement allows the algorithm to read a value of a variable from the input device (e.g., the keyboard). The value is assigned to the variable indicated. The general structure of the input statement is:

**read** ⟨ *variable_name* ⟩

For example, to read a value for variable *length*, the statement is:

**read** `length`

This is similar to an assignment statement for variable *length*, because the variable changes its value to the new value that is read from the input device.

The output statement writes the value of a variable to the output device (e.g., the video screen). The variable does not change its value. The general structure of the output statement is:

**display** ⟨ *data_list* ⟩

The data list consists of the list of data items separated by commas. For example, to print the value of variable *x* on the video screen unit, the statement is:

**display** `x`

A more practical output statement that includes a string literal and the value of variable *x* is:

```
display "value of x is:  ", x
```

### 6.6.3 Other Statements with Simple Arithmetic

The following statements are similar to the ones previously discussed, and they involve only simple arithmetic operations.

```
add 24 to x
increment j
subtract x from y
decrement counter_a
```

The first statement takes the constant value 24, and adds it to the current value of variable *x*. The result of the addition becomes the new value of variable *x*. This statement requires the keyword **add** and is equivalent to the following assignment statement:

```
set x  = x + 24
```

On the righthand side of the equal sign (the assignment operator), the current value of variable *x* is used. The variable on the lefthand side of the assignment operator changes its value; variable *x* now has a new value.

The **increment** statement, `increment j`, adds the constant 1 to the current value of variable *j*. This statement is equivalent to the following assignment statement:

```
set j = j + 1
```

The other two statements, **subtract** and **decrement**, are applied in a similar manner to the first two.

### 6.6.4 More Advanced Arithmetic Expressions

The arithmetic expressions used in the assignment statements discussed previously were very simple; only basic arithmetic operations appeared in the expressions. These are addition, subtraction, multiplication, and division.

To use a particular function of the `Math` library class, the name of the class must appear followed by a dot and then the name of the particular function invoked. For example, consider the value of the expression $\sqrt{s}$ that is assigned to variable *y*. The expression in the assignment statement must use the mathematical function *sqrt* in class `Math`; the statement is:

```
set y = Math.sqrt(s)
```

In a similar manner, to assign the value of the mathematical expression $x^2$ to the variable *interest*, the complete assignment statement is:

```
set interest = Math.pow(x, 2)
```

This statement invokes function *pow* from class `Math`, to raise the value of *x* to the power of two; the value of this expression is assigned to variable *interest*.

NOTE *Class `Math` is a predefined class and is part of the class library supplied with the Java compiler. This class provides several mathematical functions, such as square root, exponentiation, trigonometric, and other mathematical functions.*

## 6.7 SIMPLE EXAMPLES OF ALGORITHMS

Two simple examples are presented in this section. The first one consists of two classes and computes the salary increase of employees. The second example has only one class with function *main* to compute the area of a triangle. This class calls a function of the library class, `Math`. Because this is a static function, the name of the class is used instead of an object reference.

### 6.7.1 Salary Increase

The problem must compute a 4.5% salary increase for employees, and update their salary. The solution to this problem must first declare the necessary variables: *salary* of type `real`, and *increase* of type `real`.

The algorithm describes the following sequence of operations for an employee, in an informal pseudo-code notation.

1. Get the value of the employee's salary.
2. Compute the 4.5% salary increase of the current salary.
3. Add the value of this salary increase to the current salary to get the new (updated) salary.
4. Print the values of the salary increase and the updated salary.

The corresponding flowchart is shown in Figure 6.9. Because this example is very simple, it needs only two of the design structures, sequence and input/output. Note that the pseudo-code is much more compact than the flowchart in Figure 6.9; however, both are equally complete.

The solution is decomposed into two classes, `Employee` and `Memployee`. Class `Employee` defines the complete algorithm in one or more of its operations. Class `Memployee` contains function *main*, which declares and creates an object of class `Employee` and invokes operation *compute_increase* of that object.

The data description for the attributes of class `Employee` consists of two variables, *salary* and *name*. These attributes have access mode *private*, which is always enforced in KJP.

The algorithm is implemented in function *compute_increase*. This function computes the salary increase and updates the salary of the object.

ON THE CD *The complete KJP code for class* `Employee` *follows and is stored in the file* `Employee.kpl`.

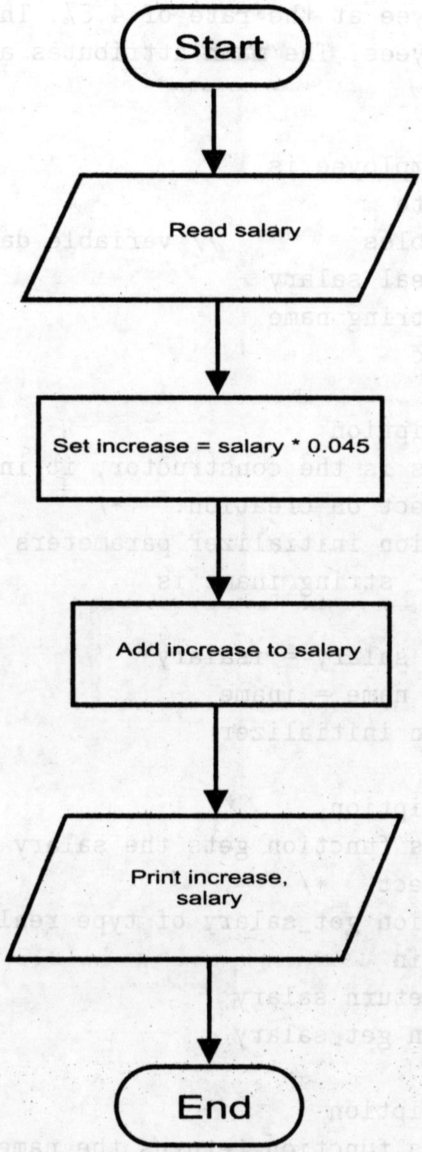


**Figure 6.9** Flowchart that shows the transformations for the simple salary problem.

```
description
  This program computes the salary increase for an
  employee at the rate of 4.5%. This is the class for
  employees. The main attributes are salary and
  name.
  */
class Employee is
  private
  variables          // variable data declarations
      real salary
      string name
  public
    //
  description
    This is the constructor, it initializes an
    object on creation.   */
  function initializer parameters real isalary,
         string iname is
  begin
    set salary = isalary
    set name = iname
  endfun initializer
  //
  description
    This function gets the salary of the employee
    object.  */
  function get_salary of type real is
    begin
      return salary
  endfun get_salary
  //
  description
    This function returns the name of the employee
    object.
    */
  function get_name of type string is
    begin
```

```
        return name
    endfun get_name
    //
    description
        This function computes the salary increase
        and updates the salary of an employee. It
        returns the increase.     */
    function compute_increase of type real is
      constants
        real percent = 0.045  //% increase
      variables
        real increase
      begin                     // body of function
        set increase = salary * percent
        add increase to salary     // update salary
        return increase
    endfun compute_increase
  endclass Employee
```

Class Memployee contains function *main*. The name and salary of the employee are read from the console, and then an object of class Employee is created with these initial values for the attributes. Function *main* invokes function *compute_increase* of the object.

ON THE CD *The complete KJP implementation of class* Memployee *follows. The code for this class is stored in the file* Memployee.kpl.

```
  description
    This program computes the salary increase for an
    employee. This class creates and manipulates the
    employee objects. */
  class Memployee is
    public
    description
        This is the main function of the application.
        */
```

```
    function main is
      variables
        real increase
        real obj_salary
        string obj_name
      objects
        object emp_obj of class Employee
      begin
        display "Enter salary: "
        read obj_salary
        display "Enter name: "
        read obj_name
        create emp_obj of class Employee using
               obj_salary, obj_name
        set increase = call compute_increase
               of emp_obj
        set obj_salary = get_salary() of emp_obj
        display "Employee name: ", obj_name
        display "increase: ", increase,
               " new salary: ", obj_salary
    endfun main
  endclass Memployee
```

ON THE CD *The Java code generated by the KJP translator for class* Employee *follows and is stored in the file* Employee.java.

```
// KJP v 1.1 File: Employee.java, Fri Dec 06
       11:22:18 2002
/**
  This program computes the salary increase for
  an employee to be 4.5%. This is the class for
  employees. The main attributes are salary and
  name.  */
public  class Employee {
   // variable data declarations
```

```
private float  salary;
private String  name;
/**
   This is the constructor, it initializes
   an object on creation.
   */
public Employee(float  isalary, String iname)
{
  salary =  isalary;
  name =  iname;
} // end constructor
/**
  This function gets the salary of the employee
  object.
  */
public float  get_salary() {
  return salary;
}  // end get_salary
/**
  This function returns the name of the
  employee object.   */
public String  get_name() {
  return name;
}  // end get_name
/**
   This function computes the salary increase
   and updates the salary of an employee. It
   returns the increase.     */
public float  compute_increase() {
   // constant data declarations
   final float  percent = 0.045F; // increase
   float  increase;
   // body of function starts here
   increase =  (salary) * (percent);
   salary += increase;  // update salary
   return increase;
}  // end compute_increase
```

```
} // end Employee
```

Figure 6.10 shows the results of executing the salary program for the indicated input data.

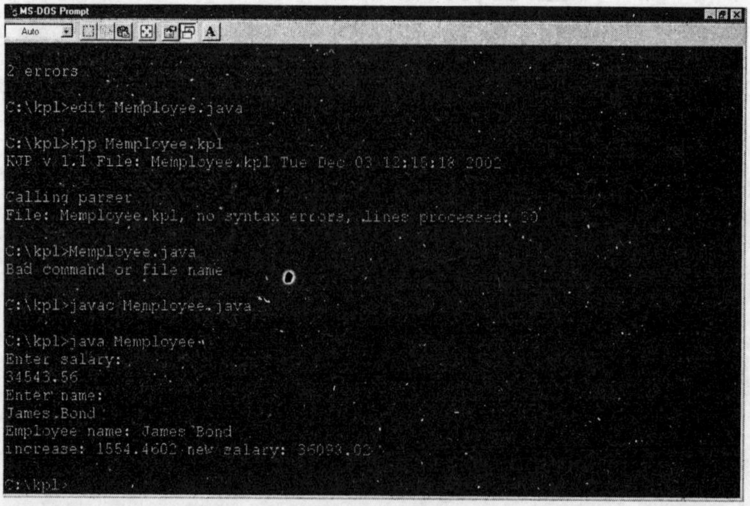


**Figure 6.10** Results on the console for salary program.

## 6.7.2 Area of a Triangle

As stated previously, this problem has the following description: Given the three sides of a triangle, calculate its area. The algorithm description in informal pseudo-code notation is:

1. Read the value of side *x* from the input device (keyboard).
2. Read the value of side *y* from the input device (keyboard).
3. Read the value of side *z* from the input device (keyboard).
4. Compute $s = 0.5(x + y + z)$, as an intermediate result.
5. Compute $area = \sqrt{s(s - x)(s - y)(s - z)}$.
6. Print the value of *area* to the output device (video screen).

The data description and the algorithm for calculating the area of a triangle in KJP notation is included in function *main*:

```
function main is
variables
  // data descriptions
  real x   // first side of triangle
  real y   // second side
  real z   // third side
  real s   // intermediate result
  double area
  //
begin
  // instructions starts here
  display "enter value of first side: "
  read x
  display "enter value of second side: "
  read y
  display "enter value of third side: "
  read z
  set s = 0.5 * (x + y + z)
  set area = Math.sqrt(s * (s - x)*(s - y)*(s - z))
  print "Area of triangle is: ", area
endfun main
```

## 6.8 SUMMARY

Data descriptions involve identifying, assigning a name, and assigning a type to every data item used in the problem solution. Data items are variables and constants. The names for the data items must be unique, because they reference a particular data item. The general data types are numeric and string. The numeric types can be integer or real.

An algorithm is a precise, detailed, and complete description of a solution to a problem. The basic design notations to describe algorithms are flowcharts and pseudo-code. Flowcharts are a visual representation of the execution flow of the various instructions in the algorithm. Pseudo-code is more convenient to describe small to large algorithms; it is closer to writing an actual program.

The building blocks for designing and writing an algorithm are called design structures. These are sequence, selection, repetition, and input-output. Several pseudo-code statements are introduced in this chapter, the assignment statements, arithmetic statements, and input/output statements.

## 6.9 KEY TERMS

| | | | |
|---|---|---|---|
| algorithm | data type | identifier | pseudo-code |
| variables | constants | declarations | flowchart |
| structure | sequence | block of instructions | process |
| selection | repetition | Input/Output | statements |
| KJP | | | |

## 6.10 EXERCISES

1. Write an algorithm in informal pseudo-code to compute the perimeter of a triangle.
2. Write the flowchart description for the problem to compute the perimeter of a triangle.
3. Write a complete KJP program for computing the area of a triangle. Use only two classes.
4. Write a complete algorithm in pseudo-code that computes the average of grades for students.
5. Write the complete KJP program for the problem that computes the grades of students.
6. Write an algorithm in informal pseudo-code that calculates a bonus

for employees; the bonus is calculated to be 1.75% of the current salary.

7. Write the complete program in KJP for the problem that calculates a bonus for employees. Use only assignment and input/output statements.
8. Write an algorithm in flowchart and in informal pseudo-code to compute the conversion from inches to centimeters.
9. Write an algorithm in flowchart and in informal pseudo-code to compute the conversion from centimeters to inches.
10. Write an algorithm in flowchart and in informal pseudo-code to compute the conversion from a temperature reading in degrees Fahrenheit to Centigrade.
11. Write a complete algorithm in form of a flowchart and informal pseudo-code to compute the conversion from a temperature reading in degrees Centigrade to Fahrenheit.
12. Write a complete program in KJP to compute the conversion from inches to centimeters.
13. Write a complete program in KJP to compute the conversion from centimeters to inches.
14. Write a complete program in KJP to compute the conversion from a temperature reading in degrees Fahrenheit to Centigrade.
15. Write a complete program in KJP to compute the conversion from a temperature reading in degrees Centigrade to Fahrenheit.
16. Write a complete program in KJP that combines the conversions from inches to centimeters and from centimeters to inches.
17. Write a complete program in KJP that combines the two types of temperature conversion.
18. Write a complete program in KJP that combines the calculation of the perimeter and the area of a triangle.

# 7 SELECTION

## 7.1 INTRODUCTION

The previous chapter presented the techniques and notations used for describing algorithms. Four design structures are used for the detailed description of algorithms. These are sequence, selection, repetition, and input/output. This chapter explains the selection design structure in algorithms and its application to simple problem solutions. Two statements are discussed, the *if* and the *case* statements.

These statements include conditions, which are Boolean expressions that evaluate to a truth-value (true or false). Simple conditions are formed with relational operators for comparing two data items. Compound conditions are formed by joining two or more simple conditions with the *logical* operators.

Two examples are discussed: the solution of a quadratic equation and the solution to a modified version of the salary problem (introduced in the previous chapter).

## 7.2 SELECTION STRUCTURE

As mentioned earlier, the selection design structure is also called alternation, because alternate paths are considered based on a condition. This design structure is easier to understand in a flowchart. Figure 7.1 shows two possible paths for the execution flow. The condition is examined (or evaluated), and a decision is made to select one of the paths. If the condition is true, then the left path is taken and the instructions on this path (Block1) are executed. If the condition is not true, then the other path is taken and the instructions on this path (Block2) are executed. Thus, the selection structure provides the algorithm capability for decision-making.

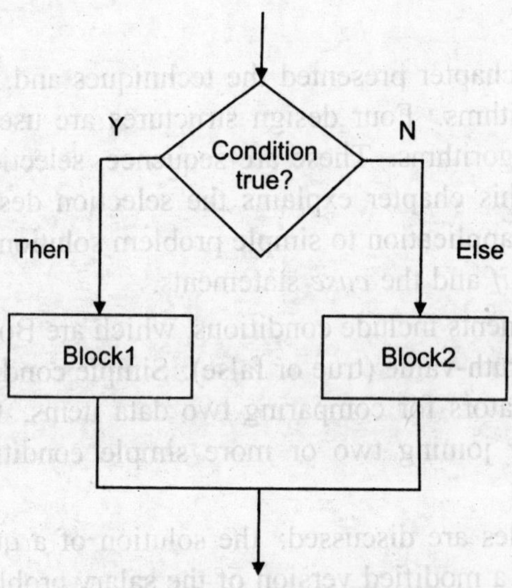


**Figure 7.1** Flowchart segment general selection structure.

### 7.2.1 Pseudo-Code and the IF Statement

In the pseudo-code notation, the selection structure is written with an *if* statement, also called an if-then-else statement. This statement includes several keywords; recall that these are reserved words because the programmer cannot use any of these words for other purposes. The keywords are: **if, then**, **else**, and **endif**.

The informal pseudo-code for the if statement that corresponds to the general selection structure illustrated in Figure 7.1 is:

```
if condition is true
   then
        perform instructions in Block1
   else
        perform instructions in Block2
endif
```

In KJP, the general structure of the *if* statement is:

```
if ⟨ condition ⟩
   then
        ⟨ statements in Block1 ⟩
   else
        ⟨ statements in Block2 ⟩
endif
```

Note that the keywords used in the pseudo-code are written in bold to clarify their usage. The **if** statement is considered a compound statement.

*All the instructions in Blockl are said to be in the then section of the* **if** *statement. In a similar manner, all the instructions in Block2 are said to be in the else section of the* **if** *statement.*

When the if statement executes, the condition is evaluated and only one of the two alternatives will be carried out: the one with the statements in *Blockl* or the one with the statements in *Block2*.

### 7.2.2 Conditions and Operators

The condition consists of an expression that evaluates to a truth-value, **true** or **false**. These types of expressions are also known as Boolean expressions. A simple Boolean expression compares the value of two data items.

A simple Boolean expression is composed of two data items and a relational operator to compare the two data items. There are six relational operators:

- Equal, ==
- Not equal, !=
- Less than, <
- Less or equal to, <=
- Greater than, >
- Greater or equal to, >=

Examples of simple conditions that can be expressed with the relational operators in KJP are:

```
x >= y
time != start_t
```

*Instead of applying the mathematical symbols shown previously for the relational operators, additional keywords can be used for the operators in KJP. For example:*

x **greater or equal to** y

time **not equal** start_t

a **greater than** b

### 7.2.3 A Simple Example of Selection

As a more concrete example, consider a portion of an algorithm in which the decision whether variable *j* should be incremented or decremented depends on the condition: $x > 0$. Figure 7.2 illustrates the flowchart portion of the algorithm that includes this selection structure for this simple example.

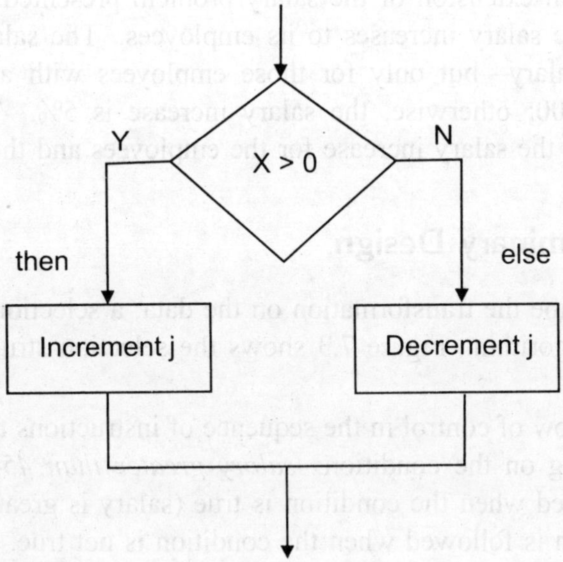


**Figure 7.2** Example of selection structure.

For this example, the portion of the algorithm written in pseudo-code is:

```
if x > 0  then
      increment j
   else
      decrement j
endif
```

In the selection statement, only one of the two paths will be taken; this means that in the example, the statement `increment j` or the statement `decrement j` will be executed. This depends on the evaluation of the condition $x > 0$.

## 7.3 THE SALARY PROBLEM WITH SELECTION

This is an extension of the salary problem presented earlier. A company is to give salary increases to its employees. The salary increase is 4.5% of the salary—but only for those employees with a salary greater than $45,000.00; otherwise, the salary increase is 5%. The solution should calculate the salary increase for the employees and the updated salary.

### 7.3.1 Preliminary Design

To describe the transformation on the data, a selection structure is needed in the algorithm. Figure 7.3 shows the selection structure applied to this problem.

The flow of control in the sequence of instructions takes alternate routes depending on the condition: *salary greater than 45,000*. The left path is followed when the condition is true (salary is greater than 45,000), the right path is followed when the condition is not true.

The first level of detail for the algorithm description in informal pseudo-code is:

```
get the salary for an employee
if salary is greater than $45,000.00
then
        calculate increase with 4.5%
else
        calculate increase with 5%
endif
update salary
show increase and updated salary for
  this employee
```

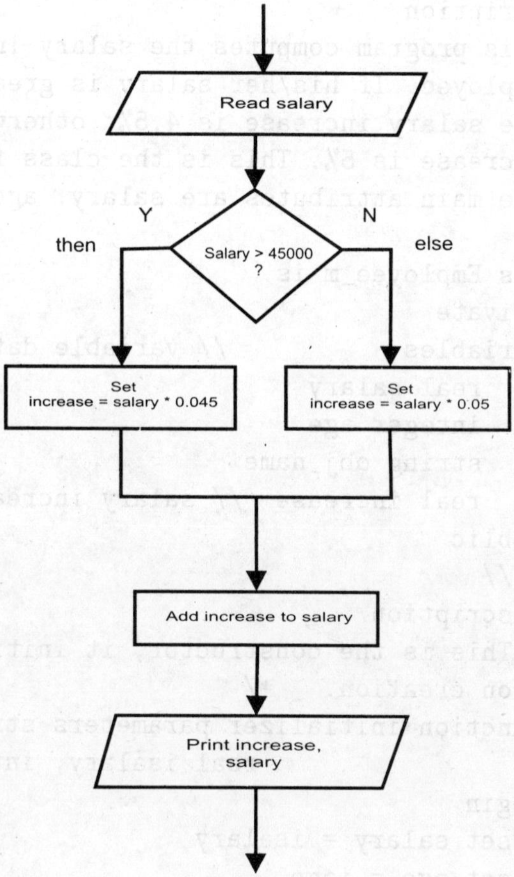


**Figure 7.3** Application of the selection structure.

Note that the flowchart shown for the salary problem is not complete, the start and the end symbols are not shown. The flowchart is only slightly more complicated than the one for the previous version of the salary problem.

## 7.3.2 Final Design and Implementation

The following class definition implements part of the solution for the salary problem. The most relevant part of the solution for this problem is found in function *sal_increase* of class `Employee_m`.

```
description
  This program computes the salary increase for an
  employee. If his/her salary is greater than $45,000,
  the salary increase is 4.5%; otherwise, the salary
  increase is 5%. This is the class for employees.
  The main attributes are salary, age, and name.
  */
class Employee_m is
  private
  variables               // variable data declarations
     real salary
     integer age
     string obj_name
     real increase  // salary increase
  public
    //
  description
    This is the constructor, it initializes an object
    on creation.   */
  function initializer parameters string iname,
                        real isalary, integer iage is
  begin
    set salary = isalary
    set age = iage
    set obj_name = iname
  endfun initializer
  //
  description
    This function gets the salary of the employee
    object.  */
  function get_salary of type real is
    begin
      return salary
  endfun get_salary
  //
  description
    This function returns the name of the
```

```
  employee object.   */
function get_name of type string is
  begin
    return obj_name
endfun get_name
//
description
   This function changes the salary of the
   Employee object by adding the change to
   current salary.
   */
function change_sal parameters real change is
begin
   add change to salary
endfun change_sal
//
description
   This function computes the salary increase
   and updates the salary of an employee.
   */
function sal_increase is
  constants
    real percent1 = 0.045 // percent
    real percent2 = 0.05
  begin                  // body starts here
    if salary > 45000 then
       set increase = salary * percent1
    else
       set increase = salary * percent2
    endif
    add increase to salary     // update salary
endfun sal_increase
//
description
   This function returns the salary increase
   for the object.  */
function get_increase of type real is
```

```
      begin
        return increase
      endfun get_increase
    endclass Employee_m
```

*The code of the KJP implementation for this class is stored in the file* Employee_m.kpl.

The following class, Comp_salary_m includes the function *main*, which creates and manipulates objects of class Employee_m.

```
    description
      This program computes the salary increase for
      an employee. If his/her salary is greater than
      $45,000, the salary increase is 4.5%; otherwise,
      the salary increase is 5%. This class creates
      and manipulates the objects of class
      Employee_m.  */
    class Comp_salary_m is
      public
      description
          This is the main function of the appli-
          cation.     */
      function main is
        variables
          real increase
          real salary
          integer age
          string oname
        objects
          object emp_obj of class Employee_m
        begin
          display "Enter salary: "
          read salary
          display "Enter age: "
          read age
```

```
            display "Enter name: "
            read oname
            create emp_obj of class Employee_m using
                    salary, age, oname
            set increase = call sal_increase of emp_obj
            // get updated salary
            set salary = get_salary() of emp_obj
            print "Employee name: ", oname
            print "increase: ", increase,
                  " new salary: ", salary
        endfun main
    endclass Comp_salary_m
```

ON THE CD

*The code for the KJP implementation is stored in the file* `Comp_salary_m.kpl`.

The following is the code for the Java implementation of class `Employee_m`.

```
// KJP v 1.1 File: Employee_m.java, Thu Dec 12
                     20:09:35 2002
/**
  This program computes the salary increase for
  an employee. If his/her salary is greater than
  $45,000, the salary increase is 4.5%; otherwise,
  the salary increase is 5%. This is the class
  for employees. The main attributes are salary,
  age, and name.
  */
public  class Employee_m  {
  // variable data declarations
  private float  salary;
  private int  age;
  private String  obj_name;
  private // salary increase
  float  increase;
  /**
```

```
     This is the initializer function (constructor),
     it initializes an object on creation.
     */
   public Employee_m(String  iname, float  isalary,
           int  iage) {
     salary =  isalary;
     age =  iage;
     obj_name =  iname;
   } // end constructor
   /**
     This function gets the salary of the employee
     object.   */
   public float  get_salary() {
     return salary;
   }  // end get_salary
   /**
     This function returns the name of the employee
     object.
     */
   public String  get_name() {
     return obj_name;
   }  // end get_name
   /**
      This function computes the salary increase
      and updates the salary of an employee.
      */
   public void  sal_increase() {
     // constant data declarations
     final float  percent1 = 0.045F;   // increase
     final float  percent2 = 0.05F;
     // body of function starts here
     if ( salary > 45000) {
        increase =  (salary) * (percent1);
     }
     else {
        increase =  (salary) * (percent2);
     } // endif
```

```
        salary += increase;     // update salary
      }  // end sal_increase
      /**
        This function returns the salary increase for
        the object.  */
      public float  get_increase() {
        return increase;
      }  // end get_increase
    }  // end Employee_m
```

ON THE CD *The implementation of class* Employee_m *is stored in the file* Employee_m.java.

The output of the execution of this program is shown in Figure 7.4. This program uses class Comp_salary_m as the main class that includes the two classes. Two runs are shown, the first with a salary less than $45,000.00, and the second with a salary higher than $45,000.00.

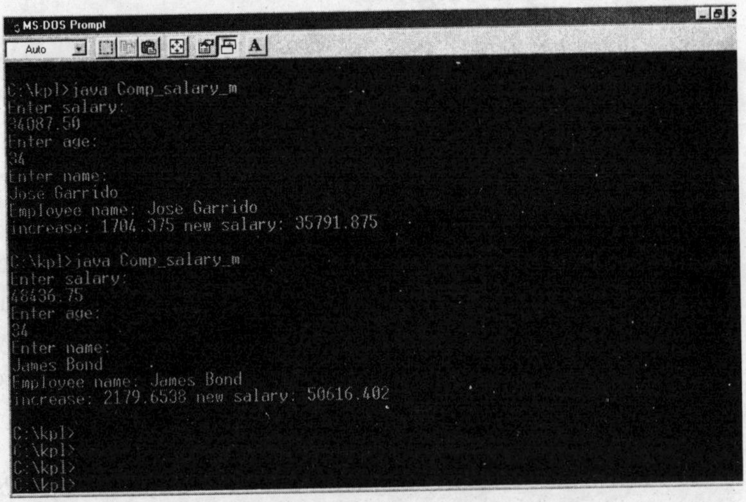


**Figure 7.4** Execution of class Comp_salary_m for the salary problem.

## 7.4 SOLVING A QUADRATIC EQUATION

A quadratic equation is a simple mathematical model of a second-degree equation. The goal of the problem is to compute the two roots of the equation.

### 7.4.1 Analysis of the Problem

Consider the problem of solving a quadratic equation (second-degree equation) of the form:

$$ax^2 + bx + c = 0$$

The input values for this problem are the values of the coefficients of the quadratic equation: *a*, *b*, and *c*. The solution of this equation gives the value of the roots, $x_1$ and $x_2$.

### 7.4.2 Preliminary Design

If the value of *a* is not zero ($a \neq 0$), the general expression for the value of the two roots is:

$$x = \frac{-b \pm \sqrt{b^2 - 4ac}}{2a}$$

The expression inside the square root is called the discriminant. It is defined as: $b^2 - 4ac$. If the discriminant is negative, the solution will involve complex roots. The solution discussed here only considers the case for real roots of the equation. Figure 7.5 shows the flowchart for the general solution.

```
Get the values of the coefficients  a,  b, and  c
Calculate value of the discriminant
If the value of the discriminant is less than zero
   Then no calculations
```

```
    Else calculate the two real roots
Show the value of the roots
```

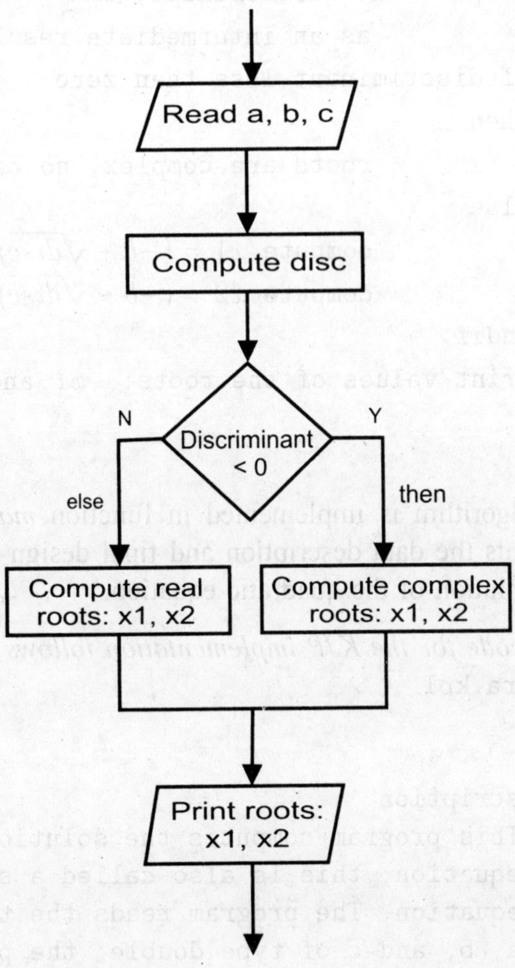


**Figure 7.5** High-level flowchart for the quadratic equation.

### 7.4.3 Next-Level Design

The algorithm in the informal pseudo-code notation for the solution of the quadratic equation is:

Read the value of $a$ from the input device
Read the value of $b$ from the input device
Read the value of $c$ from the input device
Compute the discriminant, $disc = b^2 - 4ac$,
    as an intermediate result
if discriminant less than zero
then
    roots are complex, no calculations
else
    compute $x1 = (-b + \sqrt{disc})/2a$
    compute $x2 = (-b - \sqrt{disc})/2a$
endif
Print values of the roots: *x1* and *x2*

The algorithm is implemented in function *main* of class Quadra. It implements the data description and final design of the algorithm in KJP for the solution of the quadratic equation.

ON THE CD

*The code for the KJP implementation follows and is stored in the file* Quadra.kpl.

```
description
  This program computes the solution for a quadratic
  equation; this is also called a second-degree
  equation. The program reads the three coefficients
  a, b, and c of type double; the program assumes
  a > 0. This is the main and the only class of
  this program. */
class Quadra is
  public
    description
       The control function for the program.    */
    function main is
      variables
```

```
        // coefficients: a, b, and c
        double a
        double b
        double c
        double disc       // discriminant
        double x1         // roots for the equation
        double x2
    begin
        display "Enter value of a"
        read a
        display "Enter value of b"
        read b
        display "Enter value of c"
        read c
        // Compute discriminant
        set disc = Math.pow(b,2) - (4*a*c)
        // Check if discriminant is less than zero
        if disc less than 0.0
          then
            // not solved in this program
            display "Roots are complex"
          else
            // ok, compute both roots
            display "Roots are real"
            set x1 = ( -b + Math.sqrt(disc)) /
                                   (2.0 * a)
            set x2 = ( -b - Math.sqrt(disc)) /
                                   (2.0 * a)
            print "x1: ", x1
            print "x2: ", x2
        endif
    endfun main
endclass Quadra
```

The KJP translator generates a Java file from a KJP file. In this case, the file generated is `Quadra.java`. The following code is the Java implementation of class `Quadra`.

```
// KJP v 1.1 File: Quadra.java, Fri Dec 06
              19:47:10 2002
/**
 This program computes the solution for a quadratic
 equation; this is also called a second-degree
 equation. The program reads the three coefficients
 a, b, and c of type double; the program assumes
 a > 0. This is the main and the only class of this
 program.
*/
public  class Quadra {
  /**
   The control function for the program. */
  public static void main(String[] args) {
     // coefficients: a, b, and c
     double  a;
     double  b;
     double  c;
     double  disc;     // discriminant
     // roots for the equation
     double  x1;
     double  x2;
     System.out.println("Enter value of a");
     a = Conio.input_Double();
     System.out.println("Enter value of b");
     b = Conio.input_Double();
     System.out.println("Enter value of c");
     //
     // Compute discriminant
     c = Conio.input_Double();
     // Check if discriminant is less than zero
     disc =  Math.pow(b, 2) -  (4 * a * c);
     if ( disc < 0.0) {
        // not solved in this program
        System.out.println("Roots are complex");
        // ok, compute both roots
     }
```

```
        else {
           System.out.println("Roots are real");
           x1 =   - b + Math.sqrt(disc) /( 2.0 * a);
           x2 =   - b - Math.sqrt(disc) /( 2.0 * a);
           System.out.println("x1: "+ x1);
           System.out.println("x2: "+ x2);
        } // endif
     }  // end main
  }  // end Quadra
```

ON THE CD

*The Java implementation of class* Quadra *is stored in the file* Quadra.java.

The execution of class Quadra is shown in Figure 7.6. The values for the coefficients are 2, 5, and 3 for *a*, *b*, and *c*, respectively.

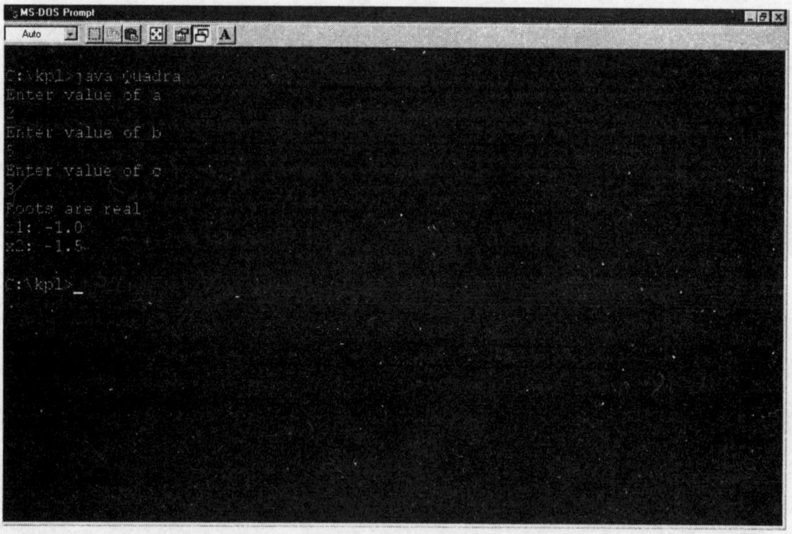


**Figure 7.6** Execution of class Quadra for the quadratic equation.

## 7.5 COMPOUND CONDITIONS

More complex expressions can be constructed with the logical operators **and**, **or**, and **not**. These logical operators help to join two or more simple conditions to construct conditions that are more complex.

The general structure of a compound condition using the **or** operator and two simple conditions, *cond1* and *cond2*, is:

```
cond1 or cond2
```

The other two logical operators are used in the same manner. For example,

```
if a != b  and x > 0
then
    ⟨ statements_1 ⟩
else
    ⟨ statements_2 ⟩
endif
```

This same compound condition can be constructed in a more verbose manner. For example:

```
if a not equal b and x greater than 0
   . . .
```

The following expression uses the **not** operator:

```
not (x <= y)
```

This expression has the following descriptive meaning: it is not true that *x* is less than or equal to *y*.

## 7.6 THE CASE STATEMENT

As mentioned in Chapter 6, the case structure is an expanded selection structure because it has more than two alternate paths. The case statement tests the value of a variable of type *integer* or of type *character*. Depending on the value of this variable, the statement selects the appropriate path to follow.

The variable to test is called the selector variable. The general structure of the *case* statement is:

```
case ⟨ selector_variable ⟩ of
  value  sel_variable_value :  ⟨ statements ⟩
  ...
endcase
```

The following example, which is widely known among students, determines the numeric value of the letter grades. Assume the possible letter grades are A, B, C, D, and F, and the corresponding numerical grades are 4, 3, 2, 1, and 0. The following case statement first evaluates the letter grade in variable *letter_grade* and then, depending on the value of *letter_grade*, it assigns a numerical value to variable *num_grade*.

```
case letter_grade of
    value 'A': num_grade = 4
    value 'B': num_grade = 3
    value 'C': num_grade = 2
    value 'D': num_grade = 1
    value 'F': num_grade = 0
endcase
```

The example assumes that the variables involved have an appropriate declaration, such as:

```
variables
    integer num_grade
    character letter_grade
    ...
```

For the next example, consider the types of tickets for the passengers on a ferry. The type of ticket determines the passenger class. Assume that there are five types of tickets, 1, 2, 3, 4, and 5. The following case statement displays the passenger class according to the type of ticket, in variable *ticket_type*.

```
variables
    integer ticket_type
    ...
    case ticket_type of
        value 1: print "Class A"
        value 2: print "Class B"
        value 3: print "Class C"
        value 4: print "Class D"
        value 5: print "Class E"
    endcase
```

The case statement supports compound statements, that is, multiple statements instead of a single statement in one or more of the selection options.

Another optional feature of the case statement is the default option. The keywords **default** or **otherwise** can be used for the last case of the selector variable. For example, the previous example only took into account tickets of type 1, 2, 3, 4, and 5. This problem solution can be enhanced by including the default option in the case statement:

```
    case ticket_type of
        value 1: print "Class A"
        value 2: print "Class B"
        value 3: print "Class C"
        value 4: print "Class D"
```

```
        value 5:  print "Class E"
    otherwise
        display "Rejected"
    endcase
```

## 7.7 SUMMARY

The selection design structure, also known as alternation, is very useful to construct algorithms for simple problems. The two statements in pseudo-code explained are the *if* and *case* statements. The first one is applied when there are two possible paths in the algorithm, depending on how the condition evaluates. The case statement is applied when the value of a variable is tested, and there are multiple possible values; one path is used for every value selected.

The condition in the *if* statement consists of a Boolean expression, which evaluates to a truth-value (true or false). It is constructed with relational operators between two data items. Conditions that are more complex are formed from simple ones using logical operators.

The KJP language (as other programming languages) includes equivalent statements for the selection structures.

## 7.8 KEY TERMS

| | | | |
|---|---|---|---|
| selection | alternation | condition | truth-value |
| if statement | relational operators | logical operators | then |
| else | endif | case statement | value |
| endcase | otherwise | | |

## 7.9 EXERCISES

1. Write a complete algorithm in flowchart and pseudo-code to compute the distance between two points. Each point, *P*, is defined by a pair of values (*x*, *y*). The algorithm must check that the point values are different than zero, and that the two points are not the same. The distance, *d*, between two points, $P_1(x_1, y_1)$ and $P_2(x_2, y_2)$ is given by the expression:

$$d = \sqrt{(x_2 - x_1)^2 + (y_2 - y_1)^2}$$

2. Given four numbers, find the largest one. Write a complete algorithm in pseudo-code that reads the four numbers and prints the largest one.

3. Given four numbers, find the smallest one. Write a complete algorithm in pseudo-code that reads the four numbers and prints the smallest one.

4. A car rental agency charges $34.50 per day for a particular vehicle. This amount includes up to 75 miles free. For every additional mile, the customer must pay $0.25. Write an algorithm in pseudo-code to compute the total amount to pay. Use the numbers of days and the total miles driven by the customer as input values.

5. Extend the salary problem to include an additional restriction, a salary increase of 5% can only be assigned to an employee if the salary is less than $45,000 and if the number of years of service is at least 5 years.

6. Write a more complete algorithm to solve the quadratic equation that includes the possibility of complex roots. In other words, include the part of the solution when the discriminant is negative.

7. Passengers with motor vehicles taken on the ferry pay an extra fare based on the vehicle's weight. Use the following data: vehicles with weight up to 800 lb pay $75.00, up to 1200 lb pay $115.55, and up to 2300 lb pay $190.25. From the data on the weight of the vehicle, calculate the fare for the vehicle.

8. Develop an algorithm in pseudo-code that reads four letter grades and calculates the average grade. Use the case statement as explained previously.

9. Expand the ferry problem to calculate the cost of the ticket per passenger. Use the following values: class A ticket costs \$150.45, class B costs \$110.00, class C costs 82.50, class D costs \$64.00, and Class E costs \$45.50. Write a complete algorithm in pseudo-code to calculate the cost of the passenger's ticket.

# 8 REPETITION

## 8.1 INTRODUCTION

Most practical algorithms require a group of operations to be carried out several times. The repetition design structure is a looping structure in which a specified condition determines the number of times the group of operations will be carried out. This group of operations is called a repetition group.

There are three variations of the repetition structure, and most programming languages include them. This chapter explains three constructs to apply the three variations of the repetition structure. The constructs for repetition are:

1. While loop
2. Loop until
3. For loop

The first construct, the while loop, is the most general one. The other two repetition constructs can be expressed with the while loop.

## 8.2 REPETITION WITH THE WHILE LOOP

The repeat structure requires a loop condition and a repeat group. With the while-loop construct, the loop condition is tested first. If the condition is true, the operations in the repeat group are carried out. This continues until the condition evaluates to false.

### 8.2.1 While-Loop Construct

Figure 8.1 shows a flowchart segment that illustrates the while loop construct. The repeat group consists of the operations in *Block1*.

If the condition is true, the operations in *Block1* are executed, then the condition is again evaluated, and the operations are carried out if the condition is still true. This continues until the condition changes to false, at which point the loop terminates, and then the control flow continues with the operation that follows the while-loop construct.

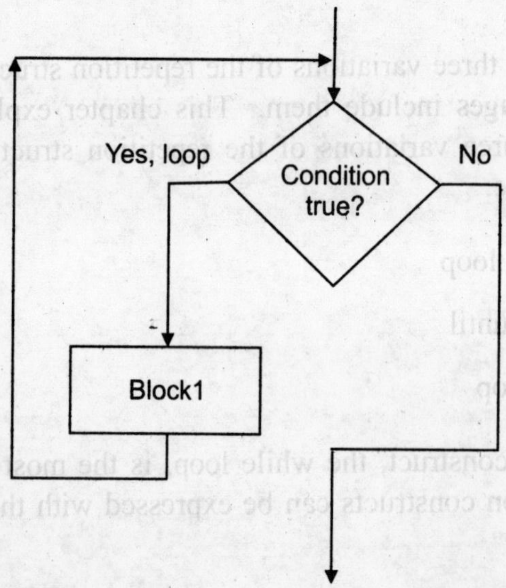


**Figure 8.1** A flowchart segment with the while-loop construct.

In KJP, the while statement is written with the keywords **while, do**, and

**endwhile**. The repeat group consists of all operations in Block1, which is placed after the **do** keyword and before the **endwhile** keyword. The following portion of code shows the general structure for the while-loop construct with the while statement in KJP that corresponds to the portion of flowchart shown in Figure 8.1.

```
while ⟨ condition ⟩ do
    ⟨  statements in Block1 ⟩
endwhile
```

## 8.2.2 Loop Condition and Loop Counter

Note that in the while-loop construct, the condition is tested first, and then the repeat group is carried out. If this condition is initially false, the operations in the repeat group are not carried out.

The number of times that the loop is carried out is normally a finite integer value. This implies that the condition will eventually be evaluated to false, that is, the loop will eventually terminate. This condition is sometimes called the *loop condition*, and it determines when the loop terminates. Only in some very special cases, the programmer can decide to write an infinite loop; this will repeat the operations in the repeat loop forever.

A counter variable has the purpose of storing the number of times (iterations) that some condition occurs in a function. The counter variable is of type integer and is incremented every time some specific condition occurs. The variable must be initialized to a given value.

*A* loop counter *is an integer variable that is incremented every time the operations in the repeat group are carried out. Before starting the loop, this counter variable must be initialized to some particular value.*

The following portion of code has a while statement with a counter variable called *loop_counter*. This counter variable is used to control the number of times the repeat group will be carried out. The counter variable is initially set to 1, and every time through the loop, its value is incremented.

```
constants
  integer Max_Num = 15   // constant, maximum number
                         // of times through the loop
  ...
variables
  integer loop_counter   // counter variable
  ...
begin
  set loop_counter = 1   // initial value of counter
  while loop_counter < Max_Num do
     increment loop_counter
     display "Value of counter: ", loop_counter
  endwhile
  ...
```

The first time the operations in the repeat group are carried out, the loop counter variable *loop_counter* has a value equal to 1. The second time through the loop, variable *loop_counter* has a value equal to 2. The third time through the loop, it has a value of 3, and so on. Eventually, the counter variable will have a value equal to the value of *Max_Num*. When this occurs, the loop terminates.

## 8.3 THE SALARY PROBLEM WITH REPETITION

This version of the salary problem includes repetition so that the same calculations for salary increase are applied to a given number of employees of a company. Assume that the sequence of instructions for calculating the salary increase is the same as the salary problem already discussed. These operations are grouped in *Block1* and are to be repeated for every employee.

In designing the algorithm for this problem, the sequence of instructions in *Block1* is placed in a loop. The while statement contains the condition that compares the loop counter with the given number of employees.

To simplify the problem, assume that the algorithm first reads a variable from the input list. This variable is an integer that represents the number of employees to compute the salary increase and update their salaries. The name of this variable is *Num_emp.* The value of this variable determines for how many employees to calculate the salary increase, and updates the salary. Figure 8.2 shows the portion of the flowchart for the algorithm for the salary problem with repetition.

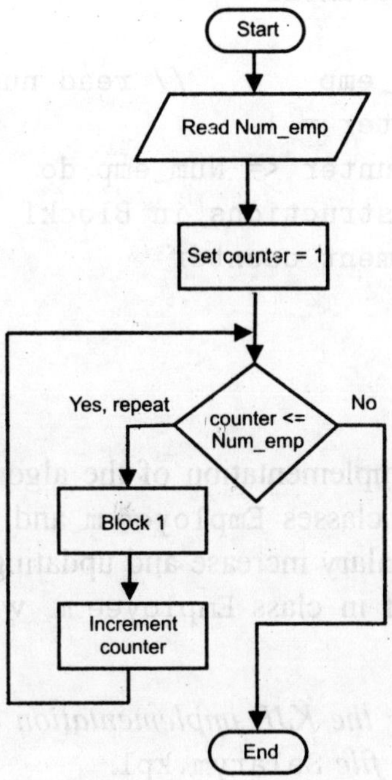


**Figure 8.2** Salary problem with repetition.

Variable *Num_emp* denotes how many times to repeat the block of instructions in *Block1*. For example, if the value of *Num_emp* is 10, this means that there are 10 employees, and the block of instructions will be repeated 10 times, once for each employee.

The condition for the repetition (loop) is: *counter* less or equal to *Num_emp.* The last instruction in the loop increments the value of variable *counter*.

The flowchart in Figure 8.2 shows only the repeat structure of the algorithm and *Block1* contain all the instructions that are repeated. This is a simple way to modularize a program, in other words, group instructions into small modules. This also helps reduce the size of the flowchart.

The corresponding code in KJP for the algorithm is:

```
integer Num_emp    // number of employees to process
integer counter
. . .
read Num_emp       // read number of employees
set counter = 1
while counter <= Num_emp do
   // instructions in Block1
   increment counter
endwhile
. . .
```

A complete implementation of the algorithm for the salary problem is implemented in classes Employee_m and Salarym. The operations for calculating the salary increase and updating the salary for every employee are implemented in class Employee_m, which is the same as discussed previously.

ON THE CD *The code for the KJP implementation of class* Salarym *follows; it is stored in the file* Salarym.kpl.

```
description
  This program computes the salary increase for a
  number of employees. If the employee's salary is
  greater than $45,000, the salary increase is 4.5%;
  otherwise, the salary increase is 5%. The program
  also calculates the number of employees with a
  salary greater than $45,000 and the total amount
  of salary increase.   */
class Salarym is
  public
    //
  description
```

```
    This function creates objects to compute the
    salary increase and update the salary. This
    calculates the number of employees with salary
    greater than $45,000 and the total salary
    increase.
    */
function main is
  variables
    integer num_emp   // number of employees
    integer loop_counter
    real salary
    string name
    integer age
    real increase
    real total_increase = 0.0
    integer num_high_sal = 0  // number employees
                 // with salary greater than 45000
  objects
    object emp_obj of class Employee_m
  begin                       // body of function
    display "enter number employees to process: "
    read num_emp
    set loop_counter = 1           // initial value
    while loop_counter <= num_emp do
      display "enter employee name:"
      read name
      display "enter salary:"
      read salary
      display "enter age:"
      read age
      create emp_obj of class Employee_m using
              name, salary, age
      if salary > 45000 then
        increment num_high_sal
      endif
      call sal_increase of emp_obj
      set increase = call get_increase of emp_obj
```

```
            // updated salary
            set salary = call get_salary of emp_obj
            display "Employee: ", name, " increase: ",
                      increase, " salary: ", salary
            increment loop_counter
            add increase to total_increase // accumulate
         endwhile
         print "Number employees with salary > 45000: ",
                      num_high_sal
         print "Total amount of salary increase: ",
                      total_increase
      endfun main
   endclass Salarym
```

*The code for Java implementation of class* Salarym *follows and is stored in the file* Salarym.java. *This file was generated by the KJP translator.*

```
   // KJP v 1.1 File: Salarym.java, Fri Dec 06
           11:28:28 2002
    /**
     This program computes the salary increase for a
     number of employees. If the employee's salary
     is greater than $45,000, the salary increase is
     4.5%; otherwise, the salary increase is 5%. The
     program also calculates the number of employees
     with a salary greater than $45,000 and the
     total amount of salary increase.        */
   public  class Salarym {
   /**
       This function creates objects to compute the
       salary increase and update the salary. This
       calculates the number of employees with
       salary greater than $45,000 and the total
       salary increase.  */
   public static void main(String[] args) {
      int  num_emp;  // number of employees to process
```

```
int  loop_counter;
float  salary;
String  name;
int  age;
float  increase;
float  total_increase = 0.0F;  // accumulator
int  num_high_sal = 0; // number employees with
                       // salary greater than 45000
Employee_m emp_obj;
// body of function starts here
System.out.println(
    "enter number of employees to process: ");
num_emp = Conio.input_Int();
loop_counter =  1;         // initial value
while ( loop_counter <= num_emp ) {
    System.out.println("enter employee name: ");
    name = Conio.input_String();
    System.out.println("enter salary: ");
    salary = Conio.input_Float();
    System.out.println("enter age: ");
    age = Conio.input_Int();
    emp_obj = new Employee_m(name, salary, age);
    if ( salary > 45000) {
        num_high_sal++;
    } // endif
    emp_obj.sal_increase();
    increase =  emp_obj.get_increase();
    // get updated salary
    salary =  emp_obj.get_salary();
    System.out.println("Employee: "+ name+
     " increase: "+increase+" salary: "+ salary);
    loop_counter++;
    total_increase += increase;    // accumulate
} // endwhile
System.out.println(
     "Number of employees with salary > 45000: "+
         num_high_sal);
```

```
            System.out.println(
                    "Total amount of salary increase: "+
                    total_increase);
        } // end main
    } // end Salarym
```

## 8.4 COUNTER AND ACCUMULATOR VARIABLES

Counters and accumulators are variables in an algorithm (and in the corresponding program), each serving a specific purpose. These variables should be well documented.

### 8.4.1 Counters

A counter variable has the purpose of storing the number of times that some condition occurs in the algorithm.

*A counter variable is of type integer and is incremented every time some specific condition occurs. The variable must be initialized to a given value, which is usually zero.*

Suppose that in the salary problem, there is a need to count the number of employees with salary greater than $45,000. The name of the variable is *num_high_sal* and its initial value is zero. The variable declaration is:

```
integer num_high_sal = 0
```

Within the while loop, if the salary of the employee is greater than $45,000.00, the counter variable is incremented. The pseudo-code statement is:

```
increment num_high_sal
```

This counter variable is included in the implementation for class `Salarym`, as described previously. After the while loop, the following KJP statement prints the value of the counter variable *num_sal*:

```
display "Employees with salary > 45000: ", num_sal
```

### 8.4.2 Accumulators

An accumulator variable stores partial results of repeated additions to it. The value added is normally that of another variable. The type of an accumulator variable depends of the type of the variable being added. The initial value of an accumulator variable is normally set to zero.

For example, assume the salary problem requires the total salary increase for all employees. A new variable of type *real* is declared, the name of this variable is *total_increase*. The data declaration for this variable is:

```
real total_increase = 0.0     // accumulator
```

The algorithm calculates the summation of salary increases for every employee. The following statement is included in the while loop to accumulate the salary increase in variable *total_increase*:

```
add increase to total_increase
```

After the *endwhile* statement, the value of the accumulator variable *total_increase* is printed. The pseudo-code statement to print the string "Total amount of salary increase" and the value of *total_increase* is:

```
display "Total salary increase: ", total_increase
```

The KJP implementation for class `Salarym` for the salary problem includes the calculation of the total amount of salary increase.

## 8.5 REPETITION WITH LOOP UNTIL

The loop-until construct is similar to the while loop. The main difference is that in the loop-until, the condition is evaluated after the repeat group. This means that the operations in the repeat group, *Block1*, will be carried out until the condition is true. Figure 8.3 shows a portion of the flowchart for the loop-until construct.

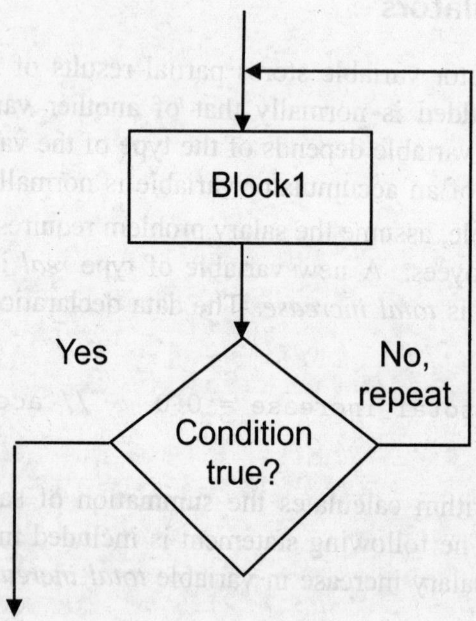


**Figure 8.3** Flowchart segment for the loop-until construct.

NOTE *Independent of the initial evaluation of the condition, the operations in the loop will be carried out at least once. If the condition is true, the operations in the repeat group will be carried out only once.*

The KJP code for the loop-until construct is written with the repeat compound statement, which uses the keywords **repeat**, **until**, and **endrepeat**. The repeat group consists of all operations after the **repeat** keyword and before the **until** keyword.

The general concepts of loop counters and loop conditions also apply to the loop-until construct. The following portion of code shows the general structure for the loop-until statement.

```
repeat
    ⟨ statements in Block1 ⟩
until ⟨ condition ⟩
endrepeat
```

As a simple example, consider a mathematical problem of calculating the summation of a series of integer numbers. These start with some given initial number, with the constraint that the total number of values added is below the maximum number of values given; for example, the summation of integer numbers starting with 10 in increments of 5 for a total of 2000 numbers. For this problem, a counter variable, *numbers*, is used to store how many of these numbers are counted. An accumulator variable is used for storing the value of the intermediate sums. Every time through the loop, the value of the increment is added to the accumulator variable called *sum*.

Class Sum computes the summation of a series of numbers. The KJP implementation of this class follows.

ON THE CD

*The KJP code that implements class* Sum *is stored in the file* Sum.kpl.

```
    description
       This class calculates summation for a series of
       numbers.  */
  class Sum is
     public
     description
        This is the main function in the program.  */
     function main is
       variables
          integer sum         // accumulates summations
          integer numbers     // number of values to sum
          integer svalue      // starting value
          integer maxnum      // maximum number of values
```

```
        integer inc_value // increment value
    begin              // body of function starts
        display "Enter starting value: "
        read svalue
        display "Enter number of values: "
        read maxnum
        display "Enter increment: "
        read inc_value
        set sum = svalue
        set numbers = 0
        repeat
           add inc_value to sum
           increment numbers
        until numbers >= maxnum
        endrepeat
        display "Summation is: ", sum, " for ",
                  numbers, " values"
    endfun main
  endclass Sum
```

ON THE CD *The code for the Java implementation of class* Sum *follows. This code is stored in the file* Sum.java *and was generated by the KJP translator.*

```
// KJP v 1.1 File: Sum.java, Fri Dec 06 14:23:54 2002
/** This class calculates summation for a series of
   numbers.   */
public  class Sum {
  /** This is the main function in the program.   */
  public static void main(String[] args) {
     // data declarations
     int  sum;       // accumulates summations
     int  numbers;   // number of values to sum
     int  svalue;    // starting value
     int  maxnum;    // maximum number of values
     int  inc_value; // increment value
     // body of function starts here
     System.out.println("Enter starting value: ");
```

```
        svalue = Conio.input_Int();
        System.out.println("Enter number of values: ");
        maxnum = Conio.input_Int();
        System.out.println("Enter increment: ");
        inc_value = Conio.input_Int();
        sum = svalue;
        numbers = 0;
        do {
            sum += inc_value;
            numbers++;
        } while (!( numbers >= maxnum) );
        System.out.println("Summation is:"+ sum+
               " for "+ numbers+ " values");
    } // end main
  } // end Sum
```

The execution of this program with the indicated input values is shown in Figure 8.4.

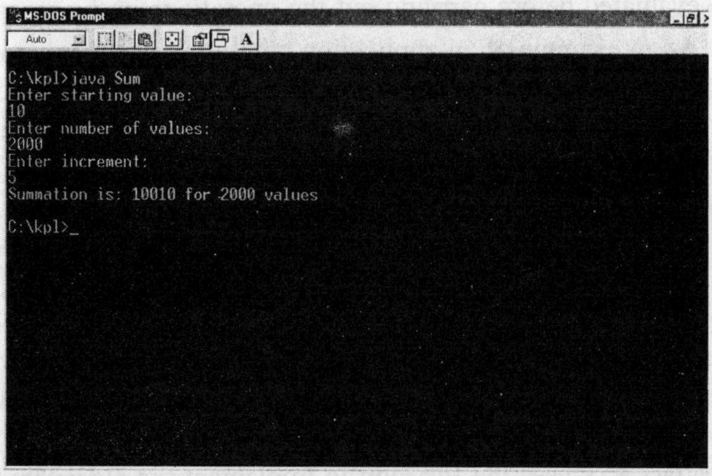


**Figure 8.4** Execution of program with class Sum.

## 8.6 REPETITION WITH FOR LOOP

The for loop is useful when the number of times that the loop is carried out is known in advance. The for loop explicitly deals with the loop counter. In the *for* statement, the initial value and the final value of the loop counter has to be indicated. The general structure of the *for* statement follows. The repeat group consists of the sequence of instructions (written as statements) in *Block1*.

```
for ⟨ counter ⟩ = ⟨ initial_value ⟩ to ⟨ final_value ⟩
  do
     Block1
endfor
```

Every time through the loop, the loop counter is automatically incremented. The last time through the loop, the loop counter has its final value allowed. In other words, when the loop counter reaches its final value, the loop terminates.

The keywords that appear in this statement are: **for**, **to**, **downto**, **do**, and **endfor**. The for loop is similar to the while loop in that the condition is evaluated before carrying out the operations in the repeat loop.

As an example of an application with a for statement, consider the problem of finding the maximum number from a list of integer numbers read one by one from the input device. The algorithm for the solution to the problem first reads the number of values to read and from which to compute the maximum.

An intermediate storage variable called *maximum* is used to hold the maximum value found so far. Its initial value is set to zero, and every time through the loop, this value is compared with the new value read. If the new value read is greater than the maximum, then this new value becomes the new maximum. After the loop terminates, the last value of maximum is the one printed.

Class `Max` uses the **for** loop to implement the algorithm with repetition. The following is the code for the KJP implementation of class `Max`.

```
description
   This class calculates the maximum of a list of
   numbers. This is the only class.  */
class Max is
  public
  description
     This is the main function in the program. */
  function main is
  variables
    real maximum                 // maximum so far
    real x
    integer num_values           // values to read
    integer lcounter             // loop counter
  begin
    set maximum = 0.0
    display "Enter number of values to read: "
    read num_values
    for lcounter = 1 to num_values do
        display "Enter value: "
        read x
        if x greater than maximum then
           set maximum = x
        endif
    endfor
    display "Maximum value found: ", maximum
  endfun main
endclass Max
```

*Class* `Max` *is stored in the file* `Max.kpl`.

The code for the Java implementation of class `Max` follows.

```
// KJP v 1.1 File: Max.java, Fri Dec 06 15:32:28 2002
/**
   This class calculates the maximum of a list of numbers.
   This is the only class.  */
```

```
public  class Max   {
/**
      This is the main function in the program. */
  public static void main(String[] args) {
    // data declarations
    float  maximum;  // maximum so far
    float  x;
    int  num_values; // number of values to read
    int  lcounter;   // loop counter
    maximum =  0.0F;
    System.out.println(
            "Enter number of values to read: ");
    num_values = Conio.input_Int();
    for (lcounter = 1 ; lcounter <= num_values;
                                  lcounter++) {
        System.out.println("Enter value: ");
        x = Conio.input_Float();
        if ( x > maximum) {
            maximum = x;
        } // endif
    } // endfor
    System.out.println("Maximum value found: "+
            maximum);
  }  // end main
} // end Max
```

*The Java implementation of class* Max *is stored in the file* Max.java *and was generated by the KJP translator.*

Figure 8.5 shows the output for the execution of the program with class Max.

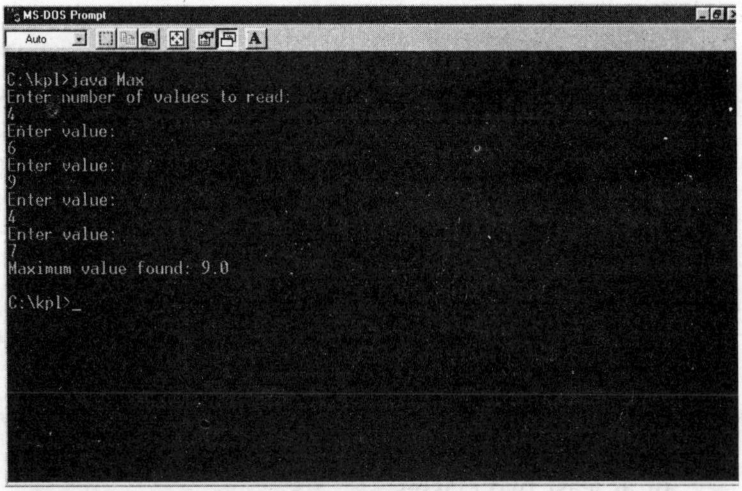


**Figure 8.5** Execution of program with class Max.

## 8.7 SUMMARY

The repetition structure is an extremely powerful design structure. A group of instructions can be placed in a loop in order to be carried out repeatedly; this group of operations is called the repetition group. The number of times the repetition group is carried out depends on the condition of the loop.

There are three loop constructs: *while loop*, *loop until*, and *for loop*. In the *while* and *for* loops, the loop condition is tested first, and then the repetition group is carried out if the condition is true. The loop terminates when the condition is false. In the *loop-until* construct, the repetition group is carried out first, and then the loop condition is tested. If the loop condition is true, the loop terminates; otherwise, the repetition group is executed again.

## 8.8 KEY TERMS

| | | | |
|---|---|---|---|
| repetition | loop | while | loop condition |
| repeat group | loop termination | loop counter | do |
| endwhile | accumulator | repeat-until | endrepeat |
| for | to | downto | endfor |

## 8.9 EXERCISES

1. Rewrite the KJP code that implements class `Sum`, which computes the summation of a series of numbers. The program should consist of at least two classes.
2. Rewrite the KJP program that includes class `Max`, which computes the maximum value of a list of numbers. The program should consist of at least two classes.
3. Write the algorithm in informal pseudo-code and KJP code for a program that is to calculate the average of a series of input values.
4. Write the complete algorithm and the KJP code for a program that finds the minimum value from a series of input values.
5. Rewrite the KJP code for Exercise 1, with a different loop statement.
6. Modify the algorithm and the KJP program of the salary problem. The algorithm should compute the average increase using 5.5% and 6% salary increases.
7. Write the algorithm and KJP code for a program that reads the grade for every student, determines his letter grade, and calculates the overall group average, maximum, and minimum grade.
8. Write the algorithm in informal pseudo-code and the KJP implementation of a program that reads rainfall data in inches for yearly quarters, for the last five years. The program should compute the average rainfall per quarter (for the last five years), the average rainfall per year, and the maximum rainfall per quarter and for each year.

9. Write the algorithm in informal pseudo-code and the KJP implementation of a program that calculates the volume of several spheres. For each sphere, the program should compute the volume. Before termination, the program should compute and display the average volume for all the spheres. After computing the volume of a sphere, the program asks the user if he wants to continue.

10. Write the algorithm in informal pseudo-code and the KJP implementation of a program that reads data for every inventory item code and calculates the total value (in dollars) for the item code. The program should also calculate the grand total of inventory value. The number of inventory data to read is not known, so the program should continue reading data until the user replies that there are no more inventory items to process. Every item includes: item code, item description, the number of items of that code in stock, and the amount for the unit value.

# 9 ARRAYS

## 9.1 INTRODUCTION

There is often the need to declare and use a large number of variables of the same type and carry out the same calculations on each of these variables. Most programming languages provide a mechanism to handle large number of values in a single collection and to refer to each value with an index.

An array is a data structure that can store multiple values of the same type. These values are stored using contiguous memory locations under the same name. The values in the array are known as *elements*. To access an element in a particular location or slot of the array, an integer value known as index is used. This index represents the relative position of the element in the array; the values of the index start from zero. Figure 9.1 illustrates the structure of an array with 10 elements.

An array is a static data structure; after the array is declared (and created), its capacity cannot change. For example, if an array is declared to hold 15 elements, it cannot be changed to hold a larger or smaller number of elements. Using arrays involves three steps:

1. Array declaration
2. Array initialization, or assigning initial values to the array elements
3. Element referencing to access and update the value of the elements

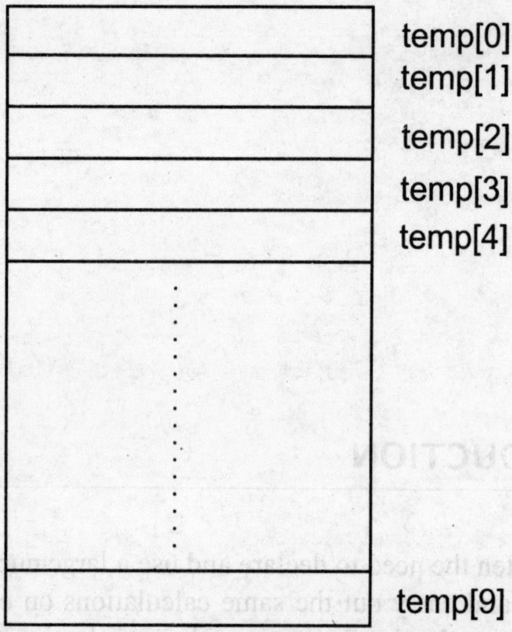


**Figure 9.1** An array named *temp* with 10 elements.

## 9.2 DECLARING ARRAYS

In an array declaration, an identifier is used for the name of the array. The type of array can be of a simple (primitive) type or a class. The capacity of the array is the number of elements it can hold. The general KJP statement to declare an array of a simple type is:

⟨ *array_type* ⟩ ⟨ *array_name* ⟩ **array** [ ⟨ *capacity* ⟩ ]

Arrays of simple types must be declared in the *variables* section for data definitions. For example, the KJP declaration of array *temp* of type *float* and with capacity of 10 elements is:

```
variables
    float temp array [10]
    . . .
```

The declaration of an array of object references is similar to the declaration of object references. The general KJP statement for declaring arrays of object references is:

**object** ⟨ *array_name* ⟩ **array** [ ⟨ *capacity* ⟩ ]
**of class** ⟨ *class_name* ⟩

Arrays of object references must be declared in the *objects* section for data definitions. For example, the KJP declaration of array *employees* of class `Employee` and with 50 elements of capacity is:

```
objects
    object employees array [50] of class Employee
    . . .
```

A more convenient and recommended manner to declare an array is to use an identifier constant with the value of the capacity of the array. For example, assume the constant *MAX_TEMP* has a value 10 and *NUM_OBJECTS* a value of 25; the declaration of the array *temp* and array *employees* is:

```
constants
    integer MAX_TEMP = 10
    integer NUM_OBJECTS = 25
variables
    float temp array [MAX_TEMP]
objects
    object employees array [NUM_OBJETS] of
                          class Employee
    . . .
```

The declaration of an array indicates the type of value that the elements of the array can hold. It also indicates the name and total number of elements of the array. In most practical problems, the number of elements manipulated in the array is less than the total number of elements. For example, an array is declared with a capacity of 50 elements, but only the first 20 elements of the array are used. Because the array is a static data structure, elements cannot be inserted or deleted from the array, only the values of the elements can be updated.

## 9.3 REFERRING INDIVIDUAL ELEMENTS OF AN ARRAY

To refer to an individual element in an array, an integer value is used that represents the relative position of the element in the array. This index value is known as the *index* for the array. The index value starts at 0, and the maximum value is the capacity of the array minus 1.

### 9.3.1 Arrays of Simple Types

A particular element in the array is denoted by the name of the array followed by the index value enclosed in rectangular brackets. For example, to assign a value of 342.65 to element 7 of array *temp*, the KJP code is:

```
set temp[6] = 342.65
```

The index value can be an integer constant, a constant identifier, or an integer variable. For example, to refer to element 7 of array *temp* using variable *j* as the index:

```
constants
    integer MAX_TEMP = 10
variables
    float temp array [MAX_TEMP]
    integer j
    . . .
    set j = 6
    set temp[j] = 342.65
```

### 9.3.2 Arrays of Object References

An array of object references is not an array of objects, because the objects are stored elsewhere in memory. To create an object of class Employee and assign its reference to the element with index *j* of array *employees*, the KJP code is:

```
create employees[j] of class Employee
```

To invoke a public function of an object referenced in an element of an array, the call statement is used as explained before and the name of the array is followed by the index value enclosed in brackets. For example, to invoke function *get_salary* of the object referenced by the element with index *j* in array *employees*, the KJP code is:

```
variables
    float obj_salary
    integer j
    . . .
    set obj_salary = call get_salary of employees[j]
```

## 9.4 SIMPLE APPLICATIONS OF ARRAYS

This section includes several simple and typical applications of arrays. Class Temp is used as an implementation for these discussions. The first part of class Temp includes the various data definitions including array *temp*.

```
class Temp is
  protected
    constants
```

```
    integer NUM_TEMP = 15    // array capacity
variables
    integer t_index
    integer num_temp_values  // number of elements
    float temp array [NUM_TEMP]
...
```

### 9.4.1 Finding Maximum and Minimum Values in an Array

To find the minimum and/or maximum values stored in an array, all the elements have to be examined. The algorithm for finding the maximum value in informal pseudo-code (as a sequence of steps) is:

1. Set the initial largest value to the value of the first element of the array.
2. Set the index value of the first element, value 0.
3. Carry out the following steps for each of the other elements of the array:
   (a) Examine the value of the next element in the array.
   (b) If the value of the current element is greater than the largest value so far, update the value found so far with this element value, and save the index of the element.
4. The result is the index value of the element value found to be the largest in the array.

The algorithm uses two intermediate (or temporary) variables that are used to store the largest value found so far, *max_val*, and the index value of the corresponding element, *jmax*.

Function *maxtemp* in class `Temp` implements the algorithm discussed. The function uses array *temp*, which is declared in the class as an array of type *float* and that has *num_temp_values* elements. The function returns the index value with the largest value found.

```
description
      This function returns the index of the element
      with the maximum value in the array.
      */
function maxtemp of type integer is
      variables
         integer j              // index variable
         // index of element with largest value
         integer jmax
         float max_val          // largest value so far
      begin
         set jmax = 0           // index first element
         set max_val = temp[0] // max value so far
         for j = 1 to num_temp_values - 1 do
            if temp[j] > max_val
            then
               set jmax = j
               set max_val = temp[j]
            endif
         endfor
      return jmax                     // result
endfun maxtemp
```

The minimum value can be found in a similar manner; the only change is the comparison in the *if* statement.

### 9.4.2 Calculating the Average Value in an Array

To find the average value in an array, all the elements have to be added to an accumulator variable, *sum*. The algorithm for computing the average value in informal pseudo-code (as a sequence of steps) is:

1. Set the accumulator variable, *sum*, to the value of the first element of the array.
2. For each of the other elements of the array, add the value of the next element in the array to the accumulator variable.

3. Divide the value of the accumulator variable by the number of elements in the array. This is the result value calculated.

The algorithm uses an accumulator variable that is used to store the summation of the element values in the array. In an array $x$ with $n$ elements, the summation of $x$ with index $j$ starting with $j = 1$ to $j = n$ is expressed mathematically as:

$$sum = \sum_{j=1}^{n} x_j.$$

The average is calculated simply as $sum/n$. Function *average_temp* in class `Temp` implements the algorithm discussed. The function uses array *temp*, which is declared in class `Temp` as an array of type *float* and that has *num_temp_values* elements. The function returns the average value calculated. The KJP code for the function follows.

```
description
  This function computes the average value of
  the array temp. The accumulator variable sum
  stores the summation of the element values.
  */
function average_temp of type float is
  variables
    float sum        // variable for summation
    float ave        // average value
    integer j
  begin
    set sum = 0
    for j = 0 to num_temp_values - 1 do
       add temp[j] to sum
    endfor
    set ave = sum / num_temp_values
    return ave
endfun average_temp
```

## 9.4.3 Searching

When the elements of an array have been assigned values, one of the problems is to search the array for an element with a particular value. This is known as searching. Not all the elements of the array need to be examined; the search ends when and if an element of the array has a value equal to the requested value. Two important techniques for searching are linear search and binary search.

### 9.4.3.1 Linear Search

Linear search is also known as sequential search, because the method starts to compare the requested value with the value in the first element of the array, and if not found, compares with the next element, and so on until the last element of the array is compared with the requested value.

A useful outcome of this search is the index of the element in the array that is equal to the requested value. If the requested value is not found, the result is a negative value. The algorithm description in informal pseudocode (as a sequence of steps) is:

1. For every element of the array and until the value is found:
   (a) Compare the current element with the requested value. If the values are equal, store the value of the index as the result and search no more.
   (b) If the values are not equal, continue the search.
2. If the value requested is not found, set the result to a negative value.

Function *searchtemp* in class `Temp` searches the array for an element with the requested temperature value. For the result, the function assigns to *t_index* the index value of the element with the value requested. If the requested value is not found, the function assigns a negative integer value to *t_index*. The code for the KJP implementation of function *searchtemp* follows.

```
description
    This function carries out a linear search of
    the array of temperature for the temperature
```

```
          value in parameter temp_val. It sets the index
          value of the element found, or -1 if not found.
          */
        function searchtemp parameters float temp_val is
          variables
            integer j
            boolean found = false
          begin
            set j = 0
            while j < num_temp_values and found
                                              not equal true do
              if temp [j] == temp_val
              then
                 set t_index = j
                 set found = true
              else
                 increment j
              endif
            endwhile
            if found not equal true
            then
              set t_index = -1
            endif
        endfun searchtemp
```

#### 9.4.3.2 Binary Search

Binary search is a more efficient search technique than linear search, because the number of comparisons is smaller. The efficiency of a search algorithm is determined by the number of relevant operations in proportion to the size of the array to search. The relevant operations in this case are the comparisons of the element values with the requested value.

For an array with $N$ elements, the average number of comparisons with linear search is $N/2$, and if the requested value is not found, the number of comparisons is $N$. With binary search, the number of comparisons is $\log_2 N$.

The binary search technique can only be applied to a sorted array. The values to be searched have to be sorted in ascending order. The part of the array elements to include in the search is split into two partitions of about the same size. The middle element is compared with the requested value. If the value is not found, the search is continues on only one partition. This partition is again split into two smaller partitions until the element is found or until no more splits are possible (not found).

Class `Temp` declares an array of temperatures named *temp*. One of the functions reads the element values from the console, another function reads the value of temperature to search, and a third function searches the array for the requested temperature value and returns the index value or a negative integer value.

The description of the algorithm, as a sequence of steps, is:

1. Set the lower and upper bounds of the array to search.
2. Continue the search while the lower index value is less than the upper index value.
   (a) Split the section of the array into two partitions. Compare the middle element with the requested value.
   (b) If the value of the middle element is the requested value, the result is the index of this element–search no more.
   (c) If the requested value is less than the middle element, change the upper bound to the index of the middle element minus 1. The search will continue on the lower partition.
   (d) If the requested value is greater or equal to the middle element, change the lower bound to the index of the middle element plus 1. The search will continue on the upper partition.
3. If the value is not found, the result is a negative value.

Function *bsearchtemp* in class `Temp` implements the binary search algorithm using array *temp*. The code for the KJP implementation for this function follows.

```
description
  This function carries out a binary search of
  the array of temperature for the temperature
  value in parameter temp_val. It sets the index
  value of the element found, or -1 if not found.
  */
function bsearchtemp parameters float temp_val is
  variables
    boolean found = false
    integer lower   // index lower bound element
    integer upper   // index upper bound element
    integer middle  // index of middle element
  begin
    set lower = 0
    set upper = num_temp_values
    while lower < upper and found not equal true
     do
      set middle = (lower + upper) / 2
      if temp_val == temp[middle]
      then
         set found = true
         set t_index =  middle
      else
         if temp_val < temp[middle]
         then
            set upper = middle -1
         else
            set lower = middle + 1
         endif
      endif
    endwhile
    if found not equal true
    then
       set t_index = -1
    endif
endfun searchtemp
```

ON THE CD

*The complete implementation of class* `Temp` *is stored in the file* `Temp.kpl`. *The Java implementation of this class is stored in the file* `Temp.java`.

### 9.4.4 Sorting

Sorting an array consists of rearranging the elements of the array in some order according to the requirements of the problem. For numerical values, the two possible sorting orders are ascending and descending. There are several sorting algorithms; however, some are more efficient than others. Some of the most widely known sorting algorithms are:

- Selection sort
- Insertion sort
- Merge sort
- Bubble sort
- Shell sort

Selection sort is the only one explained here; it is a very simple and inefficient sorting algorithm. Assume there is an array of a numerical type of size $N$; the algorithm performs several steps. First, it finds the index value of the smallest element value in the array. Second, it swaps this element with the element with index 0 (the first element). This step actually places the smallest element to the first position. Third, the first step is repeated for the part of the array with index 1 to $N-1$; this excludes the element with index 0, which is at the proper position. The smallest element found is swapped with the element at position with index 1. This is repeated until all the elements are located in ascending order. A more precise description of the algorithm, as a sequence of steps, is:

1. For all elements with index J = 0 to N-2, carry out steps 2 and 3.
2. Search for the smallest element from index J to N-1.
3. Swap the smallest element found with element with index J, if the smallest element is not the one with index J.

Class `Temp` declares an array *temp* of type *float*. The array declaration is:

```
float temp array [NUM_TEMP]
```

Function *selectionsort* in class Temp implements the algorithm for the selection sort. The code for the KJP implementation for this function follows.

```
description
  This function carries out a selection sort of
  the array of temperature.
  */
function selectionsort is
  variables
    integer N                 // elements in array
    integer Jmin              // smallest element
    integer j
    integer k
    float t_temp              // intermediate temp
  begin
    set N = num_temp_values
    for j = 0 to N - 2 do
      // search for the smallest element
      // in the index range from j to N-1
      set Jmin = j
      for k = j+1 to N - 1 do
        if temp[k] < temp[Jmin]
        then
          set Jmin = k
        endif
      endfor
      if Jmin != j then
        // swap elements with index J and Jmin
        set t_temp = temp[j]
        set temp[j] = temp[Jmin]
        set temp[Jmin] = t_temp
      endif
    endfor
 endfun selectionsort
```

The selection sort is not a very efficient algorithm. The number of element comparisons with an array size of $N$ is $N^2/2 - N/2$. The first term ($N^2/2$) in this expression is the dominant one; the order of growth of this algorithm is $N^2$. This is formally expressed as $O(N^2)$.

## 9.5 ARRAY PARAMETERS

A function can define a parameter as an array. The array can then be passed as an argument when calling the function. A copy of the array is not actually passed as an argument, only a reference to the array is passed.

To define a function with an array as a parameter, the header of the function definition must indicate this with the **parameters** KJP keyword. The general KJP syntax for a function header that includes a parameter definition is:

```
description
    . . .
  */
function ⟨ function_name ⟩ parameters
                      ⟨ parameter_list ⟩ is
    . . .
endfun ⟨ function_name ⟩
```

The *parameter_list* part of the function header can include one or more array definitions. The array name is followed by an empty pair of brackets.

```
⟨ array_name ⟩ []
```

A function definition that finds the minimum value in an array of type *float* defines the array as a parameter and an integer parameter. This second parameter is the number of elements in the array. The function returns the minimum value. The complete definition of function *minimum* in KJP follows.

```
description
   This function calculates the minimum value of
   an array parameter tarray, it then returns the
   result.
   */
function minimum of type float parameters
                float tarray[], integer numel is
variables
   real min           // local variable
   integer j
begin
   set min = tarray[0]
   for j = 1 to numel - 1 do
       if min < tarray[j] then
          set min = tarray[j]
       endif
   endfor
   return min
endfun minimum
```

To call a function and pass an array as an argument, only the name of the array is used. For example, the following KJP code calls function *minimum* and pass array *mtime*.

```
constants
    integer KNUM = 100
variables
    float mtime array [KNUM]
    float mintime
    . . .
    set mintime = minimum using mtime, KNUM
    . . .
```

The previous code with a call statement is included in another function of the same class. The call to function *minimum* is carried out in an assignment statement, because the function returns a value that is assigned to variable *mintime*.

## 9.6 ARRAYS WITH MULTIPLE DIMENSIONS

Arrays with more than one dimension can be defined to solve mathematical problems with matrices, computer games, and so on. Two-dimension arrays are easier to understand and matrices are the most common type of problems. These are mathematical structures with values arranged in columns and rows. Two index values are required, one for the rows and one for the columns.

To define a two-dimensional array, two numbers are defined, each in a pair of brackets. The first number defines the range of values for the first index (for the rows) and the second number defines the range of values for the second index (for the columns).

For example, the definition of a two-dimensional array named *matrix* with a capacity of 15 rows and 20 columns in KJP code is:

```
constants
    integer ROWS = 15
    integer COLS = 20
variables
    float matrix array [ROWS][COLS]
    . . .
```

To reference the elements of a two-dimensional array, two indices are required. For example, the following KJP code sets all the elements of array *matrix* to 0.0:

```
for j = 0 to COLS - 1 do
   for i = 0 to ROWS - 1 do
       set matrix [i][j] = 0.0
   endfor
endfor
```

For this initialization of array *matrix*, two loop definitions are needed, an outer loop and an inner loop (this is also known as nested loops). The inner loop varies the row index and outer loop varies the column index. The assignment statement sets the value 0.0 to the element at row $i$ and column $j$.

## 9.7 USING ARRAYS IN JAVA

In Java, arrays are really defined as objects. They have to be declared as an object reference, and then it must be created with the appropriate number of elements.

The general Java statement to declare and create an array is:

```
⟨ array_type ⟩ [] ⟨ array_name ⟩ =
                    new ⟨ array_type ⟩ [ ⟨ capacity ⟩ ];
```

For example, the Java declaration of array *temp* of type *float* and with a capacity of 10 elements is:

```
float[] temp = new float [10];
. . .
```

The declaration of an array of object references is the same as the declaration of object references—the array type is a class. For example, the Java declaration of array *employees* of class Employee and with 50 elements of capacity is:

```
Employee employees = new Employee [50];
. . .
```

The referencing of individual elements is carried out with an appropriate index, as explained before. For example, to assign a value of 342.65 to element 7 of array *temp*, the Java code is:

```
temp[6] = 342.65;
```

Because an array is an object in Java, there is a particular public attribute of arrays that is very useful and that stores the capacity of the array. The name of this attribute is *length*. To access this attribute, the dot notation is used with the name of the array. For example, to assign a value 0.00 to every element of array *temp*, the Java code is:

```
for (j = 0; j < temp.length; j++)
        temp[j] = 0.00;
```

To create an object of class `Employee` and assign its reference to the element with index *j* of array *employees*, the Java code is:

```
employees[j] = new Employee();
```

To invoke a public function of an object referenced in an element of an array, the dot notation is used; the name of the array is followed by a dot and followed by the name of the function. For example, to invoke the function *get_salary* of the object referenced by an element with index *j* in array *employees*, the Java code is:

```
float obj_salary;
int j;
.
obj_salary = employees[j].get_salary();
```

## 9.8 SUMMARY

Arrays are data structures capable of storing a number of different values of the same type. Each of these values is known as an element. The type of an array can be a simple type or can be a class. To refer to an individual element, an integer value, known as the index, is used to indicate the relative position of the element in the array.

Arrays are static data structures; after the array has been declared, the capacity of the array cannot be changed. Various practical problems can be solved using arrays. Searching involves finding an element in the array with a target value. Two important search algorithms are linear search and binary search. Sorting involves rearranging the elements of an array in some particular order of their values. In Java, arrays are considered objects; they need to be declared and created.

## 9.9 KEY TERMS

| | | |
|---|---|---|
| data structure | array capacity | index |
| array element | element reference | searching |
| linear search | binary search | algorithm efficiency |
| sorting | Selection sort | matrix |

## 9.10 EXERCISES

1. Design and implement a function named *mintemp* for class `Temp`. This function should find the element of array *temp* with the minimum value. The function must return the index value of the corresponding element.

2. Design and implement a function that computes the standard deviation of the temperature values in array *temp*. The standard deviation measures the spread, or dispersion, of the values in the array with respect to the average value. The standard deviation of array $X$ with $N$ elements is defined as:

$$std = \sqrt{\frac{sqdif}{N-1}},$$

where

$$sqdif = \sum_{j=0}^{N-1} (X_j - Avg)^2.$$

3. Design and implement a function for class `Temp` that sorts the array of temperature values using insertion sort. This divides the array into two parts. The first is initially empty; it is the part of the array with the elements in order. The second part of the array has the elements in the array that still need to be sorted. The algorithm takes the element from the second part and determines the position for it in the first part. To insert this element in a particular position of the first part, the elements to the right of this position need to be shifted one position to the right. Note: insertion sort is not explained in this

book; look it up on the Web.

4. Design and implement a problem that provides the rainfall data for the last five years. For every year, four quarters of rainfall are provided measured in inches. Class `Rainfall` includes attributes such as the precipitation (in inches), the year, and the quarter. Class `Mrainfall` declares an array of object references of class `Rainfall`. The problem should compute the average, minimum, and maximum rainfall per year and per quarter (for the last five years). *Hint*: use a matrix.

5. Redesign and reimplement the solution for Exercise 1 with an array parameter definition in the function. Use the appropriate call to the function.

6. Redesign and reimplement the solution for Exercise 2 with an array parameter definition in the function. Use the appropriate call to the function.

7. Redesign and reimplement the solution for Exercise 3 with an array parameter definition in the function. Use the appropriate call to the function.

8. Design and implement a problem that provides the rainfall data for the last five years. For every year, twelve months of rainfall are provided measured in inches. Class `Rainfall2` includes attributes such as the precipitation (in inches), the year, and the month. Class `Mrainfall2` declares an array of object references of class `Rainfall2`. The problem should compute the average, minimum, maximum, and standard deviation of rainfall per year and per month (for the last five years). *Hint*: use a matrix.

# 10 STRINGS

## 10.1 INTRODUCTION

Strings are special arrays with data of type *character*. Recall that type *character* is a primitive type. A string is a sequence of data items of type *character*. Most of the data manipulated by programs is either numeric or string data. Strings are used to manipulate text data.

This chapter explains and discusses the concepts related to strings and their manipulation. There are several operators that are special to strings. These string operators are explained and applied in a few examples presented in the chapter. The declaration and manipulation of strings in Java is briefly discussed.

## 10.2 DECLARING STRINGS

String variables are of type *string* and can be declared with or without their values, in a similar manner to the variables of primitive types. The following declares a string variable, *message*.

```
string message
```

A value of type *string* is a string constant enclosed in quotes. For example, the following statement assigns a string value to the string variable *message*.

```
set message = "Hello, world!"
```

A string variable can be declared with a value; the following declares string variable *s2* with the string constant "Hi, everyone!".

```
string s2 = "Hi, everyone"
```

The two string variables just declared can be displayed on the console with the following statements:

```
display message
display s2
```

When executing the program that includes these two statements, the following message will appear on the screen:

```
Hello, world!
Hi, everyone
```

## 10.3 STRING AS AN ARRAY

A string value can be thought of as a sequence of data items of type *character* and implemented as a special array of characters. Recall that type *character* is a primitive type. This section discusses additional string

| H | e | l | l | o | , | | W | o | r | l | d | ! |
|---|---|---|---|---|---|---|---|---|---|---|---|---|
| 0 | 1 | 2 | 3 | 4 | 5 | 6 | 7 | 8 | 9 | 10 | 11 | 12 |

**Figure 10.1** Structure of string variable *message*.

operators for string manipulation. Figure 10.1 illustrates the structure and contents of string variable *message*.

Strings are special variables, they are immutable. After a string has been given an assigned string value, it cannot be changed.

### 10.3.1 Length of a String

Every string has a different number of characters. The string operator **length** gets the number of characters in a string variable. This operator is normally used in an assignment statement, and the target variable should be of type *integer*. The general syntax for the assignment statement with the *length* operator follows.

**set** ⟨ *int_var* ⟩ = **length of** ⟨ *str_var* ⟩

For example, to get the number of characters in the string variable *message* and assign this to the integer variable *num*, the complete statement is:

```
set num = length of message
```

### 10.3.2 Retrieving a Character of a String

To get a copy of a character located at some specified relative position of the string, the operator *charat* is used. The relative position of a character is known as the index. The integer value of the index starts at 0 and can be up to the value given by *length - 1*. Figure 10.1 shows the index value of the characters in a string.

The *charat* operator is normally used in an assignment statement, and the target variable should be of type *character*. The general syntax for the assignment statement with the *charat* operator follows.

**set** ⟨ *char_var* ⟩ = **charat** ⟨ *index* ⟩ **of** ⟨ *str_var* ⟩

For example, to get the character at the index value 7 in string variable *message* and assign this to character variable *llchar*, the portion of code is:

```
variable
    character llchar
    ...
    set llchar = charat 7 of message
```

When this statement executes, the value of variable *llchar* becomes `'W'`, which is the character at index position 7 of the string variable *message*.

### 10.3.3 Finding the Position of a Character

To find the position of a character within a string is finding the value of the index for the given character. The *indexof* operator searches the string from left to right. This operator is also used in an assignment statement. The general structure of this statement with the *indexof* operator follows.

**set** ⟨ *int_var* ⟩ = **indexof** ⟨ *char_var* ⟩ **of** ⟨ *str_var* ⟩

For example, to get the index value in string variable *message* for the character `'r'` and assign this to integer variable *num*, the complete statement is:

```
variable
    integer num
    ...
    set num = indexof 'r' of message
```

When this statement executes, the value of variable *num* becomes 9. If the starting index value is known, it can be included after the character in the assignment statement. If the character indicated does not exist in the string, then the value assigned is −1.

### 10.3.4 Retrieving a Substring from a String

A substring is part of a string. To retrieve a substring from a string, the index position of the character that starts the substring is needed. By default, the end of the substring is also the end of the string. The *substring* operator is used in an assignment statement and gets a substring that starts at a given index position up to the end of the string. The variable that receives this value is a string variable. The general structure of the assignment statement with the *substring* operator follows.

**set** ⟨ *str_var1* ⟩ = **substring** ⟨ *index* ⟩ **of** ⟨ *str_var2* ⟩

For example, to get the substring value that starts at index position 7 in string variable *message* and assign this to string variable *yystr*, the portion of code is:

```
variable
    character yystr
    integer num = 7
    ...
    set yystr = substring num of message
```

When this statement executes, the value of variable *yystr* becomes "World!" Two index values are used for substrings that have start and end index positions. For example, to retrieve the substring located at index positions 8 to 10 of string variable *message*, the portion of code with the assignment statement should be as follows.

```
variable
    character yystr
    integer num1 = 8
    integer num2 = 10
    ...
    set yystr = substring num1 num2 of message
```

When this statement executes, the value of variable *yystr* becomes "orl".

## 10.4 FINDING THE POSITION OF A SUBSTRING

To get the position of a substring within a string is very similar to that of a character. The operator *indexof* is also used to search for substrings. This operator searches the string from left to right. This operator is also used in an assignment statement. The general structure of this statement with the *indexof* operator follows.

**set** ⟨ *int_var* ⟩ = **indexof** ⟨ *str_var1* ⟩ **of** ⟨ *str_var2* ⟩

For example, to get the index value in string variable *message* for the substring "llo" and assign this to integer variable *num*, the complete statement is:

```
variable
    integer num
    string mystr = "llo"
    ...
    set num = indexof mystr of message
```

When this statement executes, the value of variable *num* becomes 9. If the starting index value is known, it can be included after the substring in the assignment statement. If the substring indicated does not exist in the string, then the value assigned is $-1$.

## 10.5 JOINING TWO OR MORE STRINGS

Two or more strings can be joined one after the other to build a larger string. The operation of joining two strings together is called concatenation. The **concat** operator is used to join two strings. This operator must be part of an assignment statement and appears between two variables. The following presents the general syntax of the assignment statement with the **concat** operator, variables *var_2* and *var_3* are joined the second after the first. The result of the *concat* operation is assigned to variable *var_1*.

**set** ⟨ *var_1* ⟩ = ⟨ *var_2* ⟩ **concat** ⟨ *var_3* ⟩

For example, the following statement joins together the string variable *message*, the string constant " and ", and the string variable *s2*. The resulting string is assigned to string variable *s3*.

```
string s3
...
set s3 = message concat " and " concat s2
```

When this statement executes, the value of string variable *s3* becomes:

```
"Hello, World! and Hi, everyone"
```

The flexibility of the operation that joins two or more strings is that a string variable can be concatenated to a variable of a different primitive type. For example, in the following statement string, variable *s3* is joined with a blank space and joined with the integer variable *j* and assigned to string variable *s4*.

```
integer j
string s4
. . .
set s4 = s3 concat " " concat j
```

The numeric value of variable *j* is converted automatically to a string and then joined with the other string values. The blank space was joined between variables *s3* and *j* for appearance when the string variable *s4* is displayed on the console.

## 10.6 COMPARING STRINGS

In KJP, a string *s1* can be compared with another string *s2* using the **equals** operator. This operator compares two strings and evaluates to a truth-value, so it can be used with an *if* statement. The general syntax for this operator follows—variable *str_var1* is compared to *str_var2*.

**if** ⟨ *str_var1* ⟩ **equals** ⟨ *str_var2* ⟩

For example, the following statement tests if string *s1* is equal to string *s2*:

```
variables
   string s1
   string s2
   . . .
begin
   . . .
   if s1 equals s2
   then
      . . .
```

Another operator for string comparison is the **compareto** operator, which compares two strings and evaluates to an integer value. If this integer value is zero, the two strings are equal. If the integer value is greater than zero, the first string is higher alphabetically with respect to the second string. If the integer value is less than zero, the first string is lower alphabetically with respect to the second string. The **compareto** operator is used in an assignment statement. The general structure of an assignment statement with this operator follows.

**set** ⟨ *int_var* ⟩ = ⟨ *str_var1* ⟩ **compareto** ⟨ *str_var2* ⟩

For example, the following KJP code compares string variables *s1* and *s2* in an assignment statement with integer variable *test*. This integer variable is then tested in an *if* statement for various possible sets of instructions.

```
variables
   string s1
   string s2
   integer test  // result of string comparison
   . . .
begin
   . . .
   set test = s1 compareto s2
   if test == 0
   then
      . . .
   if test > 0
   then
      . . .
   else
      . . .
```

In the example, variable *test* holds the integer values with the result of the string comparison of *s1* and *s2*. Variable *test* is subsequently evaluated in an *if* statement for further processing.

## 10.7 SEARCHING STRINGS

A typical application of arrays with strings is the search of a string value in an array of strings. The most critical statements are the string comparisons. The general array techniques for searching were discussed in Chapter 9.

This string comparison with the `equals` operator only tests if two strings are equal; it is useful in carrying out linear searches. For a binary search of strings, these need to be in alphabetical order. For this search, the comparison needed is more complete in the sense that if the strings are not equal, the order of the first string with respect to the second string needs to be known.

The following problem sets up an array of objects of class `Person`. Then, it carries out a linear search of the name of the objects, looking for a specific string value (the target string). The KJP implementation consists of two classes, `Person` and `Marrayperson`. Class `Person` was described in Chapter 5 (in Section 5.7).

The array of objects is declared in function *main* of class `Marrayperson`. The KJP statement for this declaration is:

```
object parray array [NUM_PERSONS] of class Person
```

The objects of class `Person` are created in a *for* loop—not all objects of the array are created. The KJP statement is:

```
create parray[j] of class Person using lage, lname
```

The string search on the name of an object is carried out in two steps within the loop. First, function *main* accesses and gets a copy of the attribute *name* of the object (of class `Person`) with index $j$. This is done by calling the accessor function *get_name* of the object and assigning it to string variable *tname*. Second, the function compares the target string *target_name* with the name attribute (in *tname*) of the object. The *equals* operator is used in an *if* statement for the string comparison.

```
set tname = call get_name of parray[j]
if target_name equals tname  // comparison
```

The general structure of the problem is the same as the linear search of a numeric array, which was discussed in Chapter 9. The complete KJP implementation of class Marrayperson follows.

```
description
    This is the main class in the program. It
    declares an array of objects of class Person.
    It creates objects of class Person and then
    manipulates the objects.    */
class Marrayperson is
  public
  description
    This is the control function.
    */
  function main is
    constants
      integer NUM_PERSONS = 15  // array capacity
    variables
      integer n                 // number elements
      integer lage              // current age
      string lname              // current name
      string target_name        // name to search
      string tname
      integer j
      integer result_ind        // element found
      boolean found = false
    objects
      object parray array [NUM_PERSONS] of
                                        class Person
    // body of function starts here
    begin
      display "Type number of objects to process: "
      read n
```

```
        for j = 0 to n - 1 do
            display "Type age of person: "
            read lage
            display "Type name of person: "
            read lname
            create parray[j] of class Person using
                          lage, lname
        endfor
        display "Type target name: "
        read target_name
        //
        // linear search for target name
        // result is index of array element with
        // object with the name found, or -1
        //
        set j = 0
        while j < n and found not equal true do
          set tname = call get_name of parray[j]
          if target_name equals tname
          then
             set result_ind = j
             set found = true
          else
             increment j
          endif
        endwhile
        if found not equal true
        then
          set result_ind = -1  // name not found
        endif
     endfun main
  endclass Marrayperson
```

ON THE CD

*The KJP implementation for this application is stored in several files. Class* `Marrayperson` *is stored in the file* `Marrayperson.kpl`. *Class* `Person` *is stored in the file* `Person.kpl`.

## 10.8 STRINGS IN JAVA

In Java, strings are defined as objects of class `String`, which is a library class. A string variable is really an object reference to the string. A string variable can be declared with a string value:

```
String ss = "Kennesaw State";
```

This statement automatically creates an object string referenced by variable *ss*. A string variable can be declared to reference a string that is the concatenation of two other strings. The concatenation operator + is used to join strings. For example, string variable *sfn* is a string resulting from joining strings in variables *ss* and *st*.

```
String st = "University";
String sfn = ss + st;
```

### 10.8.1 Basic Methods in Class String

To get the length of a string, method `length()` in class `String` is used. For example, to get the length of a string referenced by variable *ss* and assign this value to integer variable *intlen_ss*, the Java statement is:

```
int intlen;
...
intlen_ss = ss.length();
```

The character located at a given index position in a string can be found by invoking method `charAt(...)` of the string variable. For example, to get the character at index position 5 in the string referenced by variable ss and assign this to character variable *mychar*:

```
char mychar;
...
mychar = ss.charAt(5);
```

Other similar methods defined in class String are:

- indexOf(...) gets the index position of the first occurrence in the string object of the character in the argument. For example, int intvar = ss.inexOf(mychar); tries to find the first occurrence of character variable *mychar* in string object *ss*, and assigns the value to integer variable *intvar*. If the character cannot be found, this method returns $-1$. This method can also be invoked with a substring in the argument; it gets the index position of the first character in the matching substring argument.

- substring(...) gets the substring in the string object that starts at the given index position. For example, String mysubstr = ss.substring(8); gets the substring that starts at index position 8 in the string referenced by *ss* and the substring takes the object reference *mysubstr*. When two arguments are used with this method, the substring has the first argument as the starting index position, and the second argument as the end index position.

- toLowerCase() gets a copy of the string in lowercase. For example, String mylcstr = ss.toLowerCase(); converts a copy of the string referenced by *ss* to lowercase and this new string is referenced by *mylcstr*.

- toUpperCase() gets a copy of the string in uppercase. For example, String mylcstr = ss.toUppperCase(); converts a copy of the string referenced by *ss* to uppercase and this new string is referenced by *mylcstr*.

### 10.8.2 Comparing Strings in Java

To compare strings, various functions defined in class `String` can be used. A string *s1* can be compared with another string *s2* using the *equals* function in class `String`. The expression `s1 == s2` does not really compare the two strings. It compares if the two variables are referencing the same string object. The *equals* function of the first string is invoked with the second string as the argument. This function compares two strings and evaluates to a truth-value, so it can be used with an *if* statement.

For example, the following Java statement tests if the string referenced by *s1* is equal to the string referenced by *s2*:

```
String s1;
String s2;
  . . .
if (s1.equals(s2))
      . . .
```

This string comparison only tests if two strings are equal; it is useful in carrying out linear searches. For a binary search of strings, these need to be in alphabetical order. For this search, the comparison needed is more complete in the sense that if the strings are not equal, the order of the first string with respect to the second string needs to be known.

Function *compareTo* defined in class `String` compares two strings and evaluates to an integer value. If this integer value is equal, the two strings are equal. If the integer value is greater than zero, the first string is higher alphabetically with respect to the second string. If the integer value is less than zero, the first string is lower alphabetically with respect to the second string. The *compareTo* function of the first string is invoked with the second string as the argument. This function is invoked in an assignment statement. For example, the comparison of strings *s1* and *s2* is:

```
String s1;
String s2;
int test;  // result of string comparison
```

```
    . . .
test = s1.compareTo(s2);
if (test == 0)
    . . .
if (test > 0)
    . . .
else
    . . .
```

In the example, variable *test* holds the integer values with the result of the string comparison of *s1* and *s2*. Variable *test* is subsequently evaluated in an *if* statement for further processing.

CAUTION *Because string objects cannot be modified, Java provides class* `StringBuffer`. *This library class can be instantiated by creating string objects that can be modified.*

Several methods of class `StringBuffer` are similar to the ones in class `String`. Other methods, such as *insert*(...), allow a character or a substring to be inserted at a specified index position.

## 10.9 SUMMARY

Strings are sequences of characters. Because each character has an index position in the string, this is similar to an array of characters. String variables are not variables of a primitive type. String variables have a set of operators that enable the manipulation of strings.

In Java, strings are considered objects of class `String`. This class is available in the Java class library. To manipulate strings in Java, various methods of class `String` are used.

Strings cannot be modified, Java provides the `StringBuffer`, another library class that can be instantiated to create modifiable strings. By using the various methods of this class, strings can be manipulated and modified.

## 10.10 KEY TERMS

| | | |
|---|---|---|
| character sequence | string variable | string constant |
| concatenation | string comparison | string searching |
| string length | index position | substring |
| class `String` | class `Stringbuffer` | |

## 10.11 EXERCISES

1. Design and implement a class that inputs a string and creates a copy of the input string with the characters in reverse order.
2. Design and implement a class that inputs a long string and counts the number of times that the word "and" appears; the class should display this number on the console.
3. Design and implement a class that inputs a string and checks if the string is a palindrome; if so, it displays the message "`is a palindrome`" on the console. A palindrome is a string that does not change when the characters are changed to reverse order.
4. Design and implement a class that inputs a string and checks if the string starts with the substring "Mr. " or with the string "Mrs. " Note the space after the dot. If the input string does not include any one of these substrings, the class should display a message.
5. Design and implement the solution to a problem that sets up an array of objects of class `Person`. The solution should carry out a binary search of the name of the objects looking for a specific string value (the target string). *Hint*: modify class `Marrayperson` in Chapter 9.
6. Design and implement a solution to a problem that rearranges an array of objects of class `Person`. For this, use selection sort. *Hint*: modify class `Marrayperson` in Chapter 9.
7. Redesign and reimplement the solution for Exercise 6 with an array parameter definition in the function. Use the appropriate call to the function.

# 11 BASIC OBJECT-ORIENTED MODELING

## 11.1 INTRODUCTION

Almost all phases of the software development process require definition of the model using an appropriate notation. The Unified Modeling Language (UML) is a standard graphical notation for describing the model of the problem by describing objects, classes, their relationships, and the behavior of objects.

This chapter explains basic object-oriented modeling in some detail. The models are described with various UML diagrams of the first two groups.

## 11.2 UML DIAGRAMS

The UML language provides a set of syntactic and semantic rules for representing the system in a semigraphical form. UML is an expressive visual modeling tool to help develop and express meaningful models. The UML modeling language does not include a develop methodology for constructing object-oriented applications.

The UML includes a collection of diagrams; each one describes a different view of an application or system. The diagrams are:

1. Use case diagrams
2. Class and object diagrams
3. Object interaction diagrams
   - Sequence diagrams
   - Collaboration diagrams
4. State diagrams
   - State diagrams
   - Activity diagrams
5. Implementation diagrams
   - Package diagrams
   - Component diagrams
   - Deployment diagrams

Often, only a subset of these diagrams is needed to completely model an application. The most relevant UML diagrams are described in this chapter. The UML stereotype provides an extension mechanism to the UML that allows users to extend the modeling language according to their needs. Two examples of stereotypes are ≪*actor*≫ and ≪*active*≫, which are used in the following subsections

### 11.2.1 Use Case Diagrams

These diagrams define the interactions between users and an application. The use case diagrams describe the main functionality of the application and its interactions with external entities called *actors*. A UML actor is a user, an external system, or external hardware. Such an interaction is a way that a user or an external entity can use the application. Each one of these interactions is represented by a use case.

Use cases are triggered or initiated by actors and describe the sequence of events that follow. Use case diagrams define the major processes of a system and the boundary on the problem. The diagrams also define who (or what) will use the application, and define the interactions that are allowed.

Typically, an application consists of one or more use cases, which are the processes within the application. These processes are represented as ovals, with the names inside the ovals. The application or system is represented by a rectangle, with the name of the application inside the rectangle. A line joining the actor and the use case represents the communication between each actor and its corresponding use case. An actor is shown in one of several ways; the most common is by using the stereotype ≪*actor* ≫.

Figure 11.1 shows a use case diagram for the movie rental application. There are two use cases in this example. The actors are the users of the system, who interact with the application by starting to search for a movie or by renting a movie to a customer.

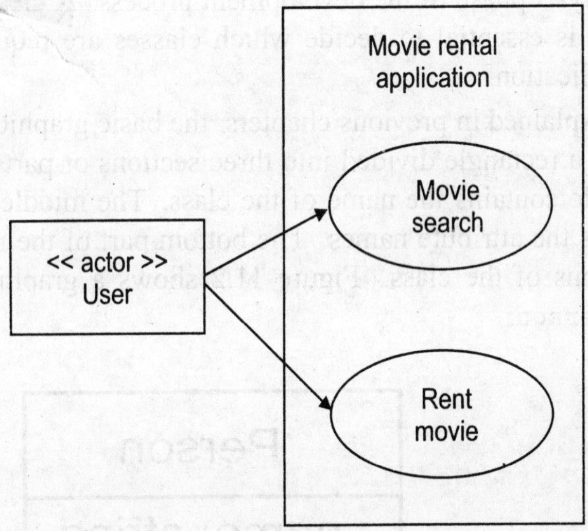


**Figure 11.1** A use-case diagram for the movie rental application.

The use cases are identified in the first part of the analysis phase of the software development process. They serve to define the user requirements.

## 11.3 STATIC MODELING DIAGRAMS

The static modeling diagrams describe the static characteristics of a system or application. These modeling UML diagrams describe the various classes in the application, the relationship among the classes, and the objects. These diagrams are also categorized as static diagrams.

### 11.3.1 Class Diagrams

The UML class diagrams describe the structure of the classes in an application model and their relationships. These diagrams are the main static descriptions of the application. These diagrams consist of the class descriptions and their relationships. These diagrams are constructed during the analysis phase of the development process. A clear idea of the problem domain is essential to decide which classes are required in the model of the application.

As explained in previous chapters, the basic graphical representation of a class is a rectangle divided into three sections or parts. The top part of the rectangle contains the name of the class. The middle part of the rectangle contains the attribute names. The bottom part of the rectangle contains the operations of the class. Figure 11.2 shows a graphical representation of class `Person`.

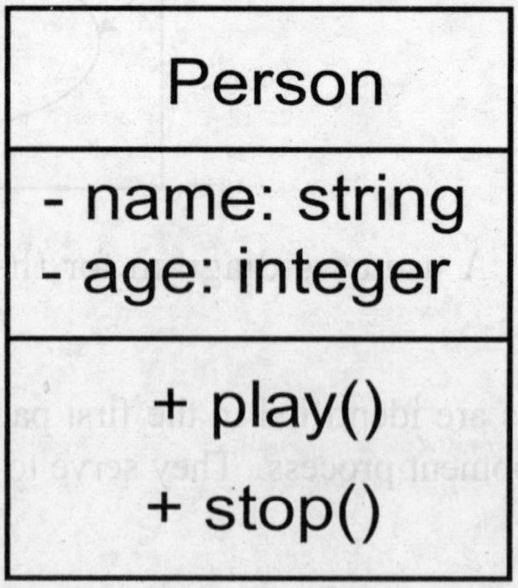


**Figure 11.2** Class `Person`.

In addition to the basic represenation of a class, the type of each attribute and the access mode of each feature is also normally shown. In Figure 11.2, the type shown for attribute *name* is *string*. The type shown for attribute *age* is *integer*. The access mode of the two attributes is *private*, shown by a – sign before the name of the attribute. The access mode for the two operationss is public, shown by + sign before the name of the operation. For features with *protected* access mode, the # sign would be included before the name of the feature.

The object diagram is often shown as a variation of the class diagram. Figure 11.3 shows a UML object diagram. The main differences of an object diagram are:

- The name of the class of the object is underlined. For example, `:Person` denotes an object of class `Person`.
- The attributes of the object include their current values. This defines the current state of the object. The types of the attributes are not included because these are defined in the class.
- The operations of the object are included. When these are left out, they are defined in the corresponding class.

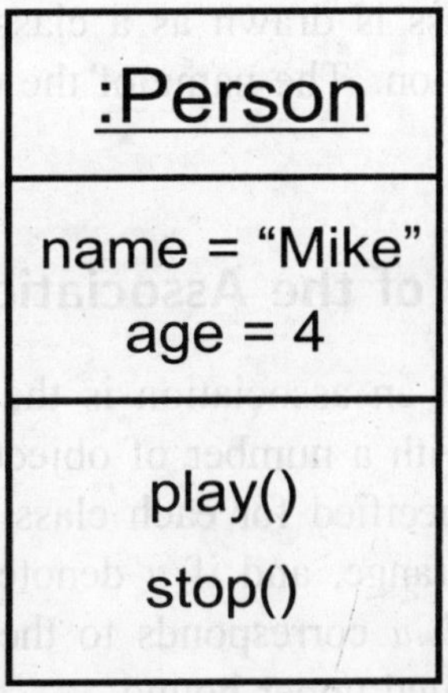


**Figure 11.3** An object of class `Person`.

### 11.3.2 Associations

An association is a relationship between two or more classes. The simplest association is the binary association, which is represented by a solid line connecting two classes in the corresponding UML diagram. The name of the association may be included just above the line. The association name may also include a solid small triangle to indicate the direction in which to read the association name. The associations can also include roles, which are shown at the ends of the line, close to the corresponding classes.

A binary association is shown in Figure 11.4. It shows a binary relation between class `Person` and class `Ball`. The name of the association here is *plays_with*, and the roles are *customer* and *provider*.

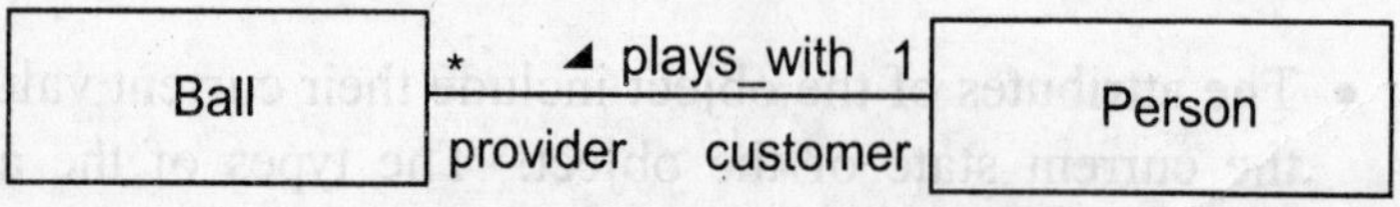


**Figure 11.4** A binary association between classes `Person` and `Ball`.

A class can be used to describe or define an association. This notation is used when it is useful to define attributes and operations to an association. An association class is drawn as a class symbol connected by a dashed line to the association. The name of the class is the name assigned to the association.

### 11.3.3 Multiplicity of the Association

The multiplicity of an association is the number of objects of one class in a relationship with a number of objects of the other class. A range of numbers can be specified for each class in the diagram. If $l$ denotes the lower bound in a range, and if $u$ denotes the upper bound in the range, then the notation $l..u$ corresponds to the range. When a star is used, it indicates an unlimited upper bound.

The star at the side of class `Ball` in Figure 11.4 denotes that there can be zero or many objects of this class in the association with class `Person`. There is only one object of class `Person`.

### 11.3.4 Aggregation

An n-ary association is a relationship that involves more than two classes. When a relationship exists among classes where some classes are contained within other classes, the relationship is known as aggregation, or *part-whole* relationship or containment. In simple aggregation, the larger class is called the *owner* class; the smaller classes are called *component* classes. Often, classes are not contained in other classes but are organized in the communication mechanism through the class representing the whole.

With UML aggregation diagrams, this relationship is denoted with a diamond at the owner class side of the association. Figure 11.5 shows an owner class `Computer`, in associations with three component classes, `CPU`, `Memory`, and `Input/Output`.

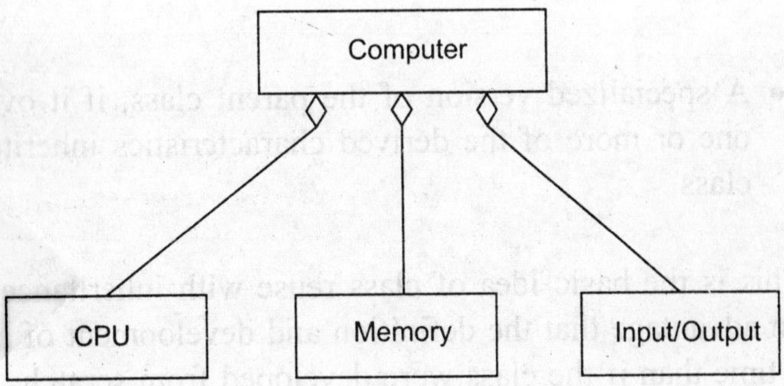


**Figure 11.5** An aggregation relationship with four classes.

*Composition* is a stronger form of aggregation in which the owner class has exclusive ownership of the contained class. In UML notation, it is shown as a solid diamond at the end of the line that represents the association.

### 11.3.5 Inheritance

Inheritance is a vertical relationship among classes. It allows for enhanced class *reuse*, that is, the ability to develop a new class using a predefined and previously developed class. This allows the sharing of some classes across several different applications. The new class inherits the characteristics of the existing and more general class, to incorporate the characteristics into the new class.

In most practical applications, classes are arranged in hierarchies, with the most general class at the top of the hierarchy. A *parent* class is also called the *super* class (or the base class). A *derived* class inherits the characteristics (all attributes and operations) of its parent class. A derived class can be further inherited to lower-level classes. In the UML class diagram, an arrow with an empty head points from a subclass (the derived class) to its parent class.

A subclass can be:

- An extension of the parent class, if it includes its own attributes and operations, in addition to the derived characteristics it inherits from the parent class

- A specialized version of the parent class, if it overrides (redefines) one or more of the derived characteristics inherited from its parent class

This is the basic idea of class reuse with inheritance, which has as its main advantage that the definition and development of a class takes much less time than if the class were developed from scratch. This is the reason why class reuse is important.

In UML terminology, generalization is the association between a general class and a more specialized class (or extended class). This association is also called *inheritance*, and it is an important relationship between classes. Therefore, in modeling, it is useful to show this in the class diagrams. In the UML class diagram, an arrow points from a class (the derived class) to its parent class.

CAUTION *When a class inherits the characteristics from more than one parent class, the mechanism is called multiple inheritance. Most object-oriented programming languages support multiple inheritance (KJP and Java do not).*

Figure 11.6 illustrates a simple class hierarchy with inheritance. The parent class is `Polygon` and the subclasses are: `Triangle`, `Rectangle`, and `Parallelogram` that inherit the features from the parent class.

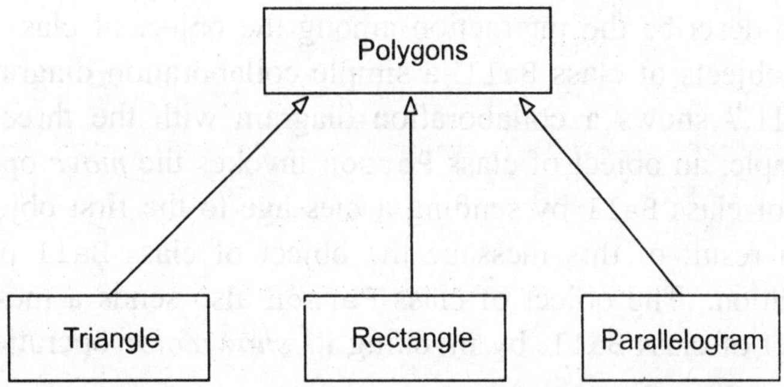


**Figure 11.6** An inheritance relationship.

## 11.4 MODELING DYNAMIC CHARACTERISTICS

In addition to the UML diagrams that describe the static characteristics of an application, UML includes a group of diagrams to describe the dynamic characteristics or behavior. These diagrams describe the individual behavior (the ordering of events and activities) of the objects and interactions among objects in an application. The sequence and collaboration diagrams describe the message communication among objects. The state diagrams show more detailed behavior of an object.

### 11.4.1 Collaboration Diagrams

The UML collaboration diagram describes the general interactions among objects. The diagram shows the overall connectivity of the objects in the application. This gives a complete high-level view of the overall communication architecture of the system. A collaboration diagram includes the notation for showing the direction of the messages by using arrows and the sequence of these messages by numbering them.

Collaboration diagrams can also be used to describe additional details of the interaction among objects. As explained before, the UML notation for an object is the rectangle. The label is written as follows: the name of the object, a colon, and the name of the class to which it belongs. The complete label must be underlined. The name of the object is optional.

To describe the interaction among the object of class `Person` with the two objects of class `Ball`, a simple collaboration diagram is drawn. Figure 11.7 shows a collaboration diagram with the three objects. In this example, an object of class `Person` invokes the *move* operation of the object of class `Ball` by sending a message to the first object of class `Ball`. As a result of this message the object of class `Ball` performs its *move* operation. The object of class `Person` also sends a message to the other object of class `Ball`, by invoking its *show_color* operation.

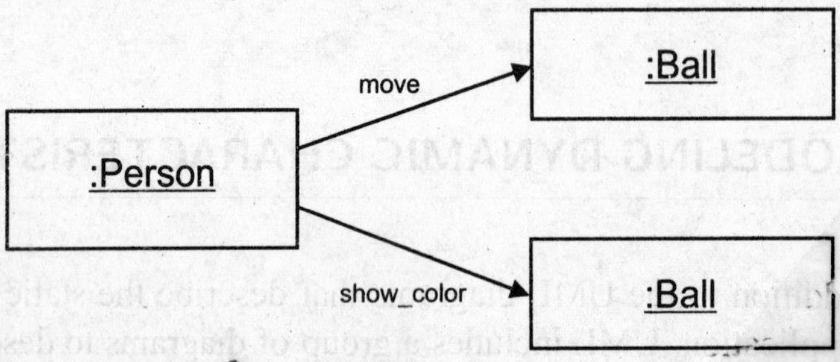


**Figure 11.7** Collaboration diagram with three objects.

### 11.4.2 Sequence Diagrams

These UML diagrams describe the interaction among objects arranged in a *time sequence*. The objects involved in the interaction are shown as rectangles arranged in a horizontal manner. In addition to the objects involved in the interaction, these diagrams have two important components: the lifelines of each object and the messages from one object to another object. The lifelines are shown as vertical dashed lines starting from each object (top). These vertical lines represent the object existence during the interaction. Each message is shown as a horizontal arrow from one object to another. Each message is labeled with a message name. Figure 11.8 shows a sequence diagram with three objects, one of class `Person` and two objects of class `Ball`.

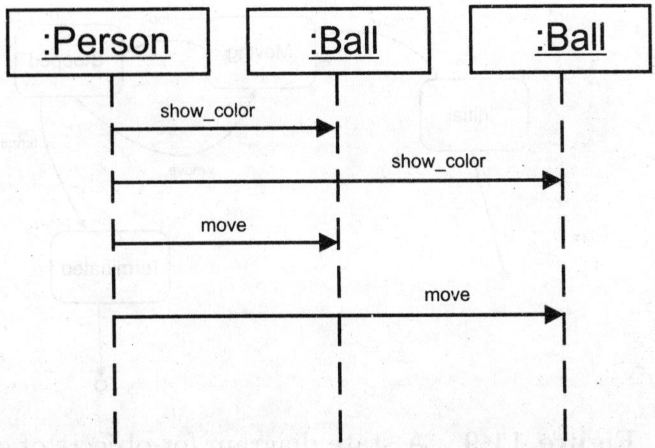


**Figure 11.8** A sequence diagram with three objects.

### 11.4.3 State Diagrams

The state diagram describes the sequence of states that an object performs in response to *events* or messages from other objects. Each state diagram describes the behavior of only one object. The state of an object is determined by the values of its attributes. The object carries out an activity while it is in a state. A *transition* is the change from one state to the next state as a result of an event or message.

The states are represented as rectangles with rounded corners, with the name of the state inside the rectangle. The transitions are represented as arrows connecting two states: the source state and the destination state. The label of the transition is the name of the message or event that triggered the transition. The transition may also include a list of arguments in parentheses for the event and an action or activity that the object must carry out as a result of the transition.

Usually, a black dot indicates the start of the transitions of an object. This transition leads to the first state. The last state is shown as the state with an arrow pointing to a black dot inside a circle. This corresponds to the last transition of the object. Figure 11.9 shows a state diagram for an object of class `Ball`.

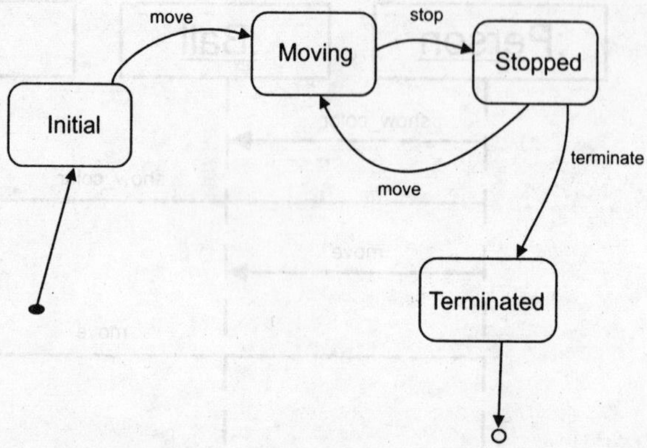


**Figure 11.9** A state diagram for objects of class `Ball`.

## 11.5 SUMMARY

The UML notation is a standard semigraphical notation for modeling a problem with various types of diagrams. These diagrams are grouped into two categories. The first group describes the static aspects of the model, and the second group describes the dynamic aspects of the model.

The class diagrams are one of the most basic and important diagrams. They show the structure of the classes in the model and the relationship among these classes. Other static modeling diagrams are object diagrams and use cases.

The UML dynamic modeling diagrams show the behavior of objects and their interactions. These are collaboration, sequence, and state diagrams.

## 11.6 KEY TERMS

| | | |
|---|---|---|
| UML diagrams | static modeling | dynamic modeling |
| class diagrams | object diagrams | use cases |
| collaboration diagrams | sequence diagrams | state diagrams |
| actor | role | multiplicity |
| cardinality | association | generalization |
| inheritance | aggregation | composition |
| extension | specialization | transition |

## 11.7 EXERCISES

1. Explain the difference between the class diagram and the object diagram. What are the similarities?

2. Explain the differences and similarities between the collaboration diagram and the sequence diagram.

3. Construct more detailed and complete UML diagrams (static and dynamic modeling) for the movies rental problem. This application must control the inventory of movies in a movie rental shop.

4. Construct the relevant UML diagrams (static and dynamic modeling) for the problem of the child playing with two balls. Explain the diagrams used in this application.

5. Construct the relevant UML diagrams (static and dynamic modeling) of a program that reads rainfall data in inches for yearly quarters, for the last five years. The program should compute the average rainfall per quarter (for the last five years), the average rainfall per year, and the maximum rainfall per quarter and for each year.

6. Construct the relevant UML diagrams (static and dynamic modeling) of a program that calculates the volume of several spheres. For each sphere, the program should compute the volume. Before termination, the program should compute and display the average volume for all the spheres. After computing the volume of a sphere, the program asks the user if he wants to continue.

7. Construct the relevant UML diagrams (static and dynamic modeling) of a program that reads data for every inventory item code and calculates the total value (in dollars) for the item code. The program also calculates the grand total inventory value. The number of inventory data to read is not known, so the program should continue reading data until the user replies that there are no more inventory items to process. Every item includes item code, item description, the number of items of that code in stock, and the unit value.

8. Consider an automobile rental office. A customer can rent an automobile for a number of days and with a finite number of miles (or kilometers). Identify the type and number of objects involved. For every type of object, list the properties and operations. Construct static and dynamic modeling diagrams for this problem.

# 12 INHERITANCE

## 12.1 INTRODUCTION

The previous chapter discussed class relationships. The two basic categories of relationship among classes are composition and inheritance. These relationships are modeled in UML diagrams, and it can be said that composition is a horizontal relationship and inheritance is a vertical relationship.

Inheritance is a mechanism provided by an object-oriented language for defining new classes from existing classes. This chapter explains the basic inheritance relationships and their applications in some detail. Inheritance enhances class reuse, that is, the use of a class in more than one application.

## 12.2 CLASSIFICATION

Classification is a modeling concept, and for a given application, it refers to the grouping of the objects with common characteristics. In this activity, the classes and their relationships are identified. Some classes of an application are completely independent—only the class with function *main* has a relationship with them. The other classes in the application are related in some manner and they form a hierarchy of classes.

In a class hierarchy, the most general class is placed at the top. This is the *parent* class and is also known as the *super* class (or the *base* class). A *derived* class inherits the characteristics (all attributes and operations) of its parent class. A derived class can be further inherited to lower-level classes. In the UML class diagram, an arrow with an empty head points from a subclass (the derived class) to its base class to show that it is inheriting the features of its base class. Because in the UML diagram, the arrow showing this relationship points from the subclass up to the base class, inheritance is seen as a vertical relationship between two classes (see Figure 12.1).

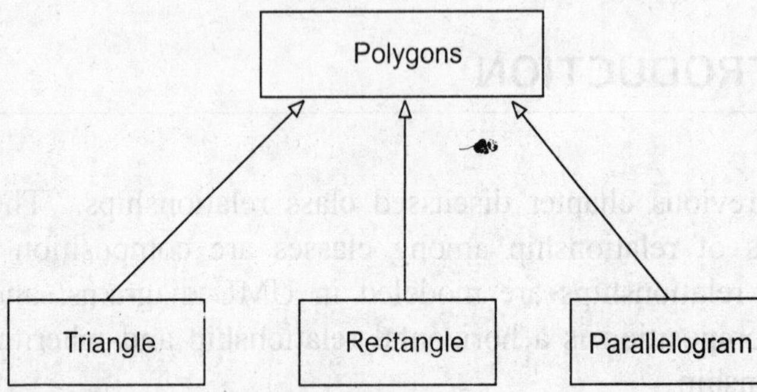


**Figure 12.1** An inheritance relationship.

## 12.3 INHERITANCE

Inheritance is a mechanism by which a new class acquires all the nonprivate features of an existing class. This mechanism is provided by object-oriented programming languages. The existing class is known as the parent class, the *base* class, or the *super* class. The new class being defined, which inherits the nonprivate features of the base class, is known as the *derived* class or *subclass*.

The new class acquires all the features of the existing base class, which is a more general class. This new class can be tailored in several ways by the programmer by adding more features or modifying some of the inherited features.

The main advantage of inheritance is that the definition and development of a class takes much less time than if the class were developed from scratch. Another advantage of inheritance is that it enhances class reuse. A subclass can be:

- An extension of the base class, if it includes its own attributes and operations, in addition to the derived characteristics it inherits from the base class
- A specialized version of the base class, if it overrides (redefines) one or more of the characteristics inherited from its parent class
- A combination of an extension and a specialization of the base class

When a class inherits the characteristics from more than one parent class, the mechanism is called multiple inheritance. Most object-oriented programming languages support multiple inheritance; however, Java and KJP support only single inheritance. Therefore, in modeling, it is useful to show this in the class diagrams.

In UML terminology, *generalization* is the association between a general class and a more specialized class or extended class. This association is also known as *inheritance*, and it is an important relationship between classes. In the UML class diagram, the arrow that represents this relationship points from a class (the derived class) to its parent class.

Figure 12.1 illustrates a simple class hierarchy with inheritance. The parent class is `Polygon` and the subclasses are: `Triangle`, `Rectangle`, and `Parallelogram` that inherit the features from the parent class. The idea of a subclass and a subtype is important. All objects of class `Parallelogram` are also objects of class `Polygon`, because this is the base class for the other classes. On the contrary, not all objects of class `Polygon` are objects of class `Parallelogram`.

### 12.3.1 Defining New Classes with Inheritance

In KJP and in Java, the subclass acquires all the public and protected features of the base class. A protected feature is only accessible to the class that defines it and to the subclasses. The only public features that are not inherited by the subclasses are the initializer functions of the base classes.

In KJP, the definition of a subclass must include the keyword **inherits** to name the base class that it inherits. The general structure of the KJP statement that defines a subclass is:

```
description
   ...
class ⟨ class_name ⟩ inherits ⟨ base_class_name ⟩ is
   private
      ...
   protected
      ...
   public
      ...
endclass ⟨ class_name ⟩
```

Because a subclass can also be inherited by another class, it often includes protected features in addition to the private and public ones. In UML class diagrams, a feature of the class is indicated with a plus (+) sign if it is public, with a minus (-) sign if it is private, and with a pound (#) sign if it is protected.

### 12.3.2 Initializer Functions in Subclasses

An initializer function of the subclass will normally need to invoke the initializer function of the base class. The special name given to the initializer function of the base class is *super*. This call must be the first statement in the initializer function of the subclass. Calling this function may require arguments, and these must correspond to the parameters defined in the initializer function of the base class.

*Initializer (constructor) functions are not inherited. A derived class must provide its own initializer functions. These are the only public features that are not inherited by the subclass.*

The KJP statement to call or invoke an initializer function of the base class from the subclass is:

**call super** ⟨ **using** *argument_list* ⟩

If the argument list is absent in the call, the initializer function invoked is the default initializer of the base class.

Suppose a new class, `Toyball`, is being defined that inherits the features of an existing (base) class `Ball`. The attributes of class `Ball` are *color* and *size*. The color attribute is coded as integer values (white is 0, blue is 2, yellow is 3, red is 4, black is 5). Class `Ball` includes an initializer function that sets initial values to these two attributes.

The subclass `Toyball` has one other attribute, *weight*. The initializer function of this class needs to set initial values to the three attributes, two attributes of the base class and the one attribute of the subclass. The two attributes of the base class (`Ball`) are set by invoking the function *super* in the initializer function of the subclass, `Toyball`.

```
class Toyball inherits Ball is
    private
    // attributes
    variables
        real weight
    // no private methods in this class
    public
        // public methods
    description
       This is the constructor, it initializes an
       object on creation.     */
    function initializer parameters real iweight,
                             integer icolor, real isize is
```

```
        begin
           // call the initializer of the base class
           call super using icolor, isize
           set weight = iweight
        endfun initializer
           . . .
    endclass Toyball
```

The attributes of a class are private, so the only way to set the initial values for the attributes of base class is to invoke its initializer function of the base class. In the previous KJP code, this is accomplished with the statement:

```
call super using icolor, isize
```

### 12.3.3 Example Using Extension

Consider revising the employee salary problem presented in previous chapters. The problem consists of three classes, as seen in Figure 12.2.

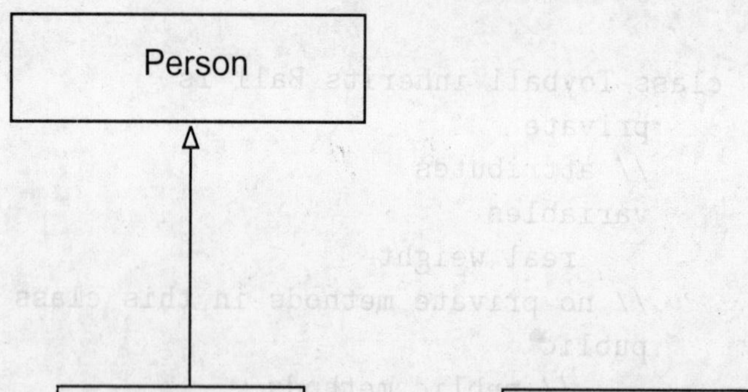


**Figure 12.2** An inheritance diagram for the Employee problem.

The base class, Person, has the basic and general characteristics of the objects in the problem. The subclass, Employeec, inherits the features of the base class and is an extension of the base class by adding two new attributes, *salary* and *years_service*, and several new functions. This class computes the salary increase for employee objects. If the object's salary is greater than \$45,000.00, the salary increase is 4.5%; otherwise, the salary increase is 5%.

ON THE CD

*The code for the KJP implementation of base class* Person *follows; this is stored in the file* Person.kpl.

```
description
  This is the complete definition of class Person.
  The attributes are age and name.  */
class Person is
  private
  // attributes
  variables            // variable data declarations
      integer age
      string obj_name
  // no private methods in this class
  public
  description
    This is the default initializer method.     */
  function initializer is
    begin
     set age = 21
     set obj_name = "None"
  endfun initializer
  //
  description
    This is a complete initializer function, it
    sets the attributes to the values given on
    object creation.    */
  function initializer parameters integer iage,
                               string iname is
  begin
```

```
         set age = iage
         set obj_name = iname
       endfun initializer
       description
         This accessor function returns the name
         of the object.
         */
       function get_name of type string is
         begin
           return obj_name
       endfun get_name
       description
         This mutator function changes the name of
         the object to the name in 'new_name'. This
         function is void.   */
       function change_name parameters
                                   string new_name is
         begin
           set obj_name = new_name
       endfun change_name
       description
         This function returns the age of the Person
         object.    */
       function get_age of type integer is
         begin
           return age
       endfun get_age
       description
         This mutator function increases the age of
         the person object when called.    */
       function increase_age is
         begin
           increment age
       endfun increase_age
     endclass Person
```

The following KJP code implements class Employeec, which is a subclass of class Person. Class Employeec computes the salary increase.

```
description
  This class computes the salary increase for
  an employee. If his/her salary is greater than
  $45,000, the salary increase is 4.5%; otherwise,
  the salary increase is 5%. This is the class
  for employees. The main attributes are salary,
  age, and name.  */
class Employeec inherits Person is
  private
  variables
      integer years_service
      real salary
  public
  description
    This is the initializer function (constructor),
    it initializes an object on creation.    */
  function initializer parameters real isalary,
                        integer iage, string iname is
  begin
    // call the initializer in the base class
    call super using iage, iname
    set salary = isalary
    set years_service = 0
  endfun initializer
  description
      This function gets the salary of the employee
      object.   */
  function get_salary of type real is
    begin
      return salary
  endfun get_salary
  description
      This accessor function gets the years of
      service of the employee object.       */
```

```
function get_years_serv of type integer is
  begin
    return years_service
endfun get_years_serv
description
   This mutator function changes the years of
   service of the object by adding change_y to
   current years. This function is void.    */
function change_yearsv parameters
                              integer change_y is
begin
   add change_y to years_service
endfun change_yearsv
description
   This function changes the salary of the
   Employee object by adding change to current
   salary.       */
function change_sal parameters real change is
begin
   add change to salary
endfun change_sal
description
    This function computes the salary increase
    and updates the salary of an employee. It
    returns the increase.          */
function sal_increase of type real is
  // constant data declarations
  constants
    // percentages of salary increase
    real percent1 = 0.045
    real percent2 = 0.05
  variables
    real increase
  begin        // body of function starts here
    if salary > 45000 then
       set increase = salary * percent1
    else
```

```
        set increase = salary * percent2
     endif
     add increase to salary  // update salary
     return increase
   endfun sal_increase
 endclass Employeec
```

ON THE CD

*Class* Employee *is stored in file* Employeec.kpl. *Class* Memployeec *includes the definition of function* main*, which creates and manipulates objects of class* Employeec. *This class is stored in the file* Memployeec.kpl *and the KJP implementation is:*

```
import Conio    // Library class for console I/O
description
  This program computes the salary increase for
  an employee. This class creates and
  manipulates objects of class Employeec.  */
class Memployeec is
  public
  description
    The main function of the application.  */
  function main is
    variables
      integer obj_age
      real increase
      real obj_salary
      string obj_name
    objects
      object emp_obj of class Employeec
    begin
      display "Enter name: "
      read obj_name
      display "Enter age:"
      read obj_age
      display "Enter salary: "
      read obj_salary
```

```
        create emp_obj of class Employeec using
                    obj_salary, obj_age, obj_name
        set increase = call sal_increase of
                                        emp_obj
        set obj_salary = get_salary() of emp_obj
        display "Employee name: ", obj_name
        display "increase: ", increase,
                        " new salary: ", obj_salary
    endfun main
endclass Memployeec
```

ON THE CD

*The Java implementation of class* Employeec *is shown next, and is stored in the file* Employeec.java.

```
// KJP v 1.1 File: Employeec.java, Sat Dec 21
                                    14:47:01 2002
/**
   This class computes the salary increase for
   an employee. If his/her salary is greater than
   $45,000, the salary increase is 4.5%; otherwise,
   the salary increase is 5%. This is the class
   for employees. The main attributes are salary,
   age, and name.  */
public  class Employeec extends Person {
   private int  years_service;
   private float  salary;
   /**
     This is the initializer function (constructor),
     it initializes an object on creation.     */
   public Employeec(float  isalary, int iage,
                                    String  iname)
     // call the initializer in the base class
     {super(iage, iname);
     salary =  isalary;
     years_service = 0;
   } // end constructor
```

```
/**
   This function gets the salary of the employee
   object.   */
public float  get_salary() {
   return salary;
}  // end get_salary
/**
   This accessor function gets the years of
   service of the employee object.      */
public int  get_years_serv() {
   return years_service;
}  // end get_years_serv
/**
   This mutator function changes the years of
   service of the object by adding change_y to
   current years. This function is void.     */
public void  change_yearsv(int  change_y) {
   years_service += change_y;
}  // end change_yearsv
/**
   This function changes the salary of the
   Employee object by adding change to current
   salary.     */
public void  change_sal(float  change) {
   salary += change;
}  // end change_sal

/**
   This function computes the salary increase
   and updates the salary of an employee. It
   returns the increase.        */
public float  sal_increase() {
   // constant data declarations
   // percentages of salary increase
   final float  percent1 = 0.045F;
   final float  percent2 = 0.05F;
   float  increase;
```

```
            // body of function starts here
            if ( salary > 45000) {
               increase =  salary * percent1;
            }
            else {
               increase =  salary * percent2;
            } // endif
            // update salary
            salary += increase;
            return increase;
        }  // end sal_increase
     }     // end Employeec
```

The resulting screen output from the execution of the program with class Memployeec is shown in Figure 12.3.

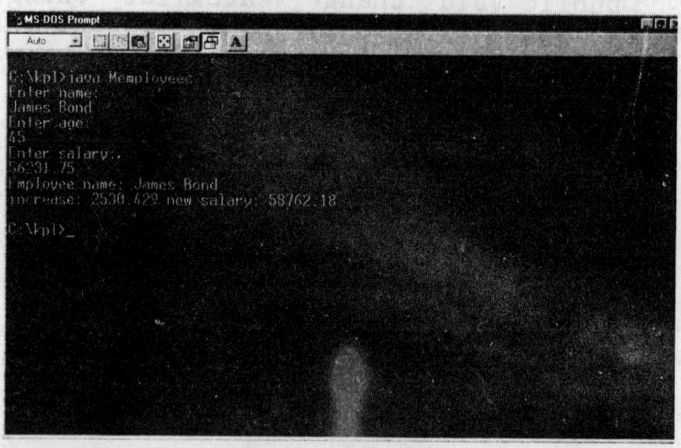


**Figure 12.3** Output of execution of problem with class Memployeec.

### 12.3.4 Inheritance with Specialization

When a subclass is a specialization of the base class, then one or more functions of the base class are redefined (or overridden) by the subclass. The subclass reimplements one or more functions of the base class.

Suppose that in the salary problem described in the previous section, a specialized class, Manager, includes a different calculation for salary increase. Objects of class Manager have similar characteristics as objects of class Employee. The only difference is that the salary increase is computed as 2.5% of the salary plus $2700.00.

*The KJP implementation of class* Manager *is stored in the file* Manager.kpl *and is shown next.*

Class Manager is a specialized version of class Employeec. Class Manager inherits class Employeec and overrides function *sal_increase.*

```
description
  This class computes the salary increase for a
    manager; the salary increase is 2.5% of the
    salary plus $2700.00. */
class Manager inherits Employeec is
  public
  description
    This is the initializer function (constructor),
      it initializes an object on creation.     */
  function initializer parameters real isalary,
                                  integer iage, string iname is
  begin
    // call the initializer of the base class
    call super using isalary, iage, iname
  endfun initializer
  description
    This function computes the salary increase
      and updates the salary of a manager object.
      It returns the increase.          */
  function sal_increase of type real is
    constants
      real MAN_PERCENT = 0.025
    variables
      real increase
      real salary
    begin                           // body of function
```

```
        set salary = call get_salary
        set increase = salary * MAN_PERCENT + 2700.00
        add increase to salary  // update salary
        return increase
    endfun sal_increase
endclass Manager
```

Class Manager does not include any attributes; the initializer function invokes the initializer of its base class to set the initial values of all the inherited attributes.

Attribute *salary* is a private attribute of the base class Employeec; to access the value of this attribute, function *get_salary* is called and is used to compute the salary increase in function *sal_increase*.

As mentioned before, a more practical case of inheritance involves the subclass as an extension and specialization of the base class.

ON THE CD

*Class* Mmanager *includes the definition of function* main, *which creates and manipulates objects of class* Manager. *Class* Mmanager *is stored in file* Mmanager.kpl.

## 12.4 SUMMARY

Inheritance is a vertical relationship among classes. This relationship enhances class reuse. A subclass (derived class) inherits all the features of its base (parent) class. Only the public and protected features can directly be accessed by the base class. The initializer (constructor) functions of the base class are not inherited; all classes are responsible for defining their initializer functions.

A subclass can be an extension and/or a specialization of the base class. If a subclass defines new features in addition to the ones that it inherits from the base class, then the subclass is said to be an extension to the base class. If a subclass redefines (overrides) one or more functions of the base class, then the subclass is said to be a specialization of the base class. The UML class diagrams show the inheritance relationships.

## 12.5 KEY TERMS

| | | |
|---|---|---|
| classification | parent class | super class |
| base class | subclass | derived class |
| horizontal relationship | vertical relationship | class hierarchy |
| inherit | extension | specialization |
| class reuse | association | generalization |
| inheritance | reuse | overiding |

## 12.6 EXERCISES

1. Explain the difference between horizontal and vertical relationships. How can these be illustrated in UML diagrams?
2. In what way does inheritance enhance class reuse? Why is this important?
3. Because attributes are private in KJP, explain the limitations in dealing with inheritance.
4. One of the examples discussed in this chapter is class `Toyball` as a subclass of class `Ball`. Draw UML diagrams, and design and write a complete KJP program for a sport using specialized objects of class `Ball`. Choose tennis or volleyball (or any other sport of your preference).
5. Repeat the previous problem with the subclass being a specialization and an extension of the base class.
6. Draw the corresponding UML diagrams, redesign, and rewrite class `Manager` for the salary problem. Provide a class that includes function *main* and that creates and manipulates objects of class `Manager` and objects of class `Employeec`. Class `Manager` should be an extension and a specialization of class `Employeec`. Explain how class reuse is being applied in this problem.
7. Refer to Figure 12.1. Design and write the class definitions for the four classes. Class `Polygon` is the base class, the most simple and

general class in the hierarchy. The other three classes are specializations and/or extensions of the base class. These three classes should provide functions to compute the perimeter and the area for the corresponding objects.

8. How would you include classes `Circle` and `Sphere` in the class hierarchy of the previous problem? Write the KJP program with the class implementations for these two classes..

9. A complex number has two attributes, the real part and the imaginary part. The two basic operations on complex numbers are complex addition and complex subtraction. Design and implement a KJP program for simple complex numbers. A slightly more advanced pair of operations are complex multiplication and complex division. Design and write the KJP program that includes an extension to the basic complex numbers. *Hint*: in addition to the rectangular representation of complex numbers (x,y), it might be useful to include attributes for the polar representation of complex numbers (module, angle).

10. Consider a class hierarchy involving motor vehicles. At the top of the hierarchy, class `Motor_vehicle` represents the most basic and general type of vehicles. `Automobiles`, `Trucks`, and `Motorcycles` are three types of vehicles that are extensions and specializations of the base class. `Sport_automobiles` are included in the class hierarchy as a subclass of `Automobile`. Design and implement a KJP program with all these classes. Include attributes such as horse power, maximum speed, passenger capacity, load capacity, and weight. Include the relevant functions.

# 13 ABSTRACT CLASSES, INTERFACES, AND POLYMORPHISM

## 13.1 INTRODUCTION

As discussed in Chapter 12, inheritance is a mechanism provided by an object-oriented language for defining new classes from existing classes. Inheritance enhances class reuse, that is, the use of a class in more than one application.

Inheritance also helps in dealing with generic modeling and programming. With generics, the more general classes are separated from the more specific or concrete classes. This separation helps to enhance reuse of the more general definitions in modeling and in programming.

Abstract classes help improve the object-oriented model of the problem. They help clarify the understanding of the model and provide good specifications. Interfaces allow the introduction to pure specifications, the complete separation between specification and implementation. Polymorphism is a mechanism that allows more flexibility in the design and provides generic programming.

This chapter discusses the three important and related concepts mentioned: abstract classes, interfaces, and polymorphism.

## 13.2 ABSTRACT CLASSES

The inheritance relationship was discussed in Chapter 12. Figure 13.1 illustrates a simple inheritance relationship with four classes `Gfigures`, `Triangle`, `Circle`, and `Rectangle`.

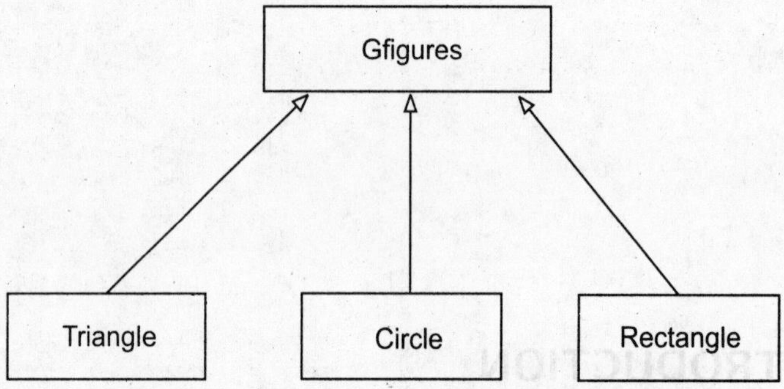


**Figure 13.1** A generic base class.

The characteristics of the geometric figures are related in some way. Assume that the relevant attributes defined in these classes are *height*, *base*, and *radius*. The relevant functions defined in the classes are *area* and *perimeter*.

An abstract class is one that includes one or more abstract methods. An abstract method has no implementation, only its declaration (also called its specification).

*An abstract class cannot be instantiated; it is generally used as a base class. The subclasses override the abstract methods inherited from the abstract base class.*

### 13.2.1 Defining an Abstract Class

To define an abstract class, the keyword **abstract** should be used before the keyword **class**. Every function that does not include its implementation is also preceded by the keyword **abstract**. An abstract class definition in KJP has the following general structure:

```
description
    . . .
abstract class ⟨ class_name ⟩ is
  private
      // private attributes
    constants
        . . .
    variables
        . . .
    objects
        . . .
    // private operations
        . . .
  public
      // public operations
        . . .
endclass ⟨ class_name ⟩
```

The attributes of derived classes `Rectangle`, `Triangle`, and `Circle` are different. Classes `Rectangle` and `Triangle` have the attributes *height* and *base*; Class `Circle` has the attribute *radius*. The calculations of area and perimeter are different in each of these subclasses. In this situation, the base class (`Gfigures`) cannot include the implementations for functions *area* and *perimeter*. It can only provide the prototypes for these functions.

A base class is an abstract class when it does not provide the implementation for one or more functions. Such base classes provide single general descriptions for the common functionality and structure of its subclasses. An abstract class is a foundation on which to define subclasses. Classes that are not abstract classes are known as concrete classes.

The base class `Gfigures` is an abstract class because it does not provide the implementation of the functions *area* and *perimeter*. The KJP code with the definition of class `Gfigures` follows.

```
description
   This abstract class has two functions. */
```

```
abstract class Gfigures is
  public
  description
    This function computes and returns the area
    of the geometric figure.    */
  abstract function area of type double
  description
    This function computes and returns the perimeter
    of the geometric figure.    */
  abstract function perimeter of type double
endclass Gfigures
```

ON THE CD

*The KJP code with the implementation of this class is stored in the file* `Gfigures.kpl`. *The Java code for class* `Gfigures` *is stored in the file* `Gfigures.java`.

CAUTION

*Because the abstract class* `Gfigures` *does not include the body of the functions area and perimeter, objects of this class cannot be created. In other words, class* `Gfigures` *cannot be instantiated.*

In Java, the structure of the abstract class is very similar. The definition of this abstract class follows.

```
// KJP v 1.1 File: Gfigures.java, Sat Jan 04
                                      19:03:07 2003
/**
  This abstract class with two functions.    */
public abstract class Gfigures {
  /**
   This function computes and returns the area of
   the geometric figure.    */
  abstract public double area();
  /**
   This function computes and returns the perimeter
   of the geometric figure.    */
  abstract public double  perimeter();
 }  // end class Gfigures
```

## 13.2.2 Using Abstract Classes

The subclasses that inherit an abstract base class need to override (redefine) the functions that are defined as abstract functions in the abstract base class. The subclasses that are shown in Figure 13.1, `Rectangle`, `Triangle`, and `Circle`, inherit class `Gfigures` and each includes the specific implementation of the functions *area* and *perimeter* and the relevant attributes.

ON THE CD

*The following KJP code includes the complete definition of class* `Triangle`. *This inherits the function from class* `Gfigures` *and redefines functions area and perimeter. The code for this class is stored in the file* `Triangle.kpl`.

```
description
      This class computes the area and perimeter
      of a triangle, given its three sides.  */
class Triangle inherits Gfigures is
  private
  variables
      double x     // first side
      double y     // second side
      double z     // third side
  public
  description
      This constructor sets values for the three
      sides of the triangle.        */
  function initializer parameters double i_x,
                            double i_y, double i_z is
    begin
      set x = i_x
      set y = i_y
      set z = i_z
  endfun initializer
  description
    This function computes the perimeter of a
    triangle. */
  function perimeter of type double is
```

```
        variables
            double lperim
        begin
            set lperim = x + y + z
            return lperim
      endfun perim
      description
          This function computes the area of a
          triangle.     */
      function area of type double is
        variables
            double s     // intermediate result
            double r
            double area
        begin
            set s = 0.5 * (x + y + z)
            set r = s * (s - x)*(s - y)*(s - z)
            set area = Math.sqrt(r)
            return area
      endfun area
  endclass Triangle
```

To construct a complete application with class `Triangle`, a new class named `Mtriangle` is defined. This class includes function *main* that reads the three values for the sides of the triangle. Then, it creates an object of class `Triangle` and invokes functions *area* and *perimeter* of the object.

```
description
    This program computes the area and peri-
    meter of a triangle, given its three sides. */
class Mtriangle is
    public
    description
        This function gets the area and perimeter
        of a triangle object.        */
    function main is
      variables
```

```
            double x    // first side
            double y    // second side
            double z    // third side
            double area
            double perim
         objects
            object my_triangle of class Triangle
         begin
           display "This program computes the area"
           display " of a triangle"
           display "enter value of first side: "
           read x
           display "enter value of second side: "
           read y
           display "enter value of third side: "
           read z
           create my_triangle of class Triangle using x,
                                                     y, z
           set area = call area of my_triangle
           display "Area of triangle is: ", area
           set perim = call perimeter of my_triangle
           display "Perimeter of triangle is: ", perim
        endfun main
     endclass Mtriangle
```

After translating the classes Triangle and Mtriangle and compiling then with the Java compiler, class Mtriangle can be executed. The output produced on the console is:

```
This program computes the area
of a triangle
enter value of first side:
2
enter value of second side:
4
enter value of third side:
5
```

```
Area of triangle is: 3.799671038392666
Perimeter of triangle is: 11.0
```

## 13.3 INTERFACES

An interface is similar to a pure abstract class. It does not include attribute definitions and all its methods are abstract methods. Constant definitions are allowed. An interface does not include constructors and cannot be instantiated.

### 13.3.1 Defining an Interface

To define an interface, the keyword **interface** must be used instead of *abstract class* and before the name of the interface. For the functions, the keyword **abstract** is not needed because all the functions are abstract functions. In a similar manner, all features of an interface are implicitly public. An interface definition in KJP has the following general structure:

**description**
. . .
**interface** ⟨ *interface_name* ⟩ **is**
  **public**
  **constants**
  . . .
  `// public operations`
  . . .
**endinterface** ⟨ *interface_name* ⟩

The following interface, named `Iball`, defines the specification for the behavior of objects of any class that implements this interface. Note that the structure of the interface is very similar to that of an abstract class.

```
description
  This is a simple interface using KJP   */
```

```
interface Iball is
  public
  description
    This method accesses the value of attribute
    color    */
  function get_color of type integer
  description
    This method reads the value of attribute size
    from the console.     */
  function get_size of type real
  description
      This function returns the value of the
      move_status.          */
  function get_m_status of type character
  description
      This function displays the color, status, and
        size of the object. */
  function show_state
  description
      This function changes the move_status of
      the object to move.  */
  function move
  description
      This function changes the move_status of
      the object to stop.       */
  function stop
 endinterface Iball
```

### 13.3.2 Using an Interface

A class makes use of an interface by implementing it. All methods declared in the interface must be implemented in the class that implements it. This class can define additional features. The class that implements an interface must use KJP statement **implements**. The header for the class definition that uses this KJP statement has the following general structure:

**description**

. . .

**class** ⟨ *cls_name* ⟩ **implements** ⟨ *interface_name* ⟩ **is**

. . .

**endclass** ⟨ *cls_name* ⟩

ON THE CD

*For example, class* Nball *implements interface* Iball, *which was defined earlier. The KJP code for this class follows and is stored in the file* Nball.kpl.

```
// Simple class using KJP
// Jan 2003, J Garrido
//
description
  This class implements an interface.  */
class Nball implements Iball is
  private
  // attributes
  variables
      integer color
      character move_status
      real size
  public
  // public methods
  description
    Constructor initializes the state.    */
  function initializer parameters integer icolor,
                                        real isize is
  begin
    set color = icolor
    set move_status = 'S'
    set size = isize
  endfun initializer
  description
    This method accesses the value of attribute
```

```
    color. */
  function get_color of type integer is
  begin
    return color
  endfun get_color
  description
    This method accesses the value of attribute size.
    */
  function get_size of type real is
  begin
    return size
  endfun get_size
  description
      This function returns the value of the
      move_status.       */
  function get_m_status of type character is
    begin
        return move_status
  endfun get_m_status
  description
      This function displays the color, status,
      and size of the object.    */
  function show_state is
    begin
      display "Color of ball object: ", color
      display "Size of ball object: ", size
      display "Status of ball object: ",
      move_status
  endfun show_status
  description
      This function changes the move_status of
      the object to move.     */
  function move is
    begin
      set move_status = 'M'
  endfun move
  description
```

```
          This function changes the move_status of
          the object to stop.         */
      function stop is
        begin
          set move_status = 'S'
      endfun stop
    endclass Nball
```

One of the significant differences between an interface and an abstract class is that multiple interfaces can be implemented by a class, whereas only one abstract base class can be inherited by a subclass. Another important difference is that no data attribute definitions are allowed in an interface, only constant definitions. It is mandatory for a class that implements an interface to implement all the functions defined in the interface.

## 13.4 SUBTYPES

Although an interface and an abstract class cannot be instantiated, both can be used as super types for object references. This implies that interfaces and abstract classes are useful for declaring object references.

For example, refer again to Figure 13.1. Class `Gfigures` is an abstract class and the other classes are subclasses. An object reference can be declared of type `Gfigures`.

```
objects
    object gen_figure of class Gfigures
    ...
```

In a similar manner, objects of the subclasses can be declared of each of their classes. The subclasses are considered subtypes of type `Gfigures`. For example, the following declaration defines three object references, *triangle_obj*, *circle_obj*, and *rect_obj*.

```
objects
    object triangle_obj of class Triangle
    object circle_obj of class Circle
    object rect_obj of class Rectangle
  ...
```

The types of these object references declared are considered subtypes in the problem domain because of the original class hierarchy represented in Figure 13.1. For this organizational structure of the problem, the object reference *triangle_obj* is declared of type `Triangle`, but is also of type `Gfigures`. In fact, any object reference of type `Triangle` is also of type `Gfigures`. The same principle applies to the object references declared with the types `Circle` and `Rectangle`. Of course, the opposite is not true; any object reference of type `Gfigures` is not also of type `Rectangle`, `Circle`, or `Triangle`.

An interface can also be used as a super type, and all the classes that implement the interface are considered subtypes.

## 13.5 POLYMORPHISM

An object reference of a super type can refer to objects of different subtypes. This is possible from the subtyping principle explained before. To illustrate this concept, the following code creates objects for the object references *triangle_obj*, *circle_obj*, and *rect_obj*. Assume there is a declaration for variables $x$, $y$, $z$, and $r$.

```
create triangle_obj of class Triangle using x, y, z
create circle_obj of class Circle using r
create rect_obj of class Rectangle using x, y
```

The object reference *gen_figure* of class `Gfigures` can be assigned to refer to any of the three objects, *triangle_obj*, *circle_obj*, and *rect_obj*, created previously. For example, the following link implements such an assignment.

```
set gen_figure = triangle_obj
```

This is perfectly legal, because the type of object reference *triangle_obj* is a subtype of the type of object *gen_figure*. After this assignment, it is possible to invoke a function of the abstract class Gfigures that is implemented in the subclass Triangle. For example, the following code invokes function *perimeter*:

```
call perimeter of gen_figure
```

The actual function invoked is the one implemented in class Triangle, because it is the type of object reference *triangle_obj*. At some other point in the program (possibly in function *main*), another similar assignment could be included. The following code assigns the object reference *circle_obj* to the object reference *gen_figure*.

```
set gen_figure = circle_obj
```

The call to function *perimeter* is the same as before, because the three subtypes represented by the three subclasses Rectangle, Circle, and Triangle implement function *perimeter*. Because the implementation for this function is different in the three classes, the runtime system of the Java compiler selects the right version of the function.

Polymorphism is a runtime mechanism of the language that allows the selection of the right version of a function to be executed depending on the actual type of the object. Only one among several possible functions is really called. This function selection is based on *late binding* because it occurs at execution time.

## 13.6 HETEROGENEOUS ARRAY

The following problem applies the concepts of arrays and of polymorphism. A list of objects is required to store geometric figures and to calculate the perimeter and area of each figure when selected from the list. The geometric figures are circles, triangles, and rectangles.

The list is designed as an array of objects of class `Gfigures`. The solution to this problem is generic by using this abstract class, the base class for all the other classes. The type of the array is `Gfigures`, this class was defined in Sections 13.2.1 and Section 13.2.2. The capacity of the array is set with constant `MAX_GEOM`.

Each element of the array is an object reference of a concrete class, `Circle`, `Triangle`, or `Rectangle`. Figure 13.2 illustrates the basic structure of this heterogeneous array.

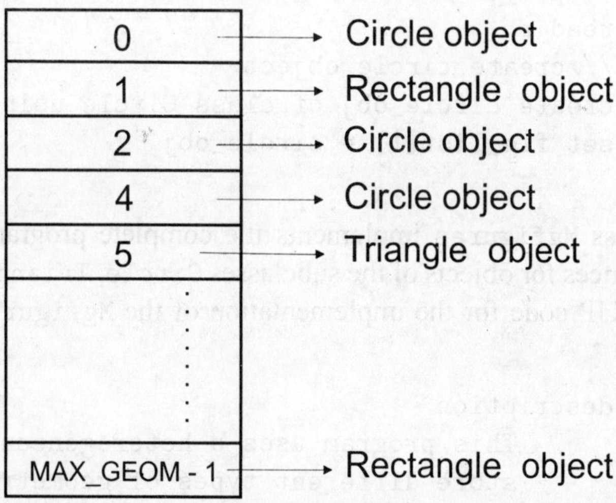


**Figure 13.2** A heterogeneous array of objects.

An object is created for every object reference in the array. To process the array, the index value is used to access the needed element and invoke the methods to compute the perimeter and the area of the geometric figure. The execution of these functions is carried out via polymorphism. The implementation of the problem solution in KJP is not too different than the one explained in the first part of this chapter. The following statements declare (and create) an array of geometric figures and declare an object of class `Circle`.

```
object fig_list array [MAX_GEOM] of class Gfigures
object circle_obj of class Circle
```

The type of array is the base class Gfigures, an abstract class. The types of the objects referred by the array elements are of the concrete classes that are subtypes of Gfigures. The following statements create an object of class Circle and assign it to an element of array *fig_list*.

```
// read value for radius
display "enter value of radius for circle: "
read r
// create circle object
create circle_obj of class Circle using r
set fig_list[1] = circle_obj
```

Class Mgfigures implements the complete program for storing object references for objects of the subclasses Circle, Triangle, and Rectangle. The KJP code for the implementation of the Mgfigures class follows.

```
description
      This program uses a heterogeneous array to
      store different types of geometric figures.
      For each element, the corresponding object
      computes the area and perimeter of the fi-
      gure.  */
class Mgfigures is
  public
  description
      This function gets the area and perimeter of
      a triangle object.   */
  function main is
    constants
       integer MAX_GEOM = 15 // array capacity
    variables
       integer i   // index for array processing
```

```
        double x    // first side
        double y    // second side
        double z    // third side
        double r    // radius
        double area
        double perim
    objects
        object geom_figure of class Gfigures
        object triangle_obj of class Triangle
        object circle_obj of class Circle
        object rect_obj of class Rectangle
        object fig_list array [MAX_GEOM] of
                                   class Gfigures
    begin
        // Read data
        display "enter value first side of triangle: "
        read x
        display "enter value second side: "
        read y
        display "enter value third side: "
        read z
        // create triangle object
        create triangle_obj of class Triangle using x,
                                                  y, z
        set fig_list[0] = triangle_obj
        // read data
        display "enter value radius of circle: "
        read r
        // create circle object
        create circle_obj of class Circle using r
        set fig_list[1] = circle_obj
        // read data
        display "Enter value first side of rectangle: "
        read x
        display "enter value of second side: "
        read y
        // create rectangle data
```

```
          create rect_obj of class Rectangle using x, y
          set fig_list[2] = rect_obj
          // invoke polymorphic functions
          for i = 0 to 2 do
             set area = call area of fig_list[i]
             display "Area of geometric fig is: ", area
             set perim = call perimeter of fig_list[i]
             display
                "Perimeter of geometric fig is: ", perim
          endfor
       endfun main
    endclass Mgfigures
```

Note that only three elements of the array are actually used, although the array has 15 elements. The Java code for class Mgfigures follows.

*The KJP code with the implementation of class* Mgfigures *is stored in the file* Mgfigures.kpl, *and the Java code implementation is stored in the file* Mgfigures.java.

```
// KJP v 1.1 File: Mgfigures.java, Thu Jan 23
                                      19:42:37 2003
/**
      This program uses a heterogeneous array
      to store different types of geometric fi-
      gures. For each element, the corresponding
      object computes the area and perimeter of
      the figure.  */
public  class Mgfigures {
/**
      This function gets the area and perimeter of
      a triangle object.    */
  public static void main(String[] args) {
    final int  MAX_GEOM = 15; // array capacity
    int i;      // index for array processing
    double  x; // first side
    double  y; // second side
```

```
double  z;  // third side
double  r;  // radius
double  area;
double  perim;
Gfigures geom_figure;
Triangle triangle_obj;
Circle circle_obj;
Rectangle rect_obj;
// body of function starts here
Gfigures fig_list[]= new Gfigures [MAX_GEOM];
// read data
System.out.println(
      "enter value first side of triangle: ");
x = Conio.input_Double();
System.out.println(
                "enter value second side: ");
y = Conio.input_Double();
System.out.println("enter value third side: ");
z = Conio.input_Double();
// create triangle object
triangle_obj = new Triangle(x, y, z);
fig_list [0] =  triangle_obj;
// read data
System.out.println(
           "enter value radius of circle: ");
r = Conio.input_Double();
// read circle object
circle_obj = new Circle(r);
fig_list [1] =  circle_obj;
// read data
System.out.println(
      "Enter value first side of rectangle: ");
x = Conio.input_Double();
System.out.println(
                  "enter value second side: ");
y = Conio.input_Double();
// create rectangle object
```

```
        rect_obj = new Rectangle(x, y);
        fig_list [2] = rect_obj;
        for (i = 0 ; i <= 2; i++) {
           area =  fig_list [i].area();
           System.out.println(
                    "Area of geometric fig is: "+area);
           perim =  fig_list [i].perimeter();
           System.out.println(
             "Perimeter of geometric fig is: "+ perim);
        } // endfor
      }  // end main
    }  // end Mgfigures
```

The output for an execution run of this class is shown next. The input values are shown in the text file as shown. Note that the values of the sides of the triangle correspond to a well-defined triangle.

```
enter value of first side of triangle:
2
enter value of second side:
4
enter value of third side:
5
enter value radius of circle:
3.5
Enter value of first side of rectangle:
4.5
enter value of second side:
7.25
Area of geometric fig is: 3.799671038392666
Perimeter of geometric fig is: 11.0
Area of geometric fig is: 38.4844775
Perimeter of geometric fig is: 21.99113
Area of geometric fig is: 32.625
Perimeter of geometric fig is: 23.5
```

## 13.7 SUMMARY

Abstract classes have one or more abstract methods. An abstract method does not include its implementation, only the function declaration, also known as the function specification. These classes cannot be instantiated; they can only be used as base classes. The subclasses redefine (override) the functions that are abstract in the base class. A pure abstract class has only abstract methods. An interface is similar to a pure abstract class, but it cannot declare attributes. An interface may include constant declarations and may inherit another interface. A class can implement several interfaces.

A base class can be used as a super type, and the subclasses as subtypes. An abstract class can be used as a type of an object variable (object reference). This object variable can be assigned object variables of a subtype. There are normally several object variables of each subtype. It is then possible to invoke a function of an object variable of a subtype. Polymorphism is a language mechanism that selects the appropriate function to execute. This selection is based on late binding. Polymorphism uses the type of the actual object and not the type of the object variable.

## 13.8 KEY TERMS

| | | |
|---|---|---|
| abstract class | concrete class | abstract method |
| function overriding | pure abstract class | interface |
| super type | subtype | polymorphism |
| late binding | heterogeneous array | |

## 13.9 EXERCISES

1. Explain the differences and similarities between interfaces and abstract classes. Give two examples.

2. Explain the differences and similarities between polymorphism and overloading. Give examples.

3. Explain the differences between implementing an interface and overriding the methods of an abstract class. Give two examples.

4. Explain the differences between function overriding and polymorphism. Give two examples.

5. Does function overriding imply polymorphism? Is it possible to override one or more functions without using polymorphism? Explain and give an example.

6. Is it possible to define an abstract base class and one or more subclasses without using polymorphism? Explain and give an example.

7. Which is the most straightforward way to overcome the Java (and KJP) limitation of only supporting single inheritance? Give an example.

8. Enhance the problem with base class `Gfigures` discussed in Section 13.2.1 and illustrated in Figure 13.1. Add the capability to the geometric figures to draw themselves on the screen using dots and dashes. Define an interface at the top of the hierarchy. Write the complete program.

9. A company has several groups of employees, executives, managers, regular staff, hourly paid staff, and others. The company needs to maintain the data for all employees in a list. Design a solution to this problem that uses a heterogeneous array of employee objects. Use an abstract base class and apply polymorphism to process the list (array). Write the complete program.

10. Repeat the previous problem defining an interface instead of an abstract base class. Compare the two solutions to the problem.

11. Design a hierarchy for animals. Find some behavior in all animals that is carried out in different manners (eat, move, reproduce, or others). Define the top-level animal category with an abstract base class and one or more interfaces. Define and implement the subclasses. Write the complete program.

# 14 BASIC GRAPHICAL USER INTERFACES

## 14.1 INTRODUCTION

Previous chapters have described development of console applications in which all input/output is carried out only through the console (video screen and keyboard). With graphical user interfaces (GUIs), the users have a much better way to interact with the programs. The user actually interacts with graphical elements, such as buttons, dialog boxes, menus, and so on.

Programs with graphical user interfaces present the user with a nice and convenient arrangement of graphical components and guide the user in a very effective manner when interacting with the application.

Java provides two important graphical libraries (or packages) of classes. The first library of classes is called the abstract windows toolkit (`AWT`) and was the only one used in early versions of Java. The second library is called `Swing`; it is an enhanced collection of graphical classes.

This chapter discusses and explains the design and construction of simple GUIs using the two graphical libraries. Most of the examples presented use mainly the `Swing` library. Also discussed in this chapter are *applets*, which are small applications that execute in a Web browser.

## 14.2 GRAPHICAL OBJECTS

When running GUI applications, a typical user looks at some graphical objects on the screen. Some of these objects display data of the program. Other graphical objects allow the user to enter data to the program. The user can also point and click with other graphical objects, and in this way, can interact with the program in execution. The most relevant objects that form part of a graphical user interface are:

- Containers
- Components
- Events
- Listeners

### 14.2.1 Components and Containers

Simple GUIs have only containers and components. Graphical interfaces that only include these objects present very limited user interaction. With *events* and *listeners*, in addition to components and containers, the full advantage of user interaction is made available.

A *container* is an object that can hold graphical components and smaller containers. A container object also allows its contained objects to be arranged in various ways. This arrangement of objects is facilitated by special objects called layout managers. Examples of container objects are *frames* and *panels*.

A *component* is a small graphical object that displays data, allows the user to enter data, or simply indicates some condition to the user. Component objects are usually arranged with other components in a container object. Examples of component objects are buttons, labels, and text fields.

Figure 14.1 shows the basic structure of a simple graphical user interface. The frame is divided into two panels, and each panel contains several graphical components.

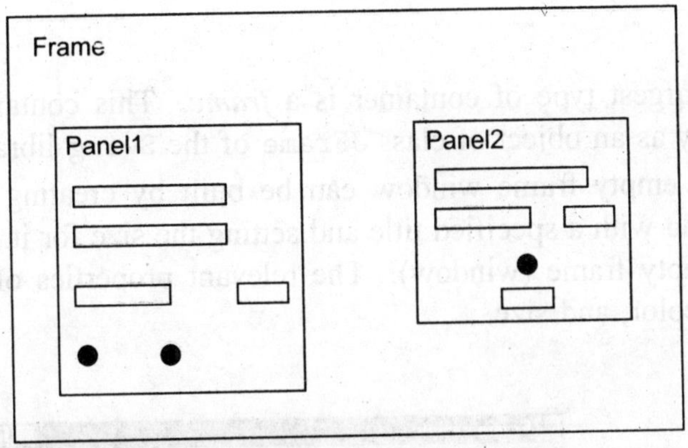


**Figure 14.1** General structure of a GUI.

### 14.2.2 Importing the AWT and Swing Libraries

A *package* is a group of related classes. A library package is a predefined group of classes that are available on the current environment.

NOTE *Several precompiled Java classes are provided in various packages with the Java compiler. Other library packages are provided by third parties.*

The *import* statement is required by any class definition that needs access to one or more classes in a library package. Most programs that include GUI, need to access the two Java class packages, `AWT` and `Swing`. In the programs, an import statement must be included at the top of a class definition.

The following two lines of code are the ones normally required by programs that access the graphical libraries `AWT` and `Swing`. The import statements shown give access to all the classes in the two packages.

```
import all java.awt
import all javax.swing
```

## 14.3 FRAMES

The largest type of container is a *frame*. This container can be created simply as an object of class `JFrame` of the `Swing` library.

An empty frame window can be built by creating an object of class `JFrame` with a specified title and setting the size for it. Figure 14.2 shows an empty frame (window). The relevant properties of this frame are its title, color, and size.

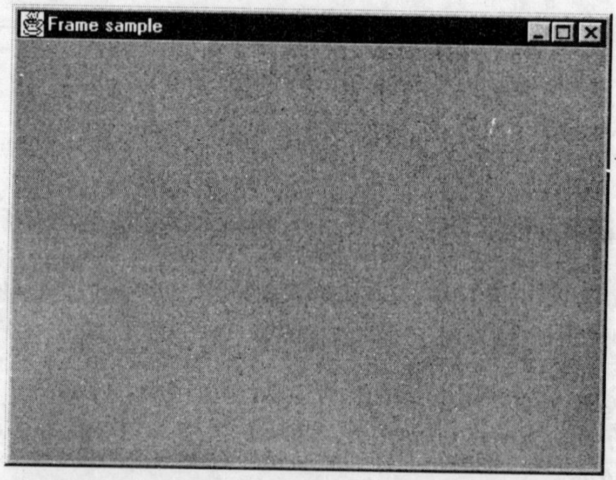


**Figure 14.2** A sample empty frame.

The KJP code in Class *Frame_sample* implements the construction of an empty frame with title "Frame sample" and size of 400 by 300 pixels. The title is set by invoking the constructor of the frame object, and the size is set by invoking the method `setSize` of object *frame_obj*. To make the frame window visible, method `setVisible` is invoked.

ON THE CD

*The KJP code that implements class* `Frame_sample` *follows. It is stored in the file* `Frame_sample.kpl`. *The Java implementation of the class is stored in the file* `Frame_sample.java`.

```
import all javax.swing       // Library for graphics
description
    This class creates and displays an empty frame
     window.    */
class Frame_sample is
  public
  description
      This is the main function of the application.
      */
  function main is
    constants
      integer WIDTH = 400
      integer HEIGHT = 300
    objects
      object frame_obj of class JFrame
    begin
      create frame_obj of class JFrame using
              "Frame sample"
      call setSize of frame_obj using WIDTH, HEIGHT
      call setVisible of frame_obj using true
    endfun main
 endclass Frame_sample
```

NOTE *The size of the graphical object on the screen is measured in* pixels. *A pixel is the smallest unit of space that can be displayed on the video screen. The total number of pixels on the screen defines the* resolution *of the screen. High-resolution screens have a larger number of pixels, and the pixels are much smaller.*

### 14.3.1 Simple Components

The simplest types of components are *labels*, which can display text titles and images. Text labels just display their text titles when they appear on a container of a window. A text label is defined as an object of class `JLabel`. The following KJP statements declare two text labels:

```
object blabel1 of class JLabel  // text label
object blabel2 of class JLabel
```

When the objects of class `JLabel` are created, their text titles are defined. The following KJP statements create the two text objects and define their associated text titles.

```
create blabel1 of class JLabel using
          "Kennesaw Java Preprocessor"
create blabel2 of class JLabel using
          "The Language for OOP"
```

Labels can also display pictures by indicating icons for the pictures. Image labels display a picture by indicating the corresponding icon. In classes using `Swing`, a picture is set up into an icon in a label, so that the classes can position the label in a container and display it. The pictures are normally in a standard format, such as `JPEG` or `GIF`.

NOTE

*A picture is defined as an icon, which is an object of class* `ImageIcon`. *The icon is then defined as part of the label. The following statements declare an object variable of class* `ImageIcon` *and an object of class* `JLabel`.

```
object kjpimage of class ImageIcon   // image
object kjplabel of class JLabel      // for image
```

ON THE CD

*The icon object is created with a picture stored in a specified picture file. The following statement creates the icon object kjpimage with a picture in the file* `kjplogo.gif`.

```
create kjpimage of class ImageIcon using
            "kjplogo2.gif"
```

Finally, with the icon object created, it can be defined as part of a label. The following statement creates the label object with the icon defined in object variable *kjpimage*.

```
create kjplabel of class JLabel using kjpimage
```

### 14.3.2 Adding Components to a Window

Components cannot be added directly to a window, which is an object of class `JFrame`. A special container called the *content pane* defines the working area for the window. All the graphical elements, components, and smaller containers are added to the content pane. The content pane is an object of class `Container`.

There are several ways to arrange graphical elements in the content pane. The type of arrangement is defined by the layout manager selected. The `AWT` package provides six layout managers:

- Border, which arranges the components in the north, east, west, center, and south positions in the container
- Flow, which arranges the components in the container from left to right
- Grid, which arranges the components in a matrix with row and column positions
- Box, which arranges the components in a single row or single column
- Card, which arranges the components in a similar manner as the stack of cards
- Gridbag, which arranges the components in a similar manner as the grid but with variable size cells

The most common layout managers are the first three: border, flow, and grid. Figure 14.3 shows the positioning of components using the border layout manager.

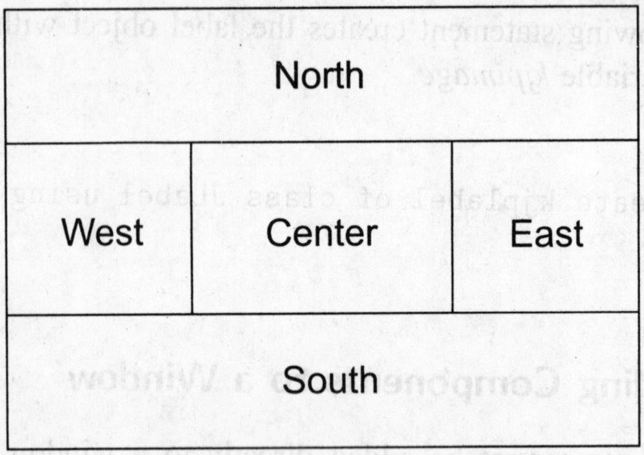


**Figure 14.3** Arrangement of the border layout manager.

As mentioned before, the content pane is an object of class `Container`. To manipulate the content pane object, a reference to this object is accessed by invoking method `getContentPane` of the window. Before adding the various graphical elements to the content pane, the layout must be set by invoking the method `setLayout` of the content pane.

ON THE CD *The following class,* `Kjplogo`*, sets up a window (an object of class* `JFrame`*) with three components: two text labels and an image label. The KJP code for class* `Kjplogo` *is implemented and stored in file* `Kjplogo.kpl`.

```
import all javax.swing     // Library for graphics
import all java.awt
description
    This class creates and displays a frame window
    with an image and two text labels.    */
class Kjplogo is
  public
  description
    This is the main function of the application. */
    function main is
```

```
constants
  integer WIDTH = 400
  integer HEIGHT = 300
objects
  object frame_obj of class JFrame // window
  // content pane
  object cpane of class Container
  object blabel1 of class JLabel  // text label
  object blabel2 of class JLabel
  object kjpimage of class ImageIcon // image
  object kjplabel of class JLabel // for image
  // layout manager
  object lmanager of class BorderLayout
begin
  create frame_obj of class JFrame using
          "KJP logo"
  create blabel1 of class JLabel using
          "Kennesaw Java Preprocessor"
  create blabel2 of class JLabel using
          "The Language for OOP"
  create kjpimage of class ImageIcon using
          "kjplogo2.gif"
  create kjplabel of class JLabel using
          kjpimage
  create lmanager of class BorderLayout
  set cpane = call getContentPane of frame_obj
  call setLayout of cpane using lmanager
  // add the text image label and text label
  //                                components
  // to the content pane of the window
  call add of cpane using kjplabel,
           BorderLayout.CENTER
  call add of cpane using blabel1,
           BorderLayout.NORTH
  call add of cpane using blabel2,
           BorderLayout.SOUTH
  call setSize of frame_obj using WIDTH, HEIGHT
```

```
        call setVisible of frame_obj using true
    endfun main
endclass Kjplogo
```

Figure 14.4 shows the window that appears on the screen when the program in class Kjplogo executes.

**Figure 14.4** A frame with three components.

### 14.3.3 Attributes of Frames

Two attributes of frames that are used in the previous examples are title and size. The title was set with the constructor of class JFrame when creating a frame object. This attribute can be set at any time by invoking method setTitle with a string argument. For example, the following statement sets a title to the frame object declared with reference *frame_obj* in the previous example:

```
call setTitle using "New Frame Title"
```

The size of the frame object is normally set before displaying it on the screen. As mentioned before, the units for size are in pixels. The previous example used two named constants: *WIDTH* and *HEIGHT*. This is the recommended manner to set the values for the size. The size is set by invoking method `setSize` with the values in pixels for width and height of the frame. For example, to set the size of the frame referenced by *frame_obj*, the statement is:

```
call setSize of frame_obj using WIDTH, HEIGHT
```

The third attribute of a frame is the color. This attribute is normally set to a container in the frame, such as the content pane of the frame or the panels defined and contained in the content pane. In other words, the color of any of these containers can directly be set. The most common method to invoke for a container is `setBackground`. The argument is normally a predefined constant in class `Color`, which is available in the `AWT` package. These constants represent various colors to apply as background color to the container. The most common constants for the colors are listed in Table 14.1.

**Table 14.1** Common colors in a frame

| | | |
|---|---|---|
| Color.blue | Color.orange | Color.green |
| Color.gray | Color.magenta | Color.pink |
| Color.red | Color.white | Color.yellow |
| Color.darkGray | Color.lightGray | |

To set the background color of a container in a frame object, method `setBackground` is invoked with the selected color. This method is defined in class `JFrame`. The following statement sets the background color to pink in frame *frame_obj* of the previous example. Recall that *cpane* is the content pane of *frame_obj*.

```
call setBackground of cpane using Color.pink
```

## 14.4 EVENTS AND LISTENERS

An *event* is a special nonvisible object that represents an occurrence or signal. This indicates that something happened during the interaction between the user and the executing program. Usually, the most important events are the ones originated by some user action.

Examples of user actions that originate events are the click of the mouse, starting of mouse movement, a keystroke on the keyboard, and so on.

NOTE *Each of these actions generates a specific type of event. A program that is dependent on events while it executes is called event-driven, because the behavior of the program depends on the events generated by user actions.*

A *listener* is an object that waits for a specific event to occur and that responds to the event in some manner. Each listener has a relationship with an event or with a group of similar events. Listener objects must be carefully designed to respond to its type of events.

### 14.4.1 Components That Generate Events

Buttons and text fields are examples of graphical components that generate events as a result of user actions. The listener object will respond when the user clicks on the button. The behavior of the listener object should be defined in a class. For a button, in addition to declaring and creating the button as an object of class `JButton`, the declaration and creation of the listener object is also required.

When a user clicks a button, the type of event generated by the button is called an *action event*. Figure 14.5 illustrates the relationship among the button object, the action event, and the listener object. Creating the action event and invoking the appropriate function of the listener object to handle the event is done automatically.

The action event generated by the button is sent to a corresponding listener object that responds to the event. For this, the listener object must

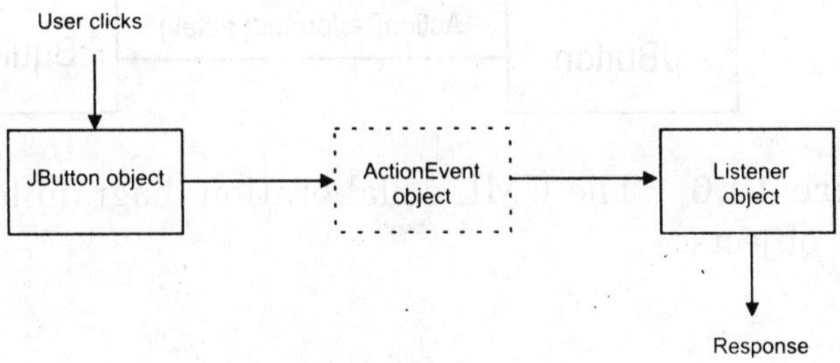


**Figure 14.5** Generation and handling of an action event.

be set to respond to an event generated by the button object—this is known as registering the listener object with the button object. The sequence of steps to set up a button is:

1. Define the class that implements the behavior of the listener object.
2. Declare the button object variable.
3. Declare the listener object for the button.
4. Create the button object with a title.
5. Create the listener object that will respond to the action event generated by the button.
6. Register the listener object for the button.
7. Add the button object to the container.

The `AWT` and `Swing` packages provide several classes and interfaces for defining listener objects. For action events, the interface `ActionListener` must be implemented by the class that defines the behavior of the listener object.

Figure 14.6 shows the UML collaboration diagram for an object of class `JButton` and a listener object of class `Bquithandler` (defined in this next section). The button object generates an action event that it sends to the listener object by invoking method `actionPerformed`. The interaction among these objects occurs automatically (behind the scenes).

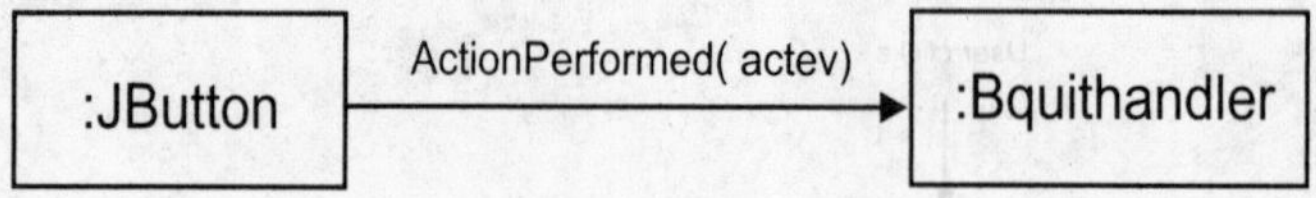


**Figure 14.6** The UML collaboration diagram for a button and listener objects.

### 14.4.2 Adding a Button to a Window

As mentioned earlier, a button is an object of class `JButton`. The following statements declare an object variable of class `JButton`.

```
object mybutton of class JButton
```

The button object is created with a title. The following statement creates the button object with the title "Push to Quit."

```
create mybutton of class JButton using
                    "Push to Quit"
```

The next two steps declare a listener object and create this object, which will respond when the user clicks the button. The actual behavior of the listener object is defined in a class that has to be defined by the programmer. The following statements declare and create the listener object of class `Bquithandler`.

```
object butthandler of class Bquithandler
...
create butthandler of class Bquithandler
```

After the button object and its corresponding listener object are created, the listener object has to be registered as the listener to the button object. Recall that a button generates an action event when pressed, which is handled by action listeners. The following statement invokes function `addActionListener` of the button to register its listener object, *butthandler*. Function `addActionListener` is defined in class `JButton`.

```
call addActionListener of mybutton using butthandler
```

The button can now be added to the content pane of the window. The following statement adds the button defined previously to the content pane with the south position. The content pane uses the border layout manager in this example.

```
call add of cpane using mybutton, BorderLayout.SOUTH
```

The following class, `Kjplogbutton`, completely implements a window with three graphical components: a text label, a label with an icon, and a button. An object listener is defined for the button. The listener object terminates the program when the user clicks the button.

ON THE CD *The KJP code that implements class* `Kjplogbutton` *is stored in the file* `Kjplogbutton.kpl`, *and the Java implementation is stored in the file* `Kjplogbutton.java`.

```
import all javax.swing   // Library for graphics
import all java.awt
//
description
  This class creates and displays a frame window
  with a text label, an image,  and a button.  */
class Fpsimbutton is
  public
  description
    This is the main function of the application. */
  function main is
    constants
```

```
        integer WIDTH = 400
        integer HEIGHT = 300
      objects
        object frame_obj of class JFrame  // window
        // content pane
        object cpane of class Container
        object blabel1 of class JLabel    // label
        object psimlabel of class JLabel  // for image
        object psimimage of class ImageIcon   // image
        object quitbutt of class JButton
        // layout manager
        object lmanager of class BorderLayout
        object butthandler of class Bquithandler
      begin
        create frame_obj of class JFrame using
                "Psim"
        create blabel1 of class JLabel using
                "The OO Simulation Package"
        create quitbutt of class JButton using "Quit"
        create psimimage of class ImageIcon
                using "psim.gif"
        create psimlabel of class JLabel
                using psimimage
        create lmanager of class BorderLayout
        create butthandler of class Bquithandler
        set cpane = call getContentPane of frame_obj
        call setLayout of cpane using lmanager
        // register the listener object with the
        //  button object
        call addActionListener of quitbutt using
                butthandler
        // add the text image label and text label
        // components to the content pane of
        // the window
        call add of cpane using psimlabel,
                BorderLayout.CENTER
        call add of cpane using blabel1,
```

```
                   BorderLayout:NORTH
          call add of cpane using quitbutt,
                   BorderLayout.SOUTH
          call setSize of frame_obj using WIDTH, HEIGHT
          call setVisible of frame_obj using true
      endfun main
  endclass Fpsimbutton
```

For every type of event object, there is a type of listener object. Therefore, the class definition that implements the behavior of listener objects depends on the type of events that these objects can handle (or respond to). For action events, the class definition must implement interface `ActionListener`, which is included in package `AWT`. The only method specified in the interface is `actionPerformed`, and it has to be completely implemented in the class defined for action listener objects.

The following class, `Bquithandler`, defines the behavior of the object listener for the button used in class *Kjplogbutton*.

```
import all javax.swing      // Library for graphics
import all java.awt.event
description
  This class defines the behavior of listener
  objects for the button. When the user clicks
  the button, the program terminates.   */
class Bquithandler implements ActionListener is
public
     description
        The only function in the class. */
     function actionPerformed parameters
                 object myev of class ActionEvent is
        begin
            call System.exit using 0
     endfun actionPerformed
 endclass Bquithandler
```

ON THE CD

*The KJP code that implements class* `Bquithandler` *is stored in the file* `Bquithandler.kpl`, *and the Java implementation is stored in the file* `Bquithandler.java`.

Figure 14.7 shows the window that appears on the screen when the program, which consists of the two classes defined previously, executes. When the user clicks the button, the program terminates.

**Figure 14.7** A frame with two labels and a button.

### 14.4.3 Data Input

A text field is a very useful component for entering data to an application. This component can also display data. When used for input, this component can generate an action event and send it to an action listener. This implies that an action listener object must be created and registered to the text field object.

When a user enters data in a text field and presses the Enter key, the text field object generates an action event and sends it to an action listener object. The text field is an object of class `JTextField`, which can be created with a given size and default text.

The following two statements declare an object reference and create the corresponding object of class `JTextField` of size 20 characters.

```
object text1 of class JTextField
. . .
create text1 of class JTextField using 20
```

To register a listener object with a text field is similar to registering a listener object to a button. The following statements declare and create a listener object, register an action event listener object with the text field object *text1*, and include the text field in the content pane.

```
object tfieldlistener of class Tlistener
create tfieldlistener of class Tlistener
. . .
call addActionListener of text1 using tfieldlistener
call add of cpane using text1
```

All data is entered and displayed as strings, so proper conversion needs to be carried out for entering and displaying numerical data. To get string data entered by a user into a text field, method `getText` of the text field object is used. To display string data in a text field, the method `setText` is used with the string as the argument. The following statement gets the string data entered by the user in the text field *text1*, and assigns the string value to variable *ss*.

```
string ss
. . .
set ss = call getText of text1
```

In a similar manner, the following statement displays string *yy* on the text field object *text1*.

```
string yy
. . .
call setText of text1 using yy
```

To convert the string value entered in a text field to numeric of type `double`, method `Double.parseDouble` is used with the string value as the argument. This is actually a static method parseDouble in class Double, which is a Java library class. The following statement converts the string *ss* to a numeric (of type *double*) variable *dd*.

```
double dd
. . .
set dd = call Double.parseDouble using ss
```

To display numeric data (of type *double*) to a text field, it must first be converted to a string value. Method String.valueOf (static method valueOf of class String) must be invoked with the numeric value as the argument. The following statement converts variable *dd* of type *double* to a string and assigns it to string variable *ss*.

```
set ss = call String.valueOf using dd
```

### 14.4.4 Decimal Formatting

For non-integer numeric output, formatting the value to be shown is important; otherwise, too many decimal digits will appear and be shown to the user. The outcome of using a decimal formatter is a string that represents the number in one of several formats. The following statements declare an object variable of class DecimalFormat (a Java library class), create the formatter object using a formatting pattern, and invoke function format of the formatter object using the numeric value to format.

```
object myformat of class DecimalFormat
...
// object for formatting output numeric data
create myformat of class DecimalFormat
                        using "###,###.##"
...
set form_increase = call format of myformat
                        using dincrease
set form_salary = call format of myformat
                        using dsalary
```

In this example, the two numeric variables of type *double*: *dincrease* and *dsalary*, are formatted with the same pattern, which allows only two decimal digits (after the decimal point). The resulting numeric value is normally rounded to the specified decimal digits.

NOTE *Formatting includes an implied conversion of the noninteger numeric value to a string. This string data can be shown in a text field in the relevant container.*

### 14.4.5 Salary Problem with GUI

This section presents a slightly different version of the solution to the salary problem presented in Chapter 4, Section 4.11.2. The problem presented here includes a GUI for I/O of data when a user interacts with the program.

The window that appears on the screen shows the user the labels to guide the user, indicating what data he needs to input. The text fields are used for data the user enters, such as the name of the person, the age, and the salary. The window also includes two buttons, one for calculating the salary increase and the other for exiting the program.

All these components are arranged on the frame with a grid layout manager. The arrangement is a grid of rows and columns, and the components are of the same size. In this problem, the content pane is divided into five rows and two columns. The following statements declare an object variable for a grid layout manager, create the object with five rows and two columns, and set the content pane of the window with the layout manager.

```
// layout manager
object gridmanager of class GridLayout
...
create gridmanager of class GridLayout using 5, 2
...
call setLayout of cpane using gridmanager
```

The main class of the problem is called `Csalarygui`. This class implements the window and sets all the components on it. The KJP code that implements this class follows.

```
import all javax.swing   // Library for graphics
import all java.awt
description
  This program computes the salary increase for
  an employee. If his/her salary is greater than
  $45,000, the salary increase is 4.5%; otherwise,
  the salary increase is 5%. The program uses the
  following components: buttons, labels, and
  text fields.  */
class Csalarygui is
  public
  description
    This is the main function of the application. */
  function main is
    constants
      integer WIDTH = 400
      integer HEIGHT = 300
    objects
      object sal_frame of class JFrame
      object cpane of class Container
      object namelabel of class JLabel
      object salarylabel of class JLabel
      object agelabel of class JLabel
      object increaselabel of class JLabel
      object nametfield of class JTextField
      object agetfield of class JTextField
      object inctfield of class JTextField
      object salarytfield of class JTextField
      // layout manager
      object gridmanager of class GridLayout
      object incbutt of class JButton
      object quitbutt of class JButton
      object actlistener of class Sal_listener
    begin
      create sal_frame of class JFrame
            using "Salary Problem"
      set cpane = call getContentPane of sal_frame
```

```
create gridmanager of class GridLayout
       using 5, 2
create namelabel of class JLabel
       using "Enter name: "
create agelabel of class JLabel
       using "Enter age: "
create salarylabel of class JLabel
       using "Enter salary: "
create increaselabel of class JLabel
       using "Salary increase: "
create nametfield of class JTextField using 20
create agetfield of class JTextField using 20
create salarytfield of class JTextField
                                     using 20
create inctfield of class JTextField using 20
create incbutt of class JButton
                             using "Increase"
create quitbutt of class JButton using "Quit"
call setLayout of cpane using gridmanager
call add of cpane using namelabel
call add of cpane using nametfield
call add of cpane using agelabel
call add of cpane using agetfield
call add of cpane using salarylabel
call add of cpane using salarytfield
call add of cpane using increaselabel
call add of cpane using inctfield
call add of cpane using incbutt
call add of cpane using quitbutt
create actlistener of class Sal_listener
           using salarytfield, inctfield
call addActionListener of incbutt
           using actlistener
call addActionListener of quitbutt
           using actlistener
call setSize of sal_frame
           using WIDTH, HEIGHT
```

```
        call setVisible of sal_frame using true
    endfun main
endclass Csalarygui
```

ON THE CD *The complete KJP code that implements class* Csalarygui *is stored in the file* Csalarygui.kpl. *The corresponding Java implementation is stored in the file* Csalarygui.java.

Class Sal_listener implements the behavior of the listener object, which responds to the buttons. Part of the code in this class calculates the salary increase and updates the salary. The KJP code that implements this class follows.

```
import all javax.swing      // Library for graphics
import all java.awt.event
import java.text.DecimalFormat // for formatting
description
  This class defines the behavior of listener objects
  for the button.
  When the user clicks the button, the
  program terminates. */
class Sal_listener implements ActionListener is
    private
        objects
            object salary of class JTextField
            object increase of class JTextField
            object myformat of class DecimalFormat
    public
    description
        Constructor that gets the salary, computes
        salary increase, and updates salary. */
    function initializer parameters
             object fsalary of class JTextField,
             object fincrease of class JTextField
             is
    begin
        set salary = fsalary
```

```
        set increase = fincrease
        // object for formatting output numeric
        create myformat of class DecimalFormat
                                    using "###,###.##"
    endfun initializer
    description
        The only function in the class. */
    function actionPerformed parameters
            object actev of class ActionEvent is
    variables
        double dsalary
        double dincrease
        string ssalary
        string form_increase
        string form_salary
        string actcomm
    begin
        // get string for salary from text field
        set ssalary = call getText of salary
        // convert to numeric double
        set dsalary = call Double.parseDouble
                using ssalary
        // get command info from action event
        set actcomm = call getActionCommand of actev
        if actcomm equals "Increase" then
            if dsalary > 45000 then
                set dincrease = dsalary * 0.045
            else
                set dincrease = dsalary * 0.050
            endif
            add dincrease to dsalary
            // convert salary and increase to strings
            // using decimal format
            set form_increase = call format
                        of myformat using dincrease
            set form_salary = call format of myformat
                        using dsalary
```

```
            // set new string data to field text
            call setText of salary using form_salary
            call setText of increase
                            using form_increase
        else
            // user pressed quit button
            call System.exit using 0
        endif
    endfun actionPerformed
endclass Sal_listener
```

ON THE CD

*The implementation of class* `Sal_listener` *is stored in the file* `Sal_listener.kpl`. *The Java implementation is stored in the file* `Sal_listener.java`.

When the program executes, the user directly interacts with the GUI presented. The data entered by the user is: "Chris D. Hunt" for attribute *name*, 45 for *age*, and 36748.50 for *salary*. The final data, after the program computes the salary increase and updates the salary, is shown in Figure 14.8.

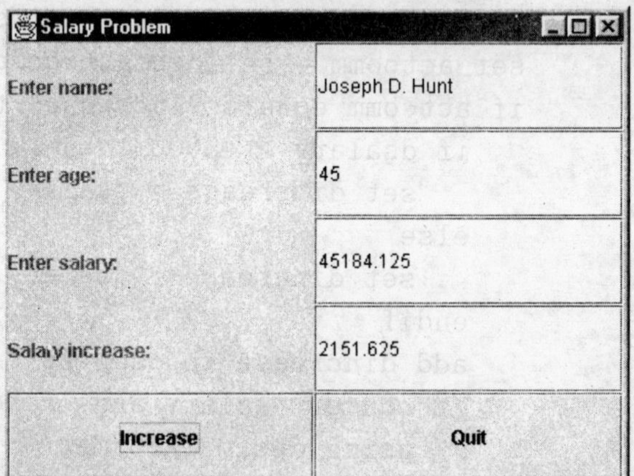


**Figure 14.8** A GUI for the salary problem.

## 14.5 APPLETS

In addition to console and graphical applications, Java and KJP support applets. These are not standalone programs, because they require a Web browser to run. The code of the compiled class for an applet is placed in an HTML file with the appropriate tags. When a user uses his Web browser to start an applet, the compiled classes of the applet in the HTML file are downloaded from the server and execute.

Suppose the class for an applet is named Akjplogo, the appropriate tags in the HTML file with the compiled class are as follows:

```
<applet
code = "Akjplogo.class" width=300 height=400>
</applet>
```

An applet normally includes graphical components in addition to any computation that may appear in a program. A Web browser displays the complete Web page, including the GUI for the applet. A small and complete HTML file with an applet embedded in it is shown next.

```
<HTML>
  <HEAD>
     <TITLE> The KJP Applet </TITLE>
  </HEAD>
<BODY BGCOLOR=blue TEXT=white>
  This is a simple applet showing the KJP logo.
  Any text included here in the HTML document.
  <CENTER>
    <H1> The KJP Applet </H1>
    <P>
       <APPLET CODE="Akjplogo.class"
       WIDTH=250 HEIGHT=150>
       </APPLET>
  </CENTER>
</BODY>
</HTML>
```

There are various aspects of an applet to consider when defining the corresponding class, and that differentiates it from a conventional class. In an applet, the class definition must inherit class `JApplet` from the Swing library, or the `Applet` class from the AWT library. As mentioned before, applets are not standalone programs, so function `main` is not used. Instead, function `init` is included. A frame for a window is not defined because the applet automatically constructs a window. The size of the applet window is set in the HTML file. The Web browser makes the applet visible.

Class `Akjplogo` defines an applet that displays the KJP logo. It defines three graphical components that are labels, in a similar manner to class `Kjplogo`. The KJP code with the implementation of the applet class `Akjplogo` is presented as follows.

```
import all javax.swing  // Library for graphics
import all java.awt
description
    This applet creates and displays a frame window
    with an image and a text label.  */
class Akjplogo inherits JApplet is
  public
  description
    This is the main function of the application. */
  function init is
    objects
      object cpane of class Container
      object blabel1 of class JLabel  // text label
      object blabel2 of class JLabel
      object kjplabel of class JLabel  // for image
      object kjpimage of class ImageIcon    // image
      object lmanager of class BorderLayout
    begin
      create blabel1 of class JLabel
           using "Kennesaw Java Preprocessor"
      create blabel2 of class JLabel
           using "The Language for OOP"
      create kjpimage of class ImageIcon
           using "kjplogo.gif"
      create kjplabel of class JLabel
```

```
            using kjpimage
        create lmanager of class BorderLayout
        set cpane = call getContentPane
        call setLayout of cpane using lmanager
        // add the text image label and text label
        // components to the content pane
        call add of cpane using
            kjplabel, BorderLayout.CENTER
        call add of cpane using
            blabel1, BorderLayout.NORTH
        call add of cpane using
            blabel2, BorderLayout.SOUTH
    endfun init
  endclass Akjplogo
```

*The KJP code with the implementation for class* `Akjplogo` *is stored in the file* `Akjplogo.kpl`. *The Java implementation is stored in the file* `Akjplogo.java`.

To execute the applet, a Web browser is used to run the applet class. To test the applet the `appletviewer` utility can be used. When the applet class `Akjplogo` executes with the appletviewer, the GUI shown in Figure 14.9 appears on the screen.

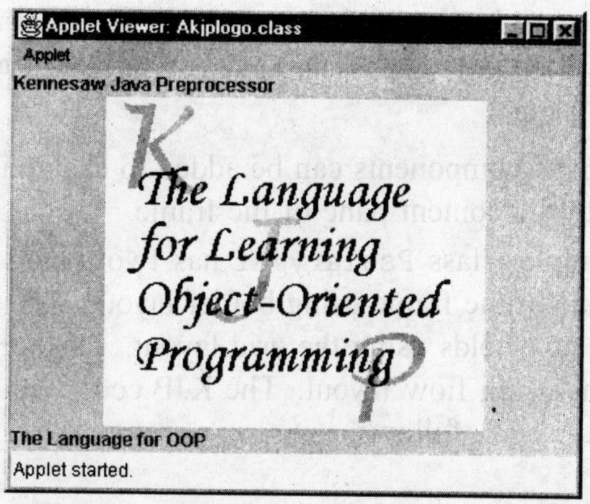


**Figure 14.9** An applet showing the KJP logo.

## 14.6 PANEL CONTAINERS

The windows discussed in previous sections placed components in the content pane of the frame. The content pane is the container where any types of components or small containers are placed.

The largest container defined is an object of class `JFrame`. The only way to add components to this object is by using its content pane. Smaller containers are objects of class `JPanel`. These objects can contain components such as labels, buttons, text fields, and other components. With panels (objects of class `JPanel`), it is possible to organize a GUI in a hierarchical manner. A GUI with several panels is structured in such a manner that all the panels and other components are placed in the content pane of the frame.

The following statements declare two panel objects, create the panels, and set the layout manager for each panel.

```
object fpanel of class JPanel
object bpanel of class JPanel
. . .
create bpanel of class JPanel
create fpanel of class JPanel
. . .
call setLayout of fpanel using gridmanager
call setLayout of bpanel using flowmanager
```

The various components can be added to each panel, and the panels can be added to the content pane of the frame.

For example, class `Psalarygui` has two panels that are placed in the content pane of the frame using border layout. The first panel contains the labels and text fields using the grid layout. The second panel contains the two buttons using flow layout. The KJP code with the implementation of class `Psalarygui` follows.

```
import all javax.swing    // Library for graphics
import all java.awt
```

```
//
description
  This program computes the salary increase
  for an employee. If his/her salary is greater
  than $45,000, the salary increase is 4.5%;
  otherwise, the salary increase is 5%.
  Two panels are used in this class. The first is
  used to place the labels and text fields, the
  second is used to place the two buttons.
  The program uses the following components:
  buttons, labels, and text fields.   */
class Psalarygui is
  public
  description
    This is the main function of the application. */
  function main is
    constants
      integer WIDTH = 400
      integer HEIGHT = 300
    objects
      object sal_frame of class JFrame
      object cpane of class Container
      object fpanel of class JPanel
      object bpanel of class JPanel
      object namelabel of class JLabel
      object salarylabel of class JLabel
      object agelabel of class JLabel
      object increaselabel of class JLabel
      object nametfield of class JTextField
      object agetfield of class JTextField
      object inctfield of class JTextField
      object salarytfield of class JTextField
      object bordermanager of class BorderLayout
      object gridmanager of class GridLayout
      object flowmanager of class FlowLayout
      object incbutt of class JButton
      object quitbutt of class JButton
```

```
        object actlistener of class Sal_listener
      begin
        create sal_frame of class JFrame using
              "Salary Problem"
        set cpane = call getContentPane of sal_frame
        create bordermanager of class BorderLayout
        create gridmanager of class GridLayout
              using 4, 2
        create flowmanager of class FlowLayout
        create bpanel of class JPanel
        create fpanel of class JPanel
        create namelabel of class JLabel
              using "Enter name: "
        create agelabel of class JLabel
              using "Enter age: "
        create salarylabel of class JLabel
              using "Enter salary: "
        create increaselabel of class JLabel
              using "Salary increase: "
        create nametfield of class JTextField using 20
        create agetfield of class JTextField using 20
        create salarytfield of class JTextField
              using 20
        create inctfield of class JTextField using 20
        create incbutt of class JButton
              using "Increase"
        create quitbutt of class JButton using "Quit"
        call setLayout of fpanel using gridmanager
        call setBackground of fpanel
              using Color.lightGray
        call setLayout of bpanel using flowmanager
        call setBackground of bpanel using Color.blue
        call setLayout of cpane using bordermanager
        call add of fpanel using namelabel
        call add of fpanel using nametfield
        call add of fpanel using agelabel
        call add of fpanel using agetfield
```

```
         call add of fpanel using salarylabel
         call add of fpanel using salarytfield
         call add of fpanel using increaselabel
         call add of fpanel using inctfield
         call add of bpanel using incbutt
         call add of bpanel using quitbutt
         create actlistener of class Sal_listener
               using salarytfield, inctfield
         call addActionListener of incbutt
               using actlistener
         call addActionListener of quitbutt
               using actlistener
         call add of cpane using
               fpanel, BorderLayout.CENTER
         call add of cpane using
               bpanel, BorderLayout.SOUTH
         call setSize of sal_frame using WIDTH, HEIGHT
         call setVisible of sal_frame using true
      endfun main
   endclass Psalarygui
```

Class `Psalarygui` is similar in functionality to class `Csalarygui`, which is discussed in Section 14.4.5. The listener class, `Sal_listener`, is the same as used in class `Csalarygui`.

ON THE CD

*The KJP code with the implementation of class* `Psalarygui` *is stored in the file* `Psalarygui.kpl`, *and the Java implementation in the file* `Psalarygui.java`.

When the program that consists of classes `Psalarygui` and `Sal_listener` executes, the window shown is similar to the program discussed in Section 14.4.5. Figure 14.10 shows the window for class `Psalarygui`.

The main difference between the two programs is noted in the two buttons located at the bottom of the frame. These buttons are smaller and on a blue background.

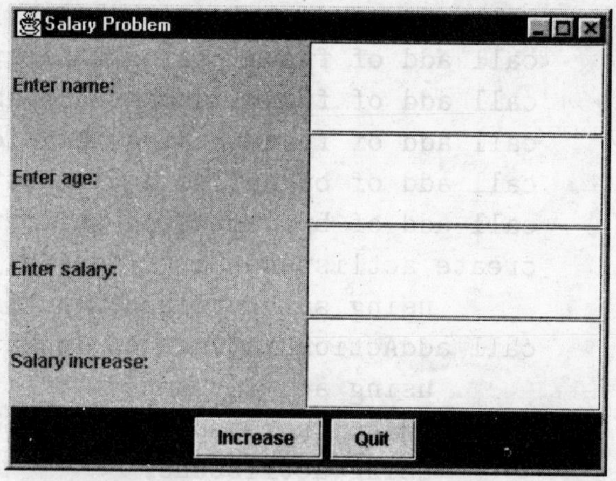


**Figure 14.10** A frame with two panels.

## 14.7 DRAWING SIMPLE OBJECTS

The *coordinate system* used in drawing objects places the *origin* of the drawing area in its upper-left corner. Figure 14.11 shows the coordinate system to represent the *position* of a point in the drawing area of the container.

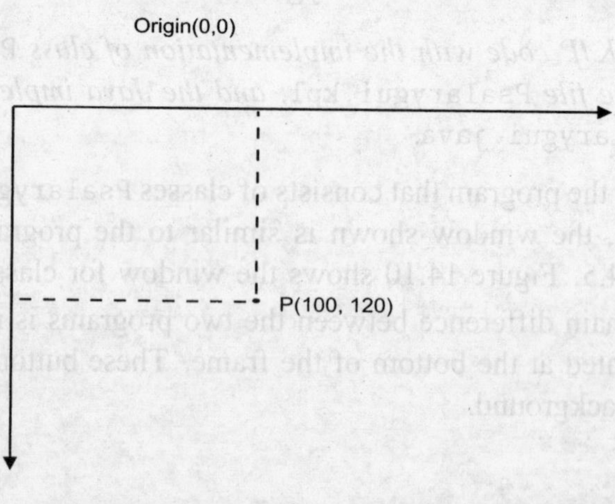


**Figure 14.11** Position of a point in the drawing area.

All measures involved in drawing use pixels as the basic unit. The position of a visible dot is measured in the number of pixels to the right of the origin and the number of pixels below the origin. This gives the position using the coordinates (x, y).

This section presents some simple tools and techniques for drawing graphics objects. The tools are provided by predefined classes in the AWT package.

### 14.7.1 General Functions for Drawing

The general technique for drawing graphics objects is to define a class that inherits class `JComponent` and redefine function `paint`. An object is created, and its reference can then be added to a frame.

Function `paint` is invoked automatically, so there is no need to explicitly call this function. Function `paint` is defined with one parameter, an object reference of class `Graphics`, which is a class in the AWT package. The functions for drawing lines, circles, polygons, and so on, are features of the parameter of class `Graphics`.

To draw a line on the drawing area, from point P1(20, 45) to point P2(75, 50), function `drawLine` is invoked with the coordinates of the two points as arguments. The following statement draws a line from point *P1* to point *P2*, using the object reference, *graph_obj*, of class `Graphics`.

```
call drawLine of graph_obj using 20, 45, 75, 50
```

This and other drawing statements must appear in function `paint`. The following statement draws a rectangle whose upper-left corner is located at point (80, 75), and with 50 pixels for width and 100 pixels for height.

```
call drawRect of graph_obj using 80, 75, 50, 100
```

The following statements draw an arc. The arc is part of an oval that is specified by an enclosing rectangle with the upper-left corner located in (*x*, *y*), and the size given by *width* and *height*. The portion of the arc to draw is specified by the starting angle and the final angle (in degrees).

```
int x = 20
```

```
int y = 50
width = 35
height = 25
startang = 0
finalang = 45
...
call drawArc of graph_obj using
          x, y, width, height, startang, finalang
```

Other drawing functions defined in class `Graphics` are listed in Table 14.2.

**Table 14.2** Common drawing functions in class `Graphics`

| | |
|---|---|
| drawOval | Draws the outline of an oval |
| draw2DRect | Draws a highlighted outline of a rectangle |
| drawPolygon | Draws a closed polygon |
| drawRoundRect | Draws a round-cornered rectangle |
| fillArc | Fills a portion of an oval with color |
| fillOval | Fills an oval with color |
| fillPolygon | Fills a polygon with color |
| fillRect | Fills a rectangle with color |
| fillRoundRect | Fills a round-cornered rectangle with color |
| fill3Drect | Fills a rectangle with color |

### 14.7.2 A GUI with Circles

This section presents an example program that shows two components on a frame: a drawing area with several circles of different sizes and a button with a listener. The program consists of several classes.

Class `DrawExample` is the main class of the application. It creates a frame with border layout manager for placing the two components. The first component is the drawing area with several circles drawn; an object of class `MydrawE` is created and placed in the center position of the frame.

The button is placed in the south position. The KJP code that implements class `DrawExample` is shown as follows.

```
import all java.awt
import all javax.swing
description
   This is the main class that presents an example
   of drawing simple objects.    */
class DrawExample is
  public
   description
     The main function.          */
   function main is
    constants
      integer WIDTH = 300
      integer HEIGHT = 250
    objects
      object dframe of class JFrame
      object cpane of class Container
      // object for drawing area
      object mdrawing of class MydrawE
      // button
      object quitbutt of class JButton
      object butthandler of class Bquithandler
      object bordermanager of class BorderLayout
    begin
      create dframe of class JFrame using
           "Drawing example"
      set cpane = call getContentPane of dframe
      create mdrawing of class MydrawE
      create quitbutt of class JButton using "Quit"
      create bordermanager of class BorderLayout
      call setLayout of cpane using bordermanager
      create butthandler of class Bquithandler
      call add of cpane using mdrawing,
             BorderLayout.CENTER
      call add of cpane using quitbutt,
```

```
                 BorderLayout.SOUTH
           // register the listener object with the
           // button object
           call addActionListener of quitbutt
                  using butthandler
           call setSize of dframe using WIDTH, HEIGHT
           call setVisible of dframe using true
        endfun main
     endclass DrawExample
```

Class MydrawE inherits class JComponent, and the relevant function is paint. This function draws 15 circles of different sizes and at different locations. The KJP code for class MydrawE is listed as follows.

```
     import all java.awt
     import all javax.swing
     description
       This class draws several ovals.  */
     class MydrawE inherits JComponent is
        public
        description
           Paint where the actual drawings are.  */
        function paint parameters object gobj of
             class Graphics is
         constants
            integer TIMES = 15 // number of circles
         variables
            // position in drawing area
            integer x
            integer y
            // width and height
            integer w
            integer h
            integer j // loop counter
         begin
            set x = 50
            set y = 20
```

```
            set w = 170
            set h = 170
            set j = 0
            for j = 0 to TIMES - 1 do
                // draw a circle
                call drawOval of gobj using x, y, w, h
                add 5 to x
                add 5 to y
                subtract 5 from w
                subtract 5 from h
            endfor
        endfun paint
    endclass MydrawE
```

Figure 14.12 shows the top part of the frame that contains the drawing area with several circles of different sizes and the bottom part of the frame that contains a single button for exiting the program when the user clicks it.

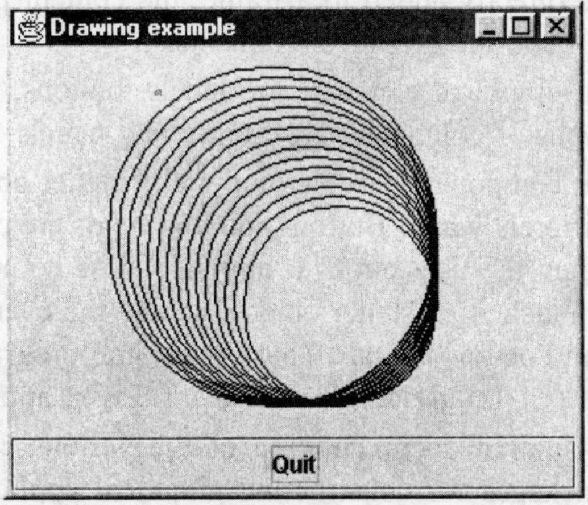


**Figure 14.12** A frame with drawing area and button.

ON THE CD *The KJP code that implement classes* DrawExample *and* MydrawE *are stored in the files* DrawExample.kpl *and* MydrawE.kpl. *The Java code are stored in the files* DrawExample.java *and* MydrawE.java.

Another way to organize the program is to define a single class that inherits class `JFrame` and include a constructor, function `main`, and function `paint`. This is a single-class application.

## 14.8 SUMMARY

For graphical applications, KJP and Java make extensive use of the Java packages AWT and Swing. These packages have a large number of predefined component and container classes for graphical user interfaces.

The purpose of a graphical user interface is to give the user a clear and attractive representation of relevant data, guide the user in the operation of the application, and facilitate his interaction with the program, and also provide some level of checking and verification of the input data.

A window is defined as a frame, which is the largest type of container. Graphical components and smaller containers are added to a frame in various manners, depending on the layout manager. Components and containers cannot be directly added to a frame; the content pane of the frame has to be used to add the graphical elements.

Typical graphical elements are labels, buttons, text fields, and drawing areas. Types of containers are frames and panels.

Various components are defined with listener objects that respond to the user in different ways. Buttons and text fields are components that generate events when the user clicks a button. These components can have object listeners attached. Listener objects handle the events that are generated by buttons and/or text fields. This is why the programs with graphical user interfaces (GUIs) are also called event-driven applications.

More detailed documentation of the various classes in the AWT and Swing packages for constructing graphical applications can be found on the Sun Microsystems Web pages. The following Web page has links to the various documentation pages for the Java packages as well as pages for tutorials.

`http://java.sun.com/docs`

## 14.9 KEY TERMS

| | | |
|---|---|---|
| window | frame | AWT |
| Swing | container | content pane |
| component | listener | pixel |
| layout manager | border | grid |
| flow | card | action event |
| picture | label | text field |
| applet | panel | drawing |
| coordinate system | origin | |

## 14.10 EXERCISES

1. Design and implement a program that carries out conversion from inches to centimeters and from centimeters to inches. The program must include a GUI for the user to select which conversion will be calculated, and then the user inputs data and gets the result on the frame.

2. Modify the salary problem with GUI, presented in this chapter. The calculations of the salary increase and updating the salary should be done in class `Csalarygui`, instead of in class `Sal_listener`.

3. Redesign the GUI for the salary problem presented. Use several panels and different layout managers and colors for the buttons than the ones included in the problem presented in this chapter.

4. Design and implement a program with two or more classes that draws a toy house and a few trees. Use lines, rectangles, ovals, and arcs.

5. Design and implement a program that converts temperature from degrees Fahrenheit to Celsius and vice versa. The program should present the appropriate GUI with the selection using two buttons, one for each type of conversion.

6. Search the appropriate Web pages for additional graphical elements. Design and implement a program that uses a GUI that includes a combo box to solve the temperature conversion problem.

7. Search the appropriate Web pages for additional graphical elements. Design and implement a program that uses a GUI that includes a combo box to solve the problem for conversion from inches to centimeters and vice versa.

8. Design and implement a program that includes a GUI for inventory data. This consists of item code, description, cost, quantity in stock, and other data. Use labels, text fields, and buttons to calculate the total inventory value for each item.

9. Redesign the previous program and implement it using text areas. Search the Web for information on these graphical elements.

10. Search the appropriate Web pages for additional graphical elements. Design and implement a program that uses a GUI that includes a slider to solve the problem for conversion from inches to centimeters and vice versa.

11. Search the appropriate Web pages for additional graphical elements. Design and implement a program that uses a GUI that includes a slider to solve the temperature conversion problem.

# 15 EXCEPTIONS AND I/O

## 15.1 INTRODUCTION

Robust programs should take specified actions when errors occur. The most common type of runtime errors are division by zero, array indexing out of bounds, variable value out of range, illegal reference, and I/O errors.

An exception is an error or an unexpected condition that occurs while the program executes. The mechanism for detecting these errors or conditions and taking some action is called exception handling.

All input/output is carried out with streams, except with GUIs. A stream is a sequence of bytes; the direction of the flow of data determines whether it is an input or an output stream—either incoming from a source or directed toward a destination.

Input and output files are associated with I/O streams. The various class packages allow the programmer to open, process, and close files.

This chapter first presents the basic concepts associated with exceptions; second, it applies exception handling in discussing I/O streams and files.

## 15.2 DEALING WITH EXCEPTIONS

The general approach used in programming for dealing with exceptions is to divide the code into two sections:

1. The first section of code detects an exception. This involves identifying some instruction sequence that might generate or throw an exception.

2. The second section of code takes some action to deal with the exception. This is called handling the exception.

There is a wide variety of exceptions, depending on the abnormal condition that occurs. By default, KJP and Java do not handle all types of exceptions. When an exception occurs, the program aborts, and the runtime system displays the type of condition detected. For example: "Exception in thread main ArithmeticException: division by zero." The runtime system also prints a trace of the function calls.

### 15.2.1 Checked and Unchecked Exceptions

There are two basic categories of exceptions: checked and unchecked. The first type of exceptions, checked, can be controlled syntactically. The compiler checks that the exception is handled in the program. These exceptions are very likely to occur in the program.

Some of the methods in the Java library packages throw various types of exceptions. These are considered checked exceptions. For example, the following function can throw an exception when invoked.

```
function mread throws IOException is
. . .
endfun mread
```

Unchecked exceptions are very difficult to detect at compile time. These exceptions do not have to be handled in the program.

### 15.2.2 Basic Handling of Exceptions

There are two blocks of statements that are needed for detection and processing of exceptions. The first block is called a `try` block and it contains statements that might generate an exception. When an exception occurs on the `try` block, the second block, called the `catch` block, begins to execute immediately.

The parameter in the `catch` block is an object reference declaration of type *Exception*. When an exception occurs, this parameter is passed and can be used in the block to get information about the exception. Method `getMessage`, defined in class `Exception`, can be used to get a description of the exception. The general syntactic structure of these two blocks of statements is:

> **try begin**
> ⟨ *statements* ⟩
> **endtry**
> **catch** ⟨ *parameters* ⟩
> **begin**
> ⟨ *statements* ⟩
> **endcatch**

The `catch` block provides a name to the object reference of the exception object that is caught. With this object reference, the message of the exception object can be displayed and/or any other action can be implemented to handle the exception.

A variation of the problem that reads data for employees follows. The solution presented includes an exception that occurs when the user types the value of the age that is zero or negative. Class `TestException` implements the solution to the problem. The KJP code for this class follows.

```
description
  This program checks for an exception in the
  value of age.  */
```

```
class TestException is
  public
  description
    This is the main function of the application.
    If the age is zero or negative, an exception
    is thrown and caught.          */
  function main is
   variables
     integer obj_age
     real increase
     real obj_salary
     string obj_name
     string lmessage // message for exception
   objects
     object emp_obj of class Employeec
     object lexecep_obj of class Exception
   begin
     display "Enter name: "
     read obj_name
     display "Enter age: "
     read obj_age
     //    Check for exception
     try begin
       if obj_age <= 0
       then
          create lexecep_obj of class Exception
               using
               "Exception: age negative or zero"
          throw lexecep_obj
       endif
     endtry
     catch parameters object excobj of
              class Exception
      begin
        set lmessage = call getMessage of excobj
        display lmessage
        display "Retrying . . . "
```

```
            display "Enter age: "
            read obj_age
        endcatch
        // continue with processing
        display "Enter salary: "
        read obj_salary
        create emp_obj of class Employeec using
            obj_salary, obj_age, obj_name
        set increase = call sal_increase of emp_obj
        set obj_salary = get_salary() of emp_obj
        display "Employee name: ", obj_name
        display "increase: ", increase,
                     " new salary: ", obj_salary
    endfun main
endclass TestException
```

In the program discussed, handling of the exception is carried by displaying information about the exception object, *lexcep_obj*, by invoking its method getMessage, and by executing the instructions that reread the value of age. All these statements appear in the catch block. If no exception occurs, the catch block does not execute, and the program proceeds normally.

ON THE CD

*The KJP code that implements class* TestException *is stored in the file* TestException.kpl, *and the Java implementation is stored in the file* TestException.java.

When the user types a zero or negative value for the age, an exception is thrown. The exception is detected in the try block. To handle the exception, the statements in the catch block are executed. These statements display the message that explains and identifies the exception and allows the user to reenter the value for the *age*.

When the program executes and the user enters a "bad" value for the *age*, the program stops, displays the message, and resumes to let the user reenter the value for the *age*. Figure 15.1 shows the values used to test this program.

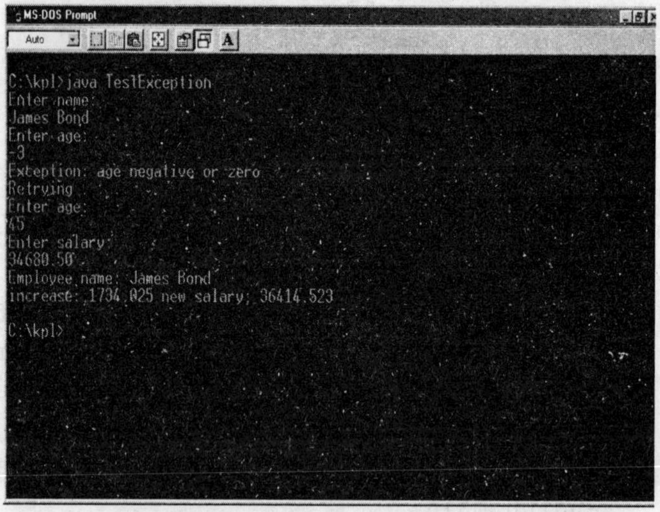


**Figure 15.1** Execution of program with exception.

## 15.3 FILES

A disk file organizes data on a massive storage device such as a disk device. The main advantage of a disk file is that it provides permanent data storage; a second advantage is that it can support a large amount of data. A third advantage of a disk file is that the data can be interchangeable among several computers, depending on the type of storage device used. On the same computer, disk files can be used by one or more different programs.

A disk file can be set up as the source of a data stream or as the destination of the data stream. In other words, the file can be associated with an input stream or with an output stream. Figure 15.2 illustrates the flow of data and the difference between an input and an output stream.

### 15.3.1 Text and Binary Files

Text files are human-readable. They contain data that is coded as printable strings. A byte is coded as a single text character. For example, a KJP source program is stored in a text file with a `.kpl` extension. In the same

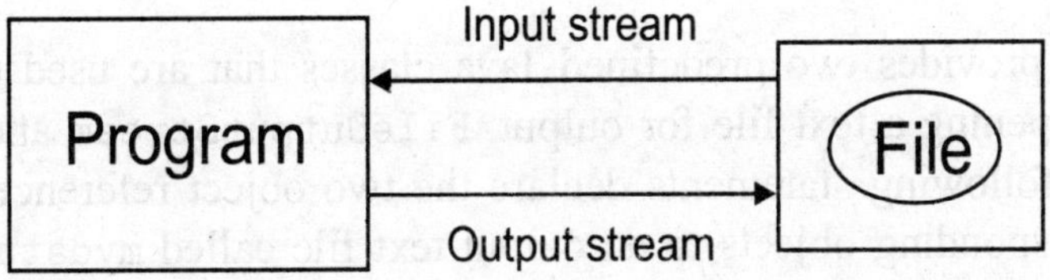


**Figure 15.2** Input and output streams.

manner, a Java source program is also stored in a text file. In simple terms, a text file consists of a sequence of characters. Lines are separated by two characters, carriage return (CR) and line feed (LF); these are placed at the end of a line by pressing the Enter key[1].

A binary file is not human-readable. Its data is stored in the same way as represented in memory. Especially for numeric data, the representation in memory is just ones and zeroes. A compiled program is stored in a binary file.

Binary files take less storage space and are more efficient to process. When reading or writing numeric data, there is no conversion from or to string format.

### 15.3.2 Handling Text Files

The normal procedure for a program that processes data on a file is the following:

1. Open the file for input or output. This step is called opening the file for input or output; it attaches the file to a stream.

2. Read data from the file or write data to the file.

3. Close the file.

For these file processing tasks, Java provides several library classes. Most of the classes for stream I/O are located in package `java.io`.

[1] In Unix, only LF is placed at the end of the line.

### 15.3.3 Output Text Files

Java provides two predefined Java classes that are used to create objects for opening a text file for output, `FileOutputStream` and `PrintWriter`. The following statements declare the two object references and create the corresponding objects to an output text file called `mydata.txt`.

```
object myoutfile of class FileOutputStream
object myoutstream of class PrintWriter
. . .
try begin
   create myoutfile of class FileOutputStream
          using "mydata.txt"
   create myoutstream of class PrintWriter
          using myoutfile
endtry
```

The previous statements have connected the disk file to an output stream, *myoutstream*. This opening of the file could generate an exception if the file cannot be created. For this reason, the statements must appear in a `try` block. To handle the exception, a `catch` block must immediately follow.

```
catch parameters object e of class
                   FileNotFoundException
  begin
    display "Error creating file mydata.txt"
    terminate
endcatch
```

If the output file cannot be created, an exception is raised (thrown) and statements in the `catch` block display an error message related to the exception and terminate the program.

The output stream created is used for all output statements in the program with methods `print` and `println` of object reference *myoutstream*.

After the output file has been created, it can be used to write string data. The numeric data must first be converted to string. For example, to convert an integer value to a string value, function valueOf of the class String is invoked. The following statements declare a variable of type *integer*, *int_val*, declare a variable of type *string*, *str_val*, convert the value of the integer variable to a string, and assign the value to the string variable, *str_val*.

```
variables
  integer int_val
  string str_val
. . .
set str_val = call String.valueOf(int_val)
```

### 15.3.4 Sample Application

The following class, Fileproc, implements the solution of the salary problem that stores data about employees in a text file. Objects of class Employeec calculate the salary increase and the updated salary.

```
import all java.io
description
  This program checks for an exception in the
  value of age, and writes data to an
  output file.  */
class Fileproc is
  public
  description
      This is the main function of the application.
      An object of class Employeec calculates the
      salary increase and updates the salary.
      If the age is zero or negative, an exception
      is thrown and caught. This data is written to
      an output text file.    */
  function main is
    variables
      integer obj_age
      character more_data
```

```
        real increase
        real obj_salary
        string obj_name
  string str_age
  string str_inc
  string str_sal
        string file_name
        string lmessage // message for exception
      objects
        object emp_obj of class Employeec
        object myoutfile of class FileOutputStream
        object myoutstream of class PrintWriter
        // exception for negative age
        object lexecep_obj of class Exception
      begin
        set myoutstream = null
        display "Enter name for output file: "
        read file_name
        // open ouput file
        try begin
           create myoutfile of class FileOutputStream
              using file_name
           create myoutstream of class PrintWriter
              using myoutfile
        endtry
        catch parameters object e of
              class FileNotFoundException
        begin
           display "Error creating file mydata.txt"
           terminate
        endcatch
        set more_data = 'Y'
        while more_data equal 'Y' do
          display "Enter person name: "
          read obj_name
          display "Enter age: "
          read obj_age
```

```
//    Check for exception
try begin
   if obj_age <= 0
   then
      create lexecep_obj of class Exception
         using
         "Exception: age negative or zero"
      throw lexecep_obj
   endif
endtry
catch parameters object excobj of
      class Exception
 begin
   set lmessage = call getMessage of excobj
   display lmessage
   display "Retrying . . . "
   display "Enter age: "
   read obj_age
endcatch
// continue with processing
display "Enter salary: "
read obj_salary
create emp_obj of class Employeec using
    obj_salary, obj_age, obj_name
set increase = call sal_increase of emp_obj
set obj_salary = get_salary() of emp_obj
display "Employee name: ", obj_name
display "increase: ", increase,
    " new salary: ", obj_salary
// write to output file
call println of myoutstream using obj_name
set str_age = call String.valueOf
    using obj_age
call println of myoutstream
    using str_age
set str_inc =call String.valueOf
    using increase
```

```
                call println of myoutstream using str_inc
                set str_sal = call String.valueOf
                    using obj_salary
                call println of myoutstream using str_sal
                display "More data? (Yy/Nn): "
                read more_data
                if more_data equal 'y'
                then
                   set more_data = 'Y'
                endif
              endwhile
              call close of myoutstream
          endfun main
        endclass Fileproc
```

ON THE CD *The KJP code that implements class* `Fileproc` *is stored in the file* `Fileproc.kpl`*, and the Java code is stored in the file* `Fileproc.java`.

The program, composed of class `Fileproc` and class `Employeec`, displays the following input/output when it executes with the data shown:

```
 ----jGRASP exec: java Fileproc
Enter name for output file:
mydata.txt
Enter person name:
James Bond
Enter age:
54
Enter salary:
51800.75
Employee name: James Bond
increase: 2331.034 new salary: 54131.785
More data? (Yy/Nn):
y
Enter person name:
Jose M. Garrido
Enter age:
```

```
48
Enter salary:
46767.50
Employee name: Jose M. Garrido
increase: 2104.5376 new salary: 48872.04
More data? (Yy/Nn):
y
Enter person name:
John B. Hunt
Enter age:
38
Enter salary:
39605.65
Employee name: John B. Hunt
increase: 1980.2825 new salary: 41585.93
More data? (Yy/Nn):
n

 ----jGRASP: operation complete.
```

The output file, mytest.txt, was created and written by the program and has one data item per line with the following structure:

```
James Bond
54
2331.034
54131.785
Jose M. Garrido
48
2104.5376
48872.04
John B. Hunt
38
1980.2825
41585.93
```

## 15.3.5 Input Text Files

Reading data from an input text file implies reading text lines from the input line. If the data items are numeric, then the source string must be converted to a numeric type. Another aspect of input text files is that the program that reads from the file has no information on the number of lines in the text file.

Java provides two predefined Java classes in the `io` package that are used to create objects for opening a text file for input, `BufferedReader` and `FileReader`. The following statements declare the two object references and create the corresponding objects for an input text file called "mydata.txt."

```
object myinfile of class BufferedReader
object myreader of class FileReader
. . .
try begin
    create myreader of class FileReader
             using "mydata.txt"
    create myinfile of class BufferedReader
             using myreader
endtry
```

Opening a text file for input can throw an exception if the file cannot be found. Therefore, the statements that create the two objects must appear in a `try` block. To handle the exception, a `catch` block must immediately follow.

```
catch parameters object excep of
              class FileNotFoundException
begin
     display "Error opening file: ", file_name
     terminate
endcatch
```

In a similar manner to dealing with the output file creation, if the input file cannot be opened, the statements shown in the `catch` block display an error message and terminate the program.

After opening the file for input, the program can read input streams from the file, line by line. The Java method `readLine`, which is defined in class `BufferedReader`, is invoked to read a line of text data. This data is assigned to a string variable. The statement to read a line of data must be placed in a `try` block because a reading error might occur. The exception is thrown by method `readLine`.

One additional complication, compared to writing a text file, is that it is necessary to check whether the file still has data; otherwise, there would be an attempt to read data even if there is no more data in the file.

When there is no more data in the file, the value of the text read is `null`. The following statements define a `try` block with a while loop, which repeatedly reads lines of text from the text file.

```
try begin
    // Read text line from input file
    set indata = call readLine of myinfile
    while indata not equal null do
          // get name
          set obj_name = indata
          . . .
          // read next line
          set indata = call readLine of myinfile
    endwhile
endtry
```

The first statement in the `try` block reads a text line from the file. All subsequent reading is placed in the `while` loop.

Because the text file can only store string values, conversion is needed for numeric variables. For example, *obj_salary* and *increase* are variables of type *double*, so the string value read from the text file has to be converted to type *double*. The following statements read the text line (a string) from the file, and then convert the string value to a value of type *double* with method `Double.parseDouble`.

```
// get salary
set indata = call readLine of myinfile
set obj_salary = call Double.parseDouble
```

```
            using indata
    // get increase
    set indata = call readLine of myinfile
    set increase = call Double.parseDouble
            using indata
```

Method `Integer.parseInt` would be invoked if conversion were needed for an integer variable.

### 15.3.6 Sample Application

The following class, `Rfileproc`, reads the text file that was written by the program presented in Section 15.3.4. This data file has one value stored per line. The values of name, age, salary, and increase are each stored in a different line. The file stores these values for every person. The class computes and displays the total accumulated value of salary and the total accumulated value of increase for several persons.

```
import all java.io
description
    Reads data from an input file, computes the
    total salary, total increase, and
    displays the data on the screen.
    */
class Rfileproc is
  public
  description
     This is the main function of the application.
     If an error occurs when opening the input
     file, an exception is thrown and caught.
     */
  function main is
    variables
      integer obj_age
      double increase
      double obj_salary
      double total_sal
```

```
    double total_inc
    string obj_name
    string str_age
    string file_name
    string indata
    string lmessage // message for exception
  objects
    object myinfile of class BufferedReader
    object myreader of class FileReader
    // exception for negative age
    object lexecep_obj of class Exception
  begin
    set myinfile = null
    set total_sal = 0.0
    set total_inc = 0.0
    display "Enter name for input file: "
    read file_name
    try begin
       // open input file
       create myreader of class FileReader
           using file_name
       create myinfile of class BufferedReader
           using myreader
    endtry
    catch parameters object e of
           class FileNotFoundException
    begin
        display "Error opening file: ", file_name
        terminate
    endcatch
    //
    try begin
        // Read text line from input file
        set indata = call readLine of myinfile
        while indata not equal null do
            // get name
            set obj_name = indata
```

```
                // get age
                set indata = call readLine of myinfile
                set str_age = indata
                // get salary
                set indata = call readLine of myinfile
                set obj_salary = call Double.parseDouble
                       using indata
                add obj_salary to total_sal
                // get increase
                set indata = call readLine of myinfile
                set increase = call Double.parseDouble
                       using indata
                add increase to total_inc
                //
                // Display and continue with processing
                display "Employee name: ", obj_name,
                       " age: ", str_age
                display "  increase: ", increase,
                       " salary: ", obj_salary
                // read next line from file
                set indata = call readLine of myinfile
            endwhile
        endtry
        catch parameters object myexc of
                class Exception
        begin
            display "Error reading file: ", file_name
            terminate
        endcatch
        display " -------------------",
                "----------------------------"
        display "Total salary: ", total_sal
        display "Total increase: ", total_inc
        try begin
            call close of myinfile
        endtry
        catch parameters object exc2 of
```

```
        class IOException
    begin
        display "Error closing file: ", file_name
        terminate
    endcatch
  endfun main
endclass Rfileproc
```

ON THE CD *The KJP code with the implementation of class* Rfileproc *is stored in the file* Rfileproc.kpl. *The corresponding Java code is stored in the file* Rfileproc.java.

When the program executes, it reads data from the text file "mydata.txt." The program gets the values for the individual data items (name, age, salary, and increase) and computes the total salary and increase. The following listing is the one displayed on the screen.

```
 ----jGRASP exec: java Rfileproc

Enter name for input file:
mydata.txt
Employee name: James Bond age: 54
  increase: 54131.785 salary: 2331.034
Employee name: Jose M. Garrido age: 48
  increase: 48872.04 salary: 2104.5376
Employee name: John B. Hunt age: 38
  increase: 41585.93 salary: 1980.2825
-----------------------------------------
Total salary: 6415.8541000000005
Total increase: 144589.755

 ----jGRASP: operation complete.
```

### 15.3.7 Files with Several Values on a Text Line

A text file usually contains lines with several values per line, each separated by white spaces or blanks. In this case, the program must read a line of text from the file, separate and retrieve the individual string values, and convert the values to the appropriate types (if needed). The program must repeat this for every line that it reads from the text file. The following text file has three lines, each with various values, some string values and some numeric values.

```
James_Bond 54  2331.034 54131.785
Jose_M._Garrido 48 2104.5376 48872.04
John_B._Hunt  38 1980.2825    41585.93
```

The Java class `StringTokenizer` facilitates separating the individual strings from a text line. The following statements declare and create an object of class `StringTokenizer`, read a line from the text file, and get two string variables, *var1* and *var2*, from the line.

```
// declare object ref for tokenizer
object tokenizer of class StringTokenizer
//

// read line from text file
set line = call readLine of input_file
//
// create tokenizer object
create tokenizer of class StringTokenizer using line
//
// get a string variable from line
set var1 = call nextToken of tokenizer
//
// get another string variable from line
set var2 = call nextToken of tokenizer
```

To get the number of substrings remaining on a line, the Java method `countTokens` can be invoked with the tokenizer object. This function returns a value of type *integer*. A similar function, `hasMoreTokens`, returns true if there are substrings on the line; otherwise, it returns false.

Class `Lfileproc` is similar to class `Rfileproc`, but it reads a line from the text file and separates the individual string variables for name, age, increase, and salary.

ON THE CD

*The KJP code that implements class* `Lfileproc` *is stored in the file* `Lfileproc.kpl`. *The Java code is stored in the file* `Lfileproc.java`.

## 15.4 SUMMARY

This chapter explains how to detect and handle exceptions. These errors indicate abnormal conditions during the execution of the program. An exception is detected in a `try` block, which encloses a sequence of statements that might throw an exception. The exception is handled in a `catch` block, which encloses the sequence of statements that implement some action in response to the exception. The simplest way to handle an exception is to display information about the exception and terminate the program.

An I/O stream is a sequence of bytes in the input direction or in the output direction, which is treated as a source of data or a destination of data. I/O streams are normally connected with files. The two general types of files are text and binary files. Only text files are explained.

Most of the statements for opening, reading, and writing files throw exceptions. Therefore, these statements must be placed in a `try` block. The input and output with text files are carried out to or from a text line, which is a string. If the data is numeric, then conversion to or from the appropriate numeric type is necessary.

## 15.5 KEY TERMS

| | | |
|---|---|---|
| error | exception | detection |
| exception handling | checked exception | unchecked exception |
| `try` block | `catch` block | throw exception |
| disk | storage device | type conversion |
| input stream | output stream | text file |
| binary file | open | close |
| read line | write line | |

## 15.6 EXERCISES

1. Explain the purpose of using exceptions in any program. If a program can be implemented without exceptions, what are the trade-offs?

2. Explain the differences between throwing an exception and catching an exception. Give examples.

3. What is the difference between detecting an exception and throwing an exception? Explain and give examples. Why do most Java classes for input/output throw exceptions?

4. Redesign and reimplement class `Fileproc` by adding exception handling for an empty name and age less than 18.

5. Redesign and reimplement class `Fileproc`. The new class must declare and create an array of objects of class `Employeec` and compute the lowest, highest, and average salary.

6. Design and implement a program with at least two classes that stores the inventory parts for a warehouse. Each inventory part has the following attributes: description, unit code, number of items in stock, and the unit cost. The program should store the data in a text file. The program should also compute the total investment per item.

7. Design and implement a program with at least two classes that reads the inventory data from the text file written by the program in the

previous exercise. The program should display the individual data on each inventory item, and print the total investment and revenue.

8. Redesign and reimplement the program in the previous exercise by adding exception handling for a negative number of parts in stock, a zero or negative unit cost, and negative unit price.
9. Redesign and reimplement the program in the previous exercise by adding exception handling for a unit price equal to or less than the unit cost.
10. Design and implement a GUI for inventory data in the inventory program in Exercise 6.

# 16 RECURSION

## 16.1 INTRODUCTION

Recursion is a design and programming technique by which a structure is defined in terms of itself. A method definition that contains a call to it is said to be recursive. This approach to design and implement functions accomplishes the same goal as using the iterative approach for problems with repetitions. Recursion can sometimes be simpler and clearer than an iterative solution to a problem. It has been used to describe complex algorithms.

This chapter introduces the basic concepts that involve recursion and includes a problem-solving application of recursion using recursive function calls.

## 16.2 BASIC RECURSIVE TECHNIQUES

Recursion is often associated with a method. A recursive method calls itself from within its own body. A recursive operation achieves exactly what an operation with iterations achieves. In principle, any problem that can be solved recursively can also be solved iteratively. With iteration, a set of instructions is executed repeatedly until some terminating condition has been satisfied. Similarly with recursion, a set of instructions, most likely a part of a method, is invoked repeatedly unless some terminating condition has been satisfied.

A recursive definition of a function consists of two parts:

1. One or more base cases define the terminating conditions. In this part, the value returned by the function is specified by one or more values of the arguments.

2. One or more recursive cases. In this part, the value returned by the function depends on the value of the arguments and the previous value returned by the function.

## 16.3 A SIMPLE RECURSIVE FUNCTION

The *exponentiation* operation, $y^n$, is an example of a function that can be defined recursively. The general, informal description of exponentiation is:

$$y^n = y \times y \times y \times y \times \ldots \times y$$

For example,

$$y^3 = y \times y \times y$$

### 16.3.1 Mathematical Specification of Exponentiation

A mathematical specification of the exponentiation function that is recursive is as follows, assuming that $n \geq 0$:

$$y^n = \begin{cases} 1, & \text{when } n = 0 \\ y \times y^{n-1}, & \text{when } n > 0 \end{cases}$$

The base case in this recursive definition is the value of 1 for the function if the argument has value zero, that is $y^n = 1$ for $n = 0$. The recursive case is $y^n = y \times y^{n-1}$, if the value of the argument is greater than zero.

### 16.3.2 Evaluating Exponentiation

To facilitate the handling of the exponentiation function, it is named *expon* with two arguments: the base and the power. For example, $y^n$ is denoted as *expon(y, n)*.

For evaluating the function $2^4$, which is denoted as *expon(2,4)*, Table 16.1 shows all the intermediate calculations necessary.

**Table 16.1** Intermediate calculations for $2^4$

| | | |
|---|---|---|
| $2^4$ | $2 \times 2^3$ | 2×*expon(2, 3)* |
| $2^3$ | $2 \times 2^2$ | 2×*expon(2, 2)* |
| $2^2$ | $2 \times 2^1$ | 2×*expon(2, 1)* |
| $2^1$ | $2 \times 2^0$ | 2×*expon(2, 0)* |
| $2^0$ | 1 | 1 |

### 16.3.3 KJP Implementation of Exponentiation

The following function is a recursive solution for the exponentiation function, *expon(y, n)*. The KJP code defines a static function that is called by function *main* in class `Rectest`.

```
description
   This function computes recursively y to the
   power of n, assuming that n > 0. */
static function expon of type double
             parameters double y, integer n is
  variables
    double result
  begin
  display "expon ", y, " power ", n
  // base case
  if n == 0 then
     set result = 1.0
```

```
      else
          // recursive case
          if n greater than 0 then
             set result = y * expon(y, n-1)
             display "y = ", y, " n = ", n,
                                   " expon ", result
          else
             // exceptional case
             display "Negative power"
             set result = 1.0
          endif
      endif
      return result
    endfun expon
```

ON THE CD *The KJP code that implements class* Rectest *is stored in the file* Rectest.kpl. *The Java implementation is stored in the file* Rectest.java.

When the program implemented in class Rectest executes, with a value 3.0 for $y$ and value 4 for $n$, the intermediate and final results are shown as follows:

```
----jGRASP exec: java Rectest

 Enter value for n:
 4
 type value for y:
 3.0
 expon 3.0 power 4
 expon 3.0 power 3
 expon 3.0 power 2
 expon 3.0 power 1
 expon 3.0 power 0
 y = 3.0 n = 1 expon 3.0
 y = 3.0 n = 2 expon 9.0
 y = 3.0 n = 3 expon 27.0
```

```
y = 3.0 n = 4 expon 81.0
Expon 3.0 power 4 is 81.0

 ----jGRASP: operation complete.
```

When analyzing the intermediate results for the computation of the recursive function *expon*, it is clear those successive calls to the function continue until it reaches the base case. After this simple calculation of the base, the function starts calculating the exponentiation of $y$ with power 1, 2, 3, and then 4. There are actually two phases in the calculation using a recursive function:

1. The recursive calls up to the base case. This represents the sequence of calls to the function; it is known as the winding phase.

2. The unwinding phase returns the values from the base case to each of the previous calls.

## 16.4 THE INTERNAL COMPUTATIONS

The implementations of the iterative and the recursive solutions to a problem are quite different. For the recursive solution, we must understand its implementation well to be able to develop and use it. We must understand the runtime stack, and to understand the runtime stack we must understand stack.

The stack has various applications in computer science. A stack is a data structure (a storage structure for data retention and retrieval) based on a last in first out (LIFO) discipline. The best example of a stack is a stack of plates. The last plate that was inserted is at the top of the stack and must be removed before any other can be removed.

In computer terminology, when a plate is put on the top of a stack, the operation is known as *push* to the stack, and the stack grows up. When a plate is taken off of the stack, the operation is known as *pop* off the stack, and the stack shrinks. In other words, a stack grows or shrinks depending upon the insertion or removal of plates from the stack. Figure 16.1 shows a stack of plates.

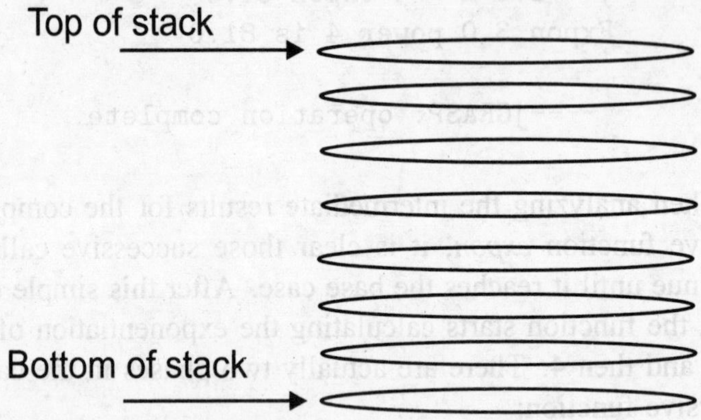


**Figure 16.1** A stack of plates.

Execution of a computer program involves two broad steps: allocating storage to hold data and then attaching a set of instructions to process the data held by the allocated storage. Some units of storage may hold data to be processed while other units may hold the results of the processing.

Generally, storage is provided for objects, constants, and methods that have local variables, constants, and parameter variables. Because recursion involves only a method, focus here is only on the associated storage of a method: local variables, constants, and parameter variables. Operating systems create a process for each program to be executed and allocate a portion of primary memory to each process. This block of memory serves as a medium for the runtime stack, which grows when a method is invoked and shrinks when the execution of a method is completed.

During the lifetime of a process, there may be many methods involved in processing; the first method is always the main method, which invokes other methods if specified by instructions. Whenever a method is invoked, the runtime system dynamically allocates storage for its local variables, constants, and parameter variables declared within the method from the allocated chunk of memory. In fact, this information is placed in a data structure known as a *frame* or activation record and *pushed* on the stack. After the execution of the invoked method is completed, the frame created for that method is *popped* from the stack.

Obviously, the first frame is always for the main method, as processing starts with this method. By using the analogy of a stack of plates, a frame that is created to provide storage for each method is a similar operation of a plate that is *pushed* on the stack and *popped* off the stack.

A runtime stack refers to a stack-type data structure (LIFO) associated with each process provided and maintained by the system. The runtime stack holds data of all the methods that have been invoked but not yet completed processing. A runtime stack grows and shrinks depending on the number of methods involved in processing and the interaction between them.

If the main method is the only method involved in processing, there is only one frame in the stack with storage for all the variables, locals and constants. If method *main* invokes another method, *A*, then the stack grows only by one frame. After the method *A* completes execution, the memory block allocated to its frame is released and returned to the system.

## 16.5 SUMMARY

A recursive method definition contains one or more calls to the function being defined. In many cases, the recursive method is very powerful and compact in defining the solution to complex problems. The main disadvantages are that it demands a relatively large amount of memory and time to build stack.

As there is a choice between using iterative and recursive algorithms, so programmers must evaluate the individual situation and make a good decision for their use.

## 16.6 KEY TERMS

| | | |
|---|---|---|
| recursive call | base case | recursive case |
| terminating condition | recursive solution | iterative solution |
| winding phase | unwinding phase | stack |
| LIFO | push operation | pop operation |
| frame | activation record | runtime stack |

## 16.7 EXERCISES

1. Write a recursive method to print the square of $n$ natural numbers.
2. Write a recursive method to print $n$ natural numbers that are even.
3. Write a recursive method to print all letters in a string in reverse order, that is, if the string is "Java," it will print "avaJ."
4. Write a recursive method that will reverse a given string, that is, it will convert "hello" to "olleh."
5. Write a recursive method that will compute the factorial of $n$ natural numbers.
6. A palindrome is a string that does not change when it is reversed. For example: "madam," "radar," and so on. Write a recursive method that checks whether a given string is a palindrome.
7. Design and implement a program that includes a recursive method for a linear search in an array of integer values. For a review on the principles of linear searches, see Section 9.4.3.1.
8. Design and implement a program that includes a recursive method for a binary search in an array of integer values. For a review on the principles of binary searches, see Section 9.4.3.2.

# 17 THREADS

## 17.1 INTRODUCTION

Practical problems include several activities that are carried out simultaneously. The solution to these problems is implemented with programs that consist of a collection of concurrent tasks, also known as *threads*.

A computer with a single CPU can actually only perform one task at a time. Concurrency is a general programming technique that allows the execution of multiple threads that appear to be running simultaneously. This simplifies the implementation of applications with multiple "simultaneous" tasks. The implementation represents an application with multiple threads.

This chapter presents a very simple and general discussion of programs with multiple threads. There are no complete programs included. More detailed concepts and techniques are treated in advanced textbooks on programming and on operating systems.

## 17.2 CONCURRENT EXECUTION

A program in execution is called a process. Modern operating systems, such as MS Windows and Unix, support multiple processes in memory. All these processes appear to be running at the "same time." This is known as concurrent execution of multiple processes.

There many applications that are required to handle multiple tasks. Within a program, each task is implemented as a *thread*. The program itself executes as a process. A thread is also known as a *light-weight* process. Figure 17.1 shows a process with three threads.

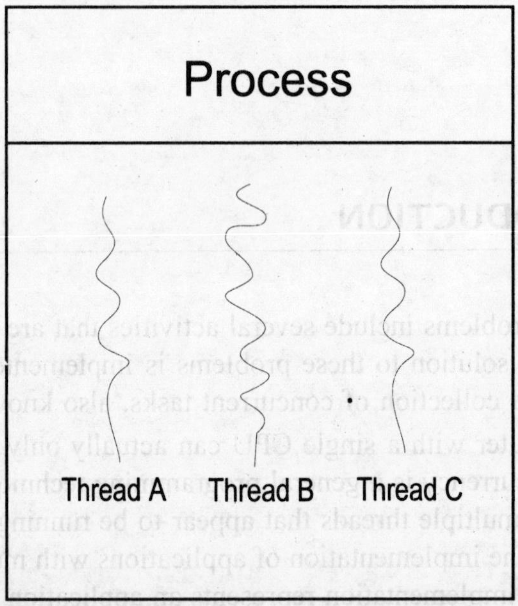


**Figure 17.1** A process with three threads.

## 17.3 PROGRAMMING WITH THREADS

Java and KJP provide to the programmer several ways to implement threads. The most relevant applications for threads are programming with GUI and animations. The Java `Thread` class allows you to create objects that have thread behavior. A thread can be started and run, can be paused and resumed, until it becomes null. The class includes the following methods: `start()`, `run()`, `sleep()`, `join()`, `yield()`, and so on.

The start() method starts the thread executing and invokes the run() method. The run() method contains the body of the code to be executed by the thread. When this method returns, the thread terminates.

A thread can be paused for a certain time period by calling the sleep() method. The statement sleep(50) means pause for 50 milliseconds. If you know your thread will be idling for an unspecified length of time, you may allow other threads with the same priority or greater priority (not lesser priority) to execute, by using method yield(). It is similar to the sleep() method, but without the specific time indication.

The join() method call waits synchronously for the thread to become inactive. This allows different threads a chance to coordinate their activities. For example, Thread *A* calls this method in Thread *B* that causes Thread *A* to block until Thread *B* has completed, and then Thread *A* can continue. When the thread is assigned with a null value, it stops at the current instruction.

## 17.4 THREAD DEFINITION

There are two ways to define threads. One way is to define a class that inherits class Thread; another way is to define a class that implements the Runnable interface. The first way to use threads is to derive a subclass from the Thread class and override the run() method. The following is a simple portion of code that illustrates the first method:

```
description
   This class defines a thread. */
class MyThread inherits Thread is
public
description
  This is the main body of the thread definition.
  */
void function run is
        //
        // do something;
        // When this method returns,
```

```
            // the thread terminates
    endfun run
    endclass MyThread
```

To create a thread and start its execution, the following portion of code is included in the main class of an application program:

```
objects
   object mt of class MyThread
   ...
begin
   ...
   create mt of class MyThread
   call start of mt    // start running the thread
   ...
```

The second technique to define a class that implements the Runnable interface and override the run() method. The following is a simple portion of code that illustrates this thechnique:

```
description
   This class also defines a thread. */
class MyThreadb inherits OtherClass
                                 implements Runnable is
public
description
   This is the main body of the thread definition.
   */
void function run is
        //
        // do something;
        // When this method returns,
        // the thread terminates
endfun run
endclass MyThreadb
```

The advantage of the second technique is that there is no need to inherit class `Thread`. To create a thread and start its execution, the following portion of code is included in the main class of an application program:

```
objects
  object ms of class MyThreadb
  object myth of class Thread
  ...
begin
  ...
  create ms of class MyThreadb
  create myth of class Thread using ms
  call start of myth
```

## 17.5 SUMMARY

This chapter presented a very simple introduction to threads and basic principles of thread programming. The thread supports concurrency inside one program. It is a necessary mechanism for event-driven programming and network programming.

## 17.6 KEY TERMS

| | | |
|---|---|---|
| threads | multithreading | processes |
| tasks | control sequence | preempt |
| animation | lightweight process | concurrent execution |

## 17.7 EXERCISES

1. Describe and explain an application with multiple threads.
2. Why are threads important?
3. Explain and give an example of concurrency.
4. What are the similarities and differences between processes and threads?
5. Investigate why is the use of threads some times necessary in event-driven programming.

# Appendix A

## A.1 INTRODUCTION

This appendix introduces and explains the use of the KJP translator and the jGRASP software development environment. There are two general procedures to follow for developing programs and using the KJP translator. These procedures are:

1. Working in a DOS window
2. Working with an integrated development environment (IDE), such as jGRASP

This appendix first explains how to set up and use the KJP translator in a DOS window. The latest information, sample files, and version of the KJP translator is available from the following Web page:

```
http://science.Kennesaw.edu/~jgarrido/kjp.html
```

In the second part of this appendix, an explanation is presented on how to configure and use the jGRASP environment, which is available from Auburn University. The Web page is:

```
http://www.eng.auburn.edu/grasp
```

The KJP translator consists of a program that provides the following functions:

1. Syntax checking of a source program in KJP; a list of errors is displayed and written to an error file with the same name as the source program
2. Conversion of the source program in KJP to an equivalent program in Java

## A.2 INSTALLING THE KJP SOFTWARE

The first general step for installing the software is to use Windows Explorer to create a folder and then to store the relevant files in the folder. A folder is a section of a disk where you can store files and other folders. This step involves copying two important files, which are the following:

1. The first file contains the KJP translator, which is an executable program called `kjp.exe`.
2. The second file contains a precompiled Java class `Conio.class`, which is required for all console I/O.

ON THE CD *These files can be copied from the CD-ROM or downloaded from the KJP Web page.*

Most versions of Windows have the Windows Explorer located in the Accessories system folder. To start Windows Explorer, from the Windows Desktop, click the Start button, select Programs, select Accessories, and then select Windows Explorer. Figure A.1 shows the Windows Explorer window. To use Windows Explorer to create a new directory (or folder), first position the mouse on the home (root) directory; this could be the drive A or drive C. Next, click the File menu, select New, and then select Folder. Type the name of the new folder in the small box that appears.

To copy a file or a folder to the new folder created previously, follow these steps:

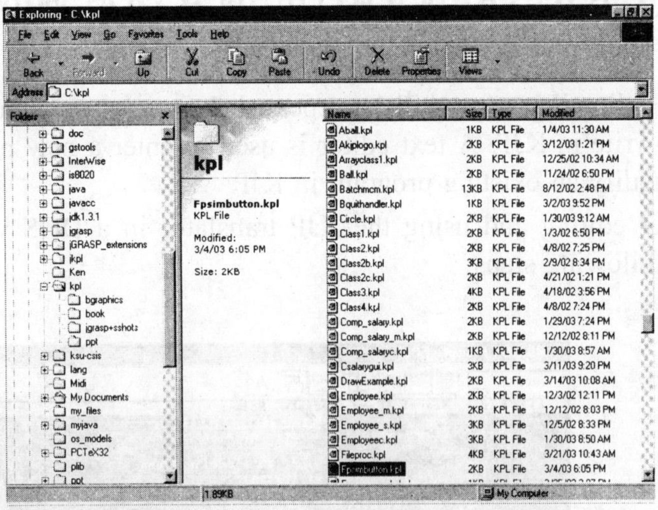


**Figure A.1** Windows Explorer.

1. Click on the icon of the file located in its original folder (or drive A). The file is now highlighted (selected).

2. Click the Edit menu and select Copy.

3. Now click on the icon of the new folder just created.

4. Click the Edit menu and select Paste. After a few seconds, the file is copied to the new folder.

The original folder is sometimes called the source folder, and the second folder is called the destination folder. Follow the procedure just explained to copy the two essential files, the KJP tool in the file `kjp.exe` and the file `Conio.class`.

## A.3 THE KJP TRANSLATOR IN A DOS WINDOW

The following steps will be repeated for every new source program that you write in KJP. A text editor is used to enter a new program in KJP or to modify an existing program in KJP.

For editing and using the KJP translator in a DOS window, complete the following steps:

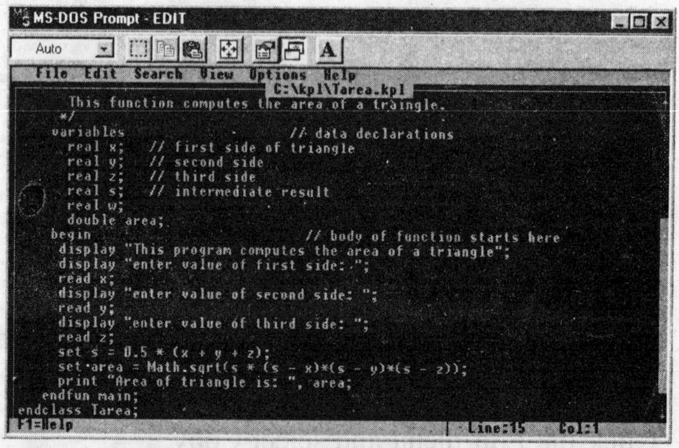


**Figure A.2** The DOS editor.

1. Start and open a DOS window. You can do this by clicking the Start button and then selecting Run. In the Run dialog box, type the word `command` and click the OK button.

2. Change the directory to the one where the KJP files are stored. Use the CD command in DOS.

3. Start the DOS editor. Figure A.2 shows a DOS window with the editor.

4. Type and edit the source program (e.g., `Cat.kpl`) in KJP with the DOS editor.

5. Invoke the KJP translator (also called the KJP compiler) to check syntax and convert your source program from KJP to Java. Type

kjp Cat.kpl, where Cat.kpl is the source program coded in KJP. Note that the filename needs the kpl extension after the dot. See Figure A.3.

6. After the KJP compiler runs, with the Windows Explorer, you will see in the current directory (or folder) two new files with the same name as your original source file. One of the files stores the syntax errors found. This file has the same name as the source program but with an err extension; for example, Cat.err.
7. The second file contains the Java program; the file has the same name but with the java extension. For example, if your source program is Cat.kpl, then the Java program created is Cat.java.
8. Use the Java compiler to compile the Java program (e.g. Cat.java) generated by the KJP translator.
9. Use the Java virtual machine (JVM) to execute the compiled program. When starting execution, enter the input data to the program, if needed.
10. Return to the Windows desktop by typing exit while in DOS.

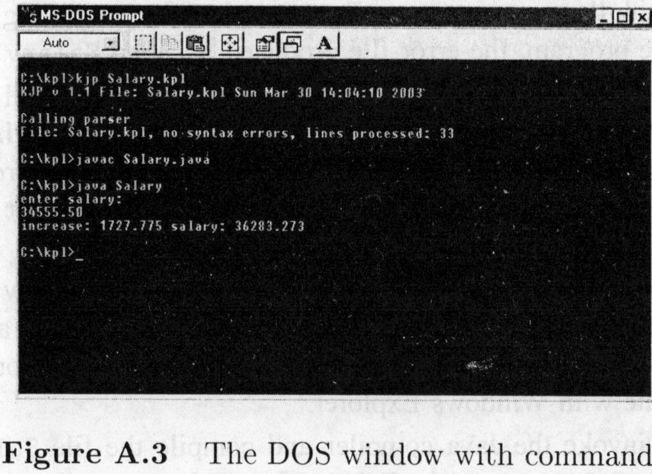


**Figure A.3** The DOS window with commands.

In step 2 (DOS window), to change the directory to the one where you have the source programs in KJP, type the following command: cd\, and then press the Enter key. If the directory with your source programs is called `my_files`, on the next line type `cd my_files` and then press the Enter key; this changes to the directory called `my_files`. To get a list of the files in the current directory, type `dir` and then press Enter.

To start the DOS editor, type `edit` at the command prompt then press the Enter key. After the editor starts and if you are typing a new source program, start typing line by line; press the Enter key at the end of every line. When you have completed entering the text, click on the File menu and select the `Save as` option. Type the name of the file (program name). It must start with a capital letter, and have a `.kpl` extension. For example, `Tarea.kpl`. Figure A.2 shows the DOS editor with some text lines already entered. To exit the DOS editor, click the File menu, and then select Exit.

To compile (step 5 above) a source program in KJP called `Salary.kpl`, type `kpl Salary.kpl` and then press the Enter key. After a few seconds, you will see a message on the screen. In this case, File `Salary.kpl, no syntax errors, lines processed: 45`. The window in Figure A.3 shows these commands.

The KJP translator produces two new files with the same name as the original source program in KJP. The first file is the corresponding Java program. The other file created contains the syntax errors that the KJP compiler detected. The name of this file is the same as the source file but with the `err` extension. For example, after compiling the `Salary.kpl` source program, the error file produced is called `Salary.err`.

The error file generated by the KJP compiler shows all the syntax errors detected in the source program. These are indicated with the line number and column number where they appear. If there are no errors detected, then the last line of this text file includes the message `no syntax errors`. The total number of lines read is also shown

In summary, after invoking the KJP compiler, the new files that appear on the current directory are `Salary.kpl`, `Salary.java`, and `Salary.err`. You can check this with the `dir` command in DOS. You can also check the date with Windows Explorer.

To invoke the Java compiler and compile the file `Salary.java`, type `javac Salary.java` in DOS. After a few seconds, the Java compiler completes and displays error messages, if any. Take note of the error messages and go back to the DOS editor to correct them, by changing the source program in KJP.

If there are no error messages, run the program by invoking the Java Virtual Machine (JVM), and then type `java Salary` at the DOS prompt. Notice that you don't need the file extension. After a few seconds, your program starts execution.

## A.4 USING JGRASP

Under Windows, jGRASP is a more flexible and powerful environment to develop programs in Java and in KJP. The tool was designed mainly for Java programs. For KJP, the jGRASP tool needs to be configured so that it will execute the KJP translator when the user issues the Compile command.

### A.4.1 Configuring KJP Translator with jGRASP

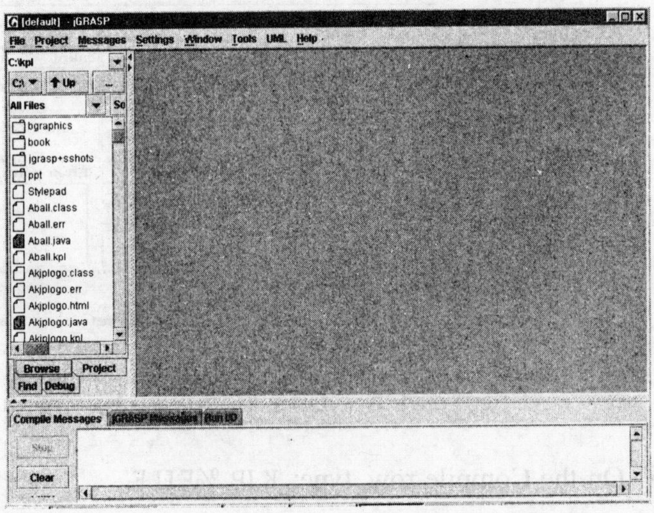

**Figure A.4** The jGRASP main window.

The following steps will guide you in configuring KJP to work with jGRASP.

1. Place the KJP translator and additional files in an appropriate directory, such as 'c:\kjp'.
2. Start jGRASP; the main window appears on the screen as shown in Figure A.4.
3. On the Settings menu, select Compiler Settings.
4. Choose Global, click on Language, and select Plain Text.
5. Click the Environment button, and select Empty.
6. Click the New button.
7. A new dialog box appears on the screen with the title: User Compiler Environment (Plain Text). On the top bar of the window, type: `KJP`. Figure A.5 shows this window.

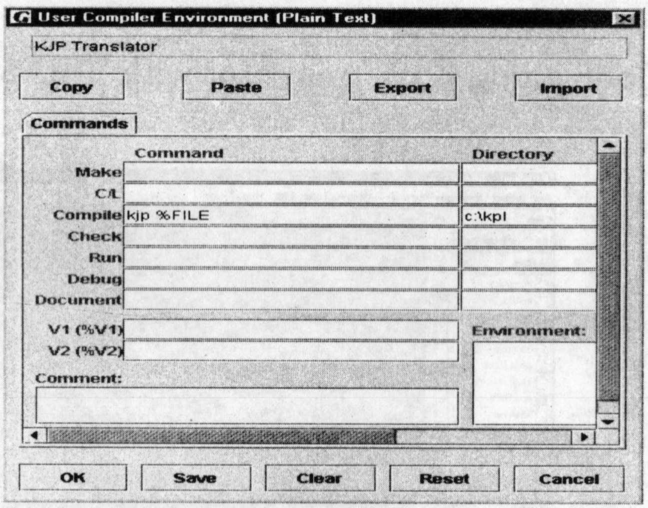


**Figure A.5** User Compiler Environment.

8. On the Compile row, type: `KJP %FILE`.
9. On the directory column, type: `C:\KJP`, or any other folder that contains the KJP translator.
10. Click the Save button.
11. Click the OK button.

12. Back on the Global Settings window, click `User:kjp`. Figure A.6 shows this window.

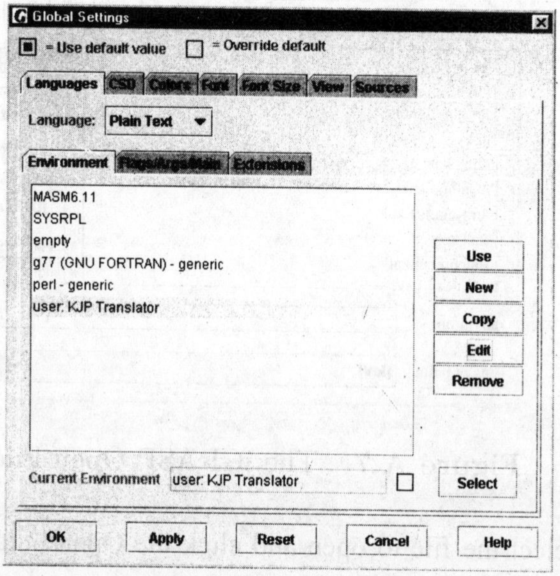


**Figure A.6** The jGRASP Global Settings window.

13. Click the Use button.

## A.4.2 Translating KJP Programs with jGRASP

To use KJP with jGRASP for translating programs from KJP to Java, follow the sequence of steps:

1. Start jGRASP.
2. The jGRASP main window appears on the screen, as shown in Figure A.4. On the left pane, select the folder where the KJP program files are located.
3. Click the File menu, and select Open. Figure A.7 shows the Open File window.
4. In the Open File, type `kpl` in the File Extension text-box (far right side), and press the Enter key.

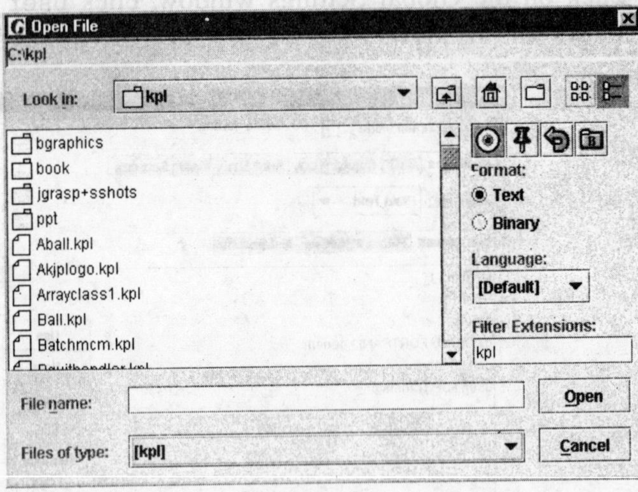


**Figure A.7** The jGRASP Open File window.

5. Select the file to open and click the Open button.

6. The KJP file (with extension `kpl`) appears on the screen. Edit the file and save, if necessary. Figure A.8 shows the jGRASP edit window.

7. Click the Compiler menu and select Compile or click the button with the green cross.

8. On the bottom pane of the screen, all the messages appear, including any compiler error messages. If there are no errors, the message `No syntax errors found` appears as the last message.

9. Edit the file if any errors were found.

10. Save the file and recompile, if necessary.

11. To close the file, click the File menu and select Clear.

### A.4.3 Compiling Java Programs with jGRASP

After the translation of a KJP program, the corresponding Java program must be compiled with the Java compiler. To compile and execute a Java program, carry out the following sequence of steps:

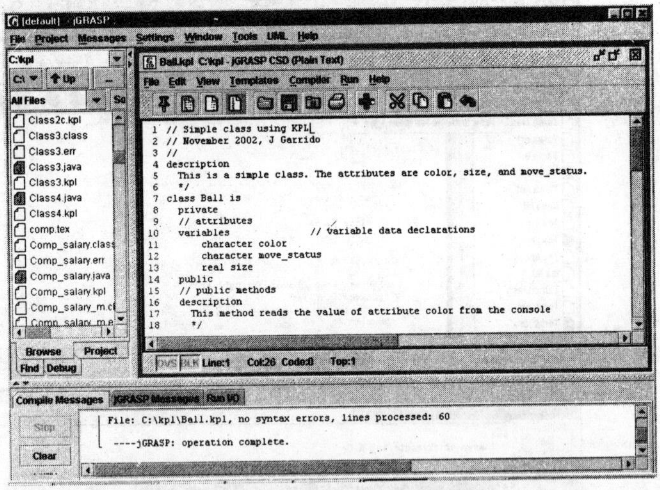

**Figure A.8** The jGRASP edit window.

1. Click the File menu and select Open.

2. Select `java` for the type of file.

3. Select the desired Java file.

4. Click the Compiler menu and select Compile, or click the button with the green cross.

5. The bottom window will display jGRASP: Operation complete.

6. Click the Run menu, and if desired, select the option Run in MSDOS window.

7. Click the Run selection, or click the button with the red man running.

8. If necessary, type the appropriate input data values required by the program when it executes.

## A.4.4 Capturing the I/O

This section explains how to capture the console output of an application program running in the jGRASP development environment.

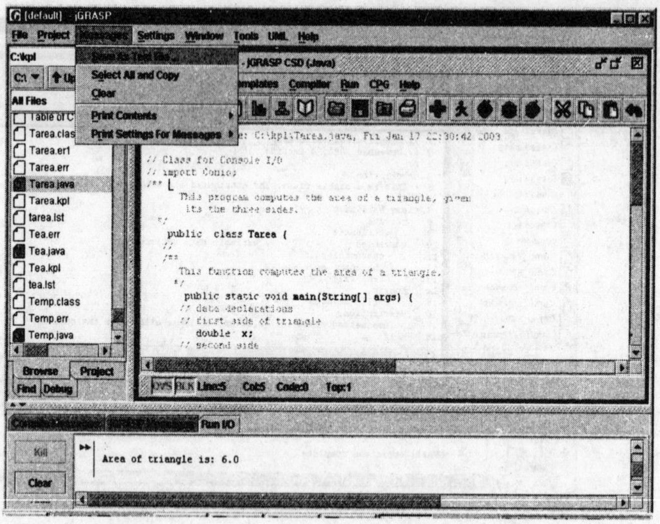

**Figure A.9** The jGRASP Messages menu.

1. First, load all files and compile the software as you normally would. Any compile errors or "successful" message(s) will appear in the Messages View along the bottom of the screen.

2. Run the code with the `Run in MS-DOS Window` selection unchecked. This keeps the output within the jGRASP window's environment and sends the output to the Messages View at the bottom of the screen. You will see the output scrolling while the program is executing.

3. After the program runs, select the `Messages` menu bar, and select `Save as Text File` option. The menu that appears is shown in Figure A.9.

4. Complete the dialog box, and click `save`. The resulting text file can be viewed by opening the file in jGRASP (select `All files` to see it in the dialog box). Of course, it can also be viewed and manipulated in other applications as any text file. Figure A.10 shows the dialog box saving the Run I/O panel.

   This method can be used to generically send any Messages View output, including compiler error logs, to a text file.

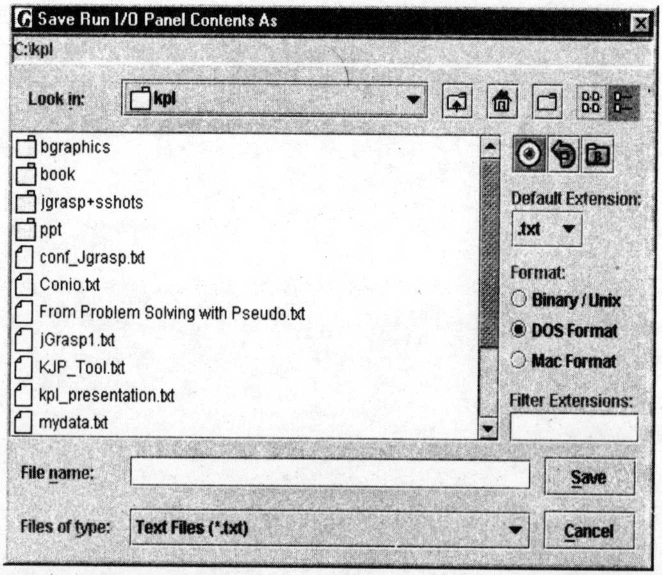


**Figure A.10** The jGRASP Save Run I/O dialog box.

# Appendix B

## B.1 ABOUT THE CD-ROM

The CD-ROM included with this book contains all the files that are used as source programs in KJP and in Java. It also includes the program file necessary for using the KJP translator and the binary file for console input/output.

## B.2 CD FOLDERS

The CD-ROM contains the following folders:

- *KJP_source*: This folder contains all of the KJP sample programs from within the book. These files are set up by chapter. These files are all in text format that can be read by most text editors.
- *Java_source*: This folder contains all of the Java files that correspond to the examples presented in the book. These files are all in text format that can be read by most text editors.
- *KJP_translator*: This folder includes the KJP translator program file, which is an executable file, and the Conio class.

## B.3 SYSTEM REQUIREMENTS

The overall system requirements are:

- The appropriate Sun Software Development Kit (SDK, 1.3x or 1.4x)
- jGRASP (Auburn University) version 1.5.x
- Windows Operating System (9.x, Me, 98, NT, 2000, XP)
- Appropriate computer with an Intel Pentium processor or equivalent
- At least 32 MB of RAM
- A CD device for reading the files in the CD-ROM provided

## B.4 INSTALLATION

To use this CD-ROM, you just need to make sure that your system matches at least the minimum system requirements. Detailed instructions for the installation are explained in Appendix A of this book.

# INDEX